MONOGRAPHS OF THE
SOCIETY FOR RESEARCH IN
CHILD DEVELOPMENT

Serial No. 255, Vol. 63, No. 4, 1998

SOCIAL COGNITION, JOINT ATTENTION, AND COMMUNICATIVE COMPETENCE FROM 9 TO 15 MONTHS OF AGE

Malinda Carpenter
Katherine Nagell
Michael Tomasello

WITH COMMENTARY BY

George Butterworth
Chris Moore

MONOGRAPHS OF THE SOCIETY FOR RESEARCH IN CHILD DEVELOPMENT
Serial No. 255, Vol. 63, No. 4, 1998

CONTENTS

COMMENTARY

ABSTRACT

CARPENTER, MALINDA, NAGELL, KATHERINE, and TOMASELLO, MICHAEL. Social
Cognition, Joint Attention, and Communicative Competence from 9 to
15 Months of Age. *Monographs of the Society for Research in Child Development,* 1998, **63**(4, No. 255).

At around 1 year of age, human infants display a number of new behaviors that seem to indicate a newly emerging understanding of other persons
as intentional beings whose attention to outside objects may be shared, followed into, and directed in various ways. These behaviors have mostly been
studied separately. In the current study, we investigated the most important
of these behaviors together as they emerged in a single group of 24 infants
between 9 and 15 months of age. At each of seven monthly visits, we measured
joint attentional engagement, gaze and point following, imitation of two different kinds of actions on objects, imperative and declarative gestures, and
comprehension and production of language. We also measured several non-
social-cognitive skills as a point of comparison.

We report two studies. The focus of the first study was the initial emergence of infants' social-cognitive skills and how these skills are related to one
another developmentally. We found a reliable pattern of emergence: Infants
progressed from *sharing* to *following* to *directing* others' attention and behavior.
The nonsocial skills did not emerge predictably in this developmental sequence. Furthermore, correlational analyses showed that the ages of emergence of all pairs of the social-cognitive skills or their components were interrelated. The focus of the second study was the social interaction of infants
and their mothers, especially with regard to their skills of joint attentional
engagement (including mothers' use of language to follow into or direct infants' attention) and how these skills related to infants' early communicative
competence. Our measures of communicative competence included not only
language production, as in previous studies, but also language comprehension and gesture production. It was found that two measures—the amount
of time infants spent in joint engagement with their mothers and the degree

to which mothers used language that followed into their infant's focus of attention—predicted infants' earliest skills of gestural and linguistic communication.

Results of the two studies are discussed in terms of their implications for theories of social-cognitive development, for theories of language development, and for theories of the process by means of which human children become fully participating members of the cultural activities and processes into which they are born.

Human cognition is in many ways a collective enterprise. Indeed, in one view, the major characteristic distinguishing the cognitive skills of human beings from those of other primate species is the ability to take advantage of the knowledge and skills of conspecifics, both present and past (Vygotsky, 1978; Vygotsky & Luria, 1993). It is highly unlikely that a human infant, or even a group of human infants, raised in isolation from adults would invent for itself many of the material and symbolic artifacts or collective social practices, including language, that constitute the truly unique aspects of human cognition. A central question of developmental psychology, therefore, is how it is that human children come initially to participate in the artifacts and social practices that constitute the collectivity of human cognition (Tomasello, Kruger, & Ratner, 1993).

Recent developmental theory and research has identified 1 year of age as an important milestone in this process. It is at around 1 year of age that infants for the first time begin to look where adults are looking flexibly and reliably, use adults as social reference points, and act on objects in the way adults are acting on them. At around this same age, infants also begin actively to direct adult attention to outside entities using intentionally communicative gestures; this achievement is soon followed by the acquisition of skills of linguistic communication. What all these skills have in common is that they involve the referential triangle of child, adult, and some third event or entity to which the participants share attention. The term *joint attention* has often been used to characterize this whole complex of social skills and interactions, and joint attention has been hypothesized to underlie the earliest forms of human cultural learning (see Tomasello, 1995a, and other papers in Moore & Dunham, 1995). Relatedly, researchers interested in children's later skills of social cognition and theory of mind have come to see skills of joint attention as precursors to the understanding of the thoughts and beliefs of others that emerges at around 4–5 years of age (see Baron-Cohen & Ring, 1994, and other papers in Lewis & Mitchell, 1994).

Historically, the study of joint attention has been approached by researchers from two points of view, one based on ontogenetically earlier phe-

1

nomena of infant social interaction and one based on ontogenetically later phenomena of intentional communication and language. From the point of view of earlier phenomena of infant social interaction, joint attention is the capstone of a long process that begins as newborn infants interact with adults face to face in "primary intersubjectivity" and ends as they begin to participate in bouts of "secondary intersubjectivity" with adults (Trevarthen, 1979a). Secondary intersubjectivity, or joint attention, allows infants to incorporate a third element into their dyadic interactions with other persons, thus making possible many kinds of triadic social interactions with people and objects.

On the other hand, from the point of view of later phenomena of intentional communication and language during the second year of life and beyond, joint attention represents not a capstone but a beginning point. Joint attentional interactions with other persons represent the initial "meeting of minds" that provides the foundation for all subsequent acts of communication and cultural learning involving reference to the outside world (Bruner, 1975a, 1975b, 1983). Once they are capable of entering into joint attentional interactions, infants begin to learn from and through others about the environment and about the artifacts used by members of their culture to mediate interactions with the environment (Cole, 1996; Rogoff, 1990). Viewed from both these perspectives simultaneously, then, the emergence of joint attention may be seen as the crossroads where human infants meet the world of collective cognition in which they will reside for the rest of their lives (for an interesting discussion, see Adamson, 1995).

In this *Monograph*, we are concerned with joint attention from both these points of view. We report two studies, both derived from our observations of 24 infants who visited our laboratory at monthly intervals from 9 to 15 months of age. At each of these monthly visits, we obtained various measures of the infant's social-cognitive skills, we observed the infant and mother's social interactions, and we obtained maternal reports of the infant's communication and language skills. The focus of the first study was the initial emergence of infants' social-cognitive and joint attentional skills and how these related to one another developmentally. The focus of the second study was infant and adult joint attentional skills in social interaction (joint engagement) and how these related to the infant's cultural learning of gestural communication and linguistic skills. The remainder of this introduction is aimed at setting in context our specific research questions and hypotheses for each of the two studies in turn.

JOINT ATTENTION AS SOCIAL COGNITION

Human infants are social creatures from birth. From the first hours of life, infants look selectively at pictures of schematic human faces over other patterns (Fantz, 1963; Morton & Johnson, 1991) and actively reproduce adults' facial and manual gestures (Meltzoff & Moore, 1977, 1989). There is even some evidence that infants are socially attuned before birth (Decasper & Fifer, 1980). Active social behavior increases dramatically at around 1–2 months of age as infants begin to engage in direct face-to-face interactions with adults (Trevarthen, 1979a; Tronick, 1989), perhaps involving active turn taking (Murray & Trevarthen, 1985). Despite this high degree of sociality, however, in none of these interactive behaviors do infants demonstrate overtly a clear understanding that other persons are psychological agents with their own interests and attention to outside entities. Overt evidence for this understanding first emerges in the latter half of the first year of life as infants begin to incorporate outside objects into their social interactions with adults.

Brief History and Definition

During the mid- and late 1970s, researchers began to focus on three ways in which human infants begin to incorporate outside entities into their social interactions with others. These may be characterized as *sharing attention, following attention,* and *directing attention.* First, Trevarthen and Hubley (1978) studied how infants went from their early dyadic interactions, with either persons or objects, to triadic interactions in which they *share* attention to an object with another person. These triadic interactions typically emerge at around 9 months of age and include such things as actively giving and requesting objects from the mother. Second, Scaife and Bruner (1975) studied the extent to which infants 2–14 months of age *follow* the gaze direction of an adult to an object, with the purpose of determining at what age infants understand that other persons have interest and attention into which they might follow. Third, Bates, Camaioni, and Volterra (1975) studied 8–12-month-old infants' use of nonverbal gestures to *direct* another person to objects in which they themselves were interested. These researchers distinguished between gestures designed to get adults to do something (imperatives) and those simply designed to direct adults' attention to an entity of potential common interest (declaratives).

There is currently much controversy over the nature of the infant social cognition that underlies these emerging triadic behaviors. Some theorists believe that human infants have adult-like social cognition from birth and that the emergence of these triadic behaviors at 9–12 months of age simply reflects the development of behavioral performance skills for manifesting this cognition in overt behavior (e.g., Trevarthen, 1979b). Other theorists believe that infants are preprogrammed with several independent social-cognitive modules—including an eye direction detector, an intention detector, and a shared attention mechanism—each with its own predetermined developmental timetable that is affected neither by the ontogeny of the other modules nor by the organism's interactions with the social environment (e.g., Baron-Cohen, 1995). Finally, still other theorists believe that infants' triadic interactions at 9–12 months of age represent learned behavioral sequences, at least somewhat independent of one another (although underlain by a common information-processing mechanism), that do not initially rest on deep social-cognitive understandings of other persons at all (e.g., Moore, 1996).

Our theoretical perspective will follow the lead of Tomasello (1995a), who attempted to provide a single theoretical foundation for the different manifestations of joint attention by positing that infants engage in joint attentional interactions when they understand other persons as intentional agents. Intentional agents are animate beings with the power to control their spontaneous behavior, but they are more than that. Intentional agents have goals and make active choices among behavioral means for attaining those goals. Also, and novel to this account, intentional agents make active choices about what they pay attention to in pursuing those goals (for the argument that attention is intentional perception, see Gibson & Rader, 1979). All the specific joint attentional behaviors in which infants share, follow, or direct adult attention and behavior are simply different manifestations of this underlying understanding of other persons as intentional agents (for a similar account based on the notion of *intersubjective awareness,* see Baldwin, 1995). At least some support for this view is provided by developmental synchronies in the emergence of the different overt manifestations of joint attention at 9–12 months as well as by habituation studies indicating that infants first discriminate goal-directed behavior from other types of behavior at 9 months of age (Csibra, Gergely, Biró, & Koos, in press; Gergely, Nádasdy, Csibra, & Biró, 1995).

How to identify joint attentional behaviors in practice is not a question that has enjoyed as much discussion. Operationally, a key feature of each of the three types of joint attentional behavior is that at some point the infant alternates gaze between person and object, for example, looking back to the adult for a reaction as she points to a salient event. But gaze alternation is not an infallible indicator of joint attention if one is interested in the infant's ability to monitor the adult's attention to an outside entity. For example, it would not be considered joint attention if an infant playing with a toy was suddenly startled by an adult's voice or movement and so looked up to the adult's face. There is no monitoring of attention here, only a case of two entities grabbing the infant's attention alternately.

A similar interpretation might be applicable to many cases in which infants "check back" with adults as if to assure themselves of the adults' presence, as has been described so often in studies of infants' attachment to adults (e.g., Ainsworth, 1973). These checking-back behaviors may not be triadic in many cases because the infant is not integrating attention to the object and the person in one interaction, or monitoring the adult's attention, but only switching attention from the one to the other. More convincing in these types of situations from the point of view of joint attention is social referencing behavior in which the infant seeks to determine the adult's reaction to an object and then uses this reaction in deciding how to interact with that object; this would seem to incorporate much more clearly a triadic dimension in which there is a monitoring of the adult's psychological relation to the object (Campos & Stenberg, 1981; Walden & Ogan, 1988).

In the three different types of joint attentional interaction, therefore, there may be precursor forms of the behaviors that involve some key operational features (e.g., gaze alternation) but that do not involve the most important feature from a social-cognitive point of view: the infant's understanding that the other person is an intentional being like me whose attention to the world may be shared, followed into, or directed. We will examine each of these three major manifestations of early joint attention in turn, with the aim in each case of identifying the age at which infants first show evidence of this understanding.

Sharing Attention

By definition, all joint attentional skills involve infants sharing attention with a partner in some manner. We are concerned here, however, with relatively extended episodes of joint attentional engagement in which adult and infant share attention to an object of mutual interest over some measurable period of time (at least a few seconds). The prototypical example of an episode of joint attentional engagement is a situation in which adult and infant are playing with a toy and the infant looks from the toy to the adult's face and back to the toy. Such joint-engagement episodes may also include other joint attentional behaviors, such as pointing or following the adult's gaze to another object, but our concern here is with these extended periods of shared attention themselves, as characterized mainly by the infant's gaze alternation between object and adult. To avoid terminological confusion, we use the term *joint attentional engagement,* or simply *joint engagement,* for this basically interactive form of sharing attention; we use the terms *joint attentional behaviors* or *joint attentional skills* (or *social-cognitive skills*) to refer to the whole complex of infant abilities involving the sharing of attention, including such things as gaze following, imitative learning, and gestural communication.

In practice, because the adult's attention to and awareness of infant attention may be taken for granted, and because visual attention is the most directly observable measure of attention, joint-engagement episodes are typically operationally defined by the infant's alternation of gaze between an object and the adult's face, especially the eyes. Minimally, the infant must be engaged with an object on which the adult is also focused, then demonstrate her awareness of the adult's focus by looking to her face, and then return to engagement with the object. This last step is important because it demonstrates that the infant has not simply switched attention from the object to the adult but rather incorporated her attention to the adult in the context of her engagement with the object.

Yet, as previously argued, gaze alternation is neither the only indicator nor an automatic indicator of joint engagement. That is, in the first case, joint engagement with an object and another individual does not have to be visual joint engagement; infants could conceivably be visually focused on an object while attending only auditorily to the other individual. This is typically not measured in studies of joint engagement. Nor, in the second case, is gaze alternation a definitive indicator of joint engagement; infants could look to an adult's face in direct response to a noise, utterance, or movement by the adult and then return to the object. In this case, their look would be more accurately described as alternation of attention rather than as coordination of attention, in which the infant actively monitors and assesses the attention of the other to the object (for further discussion of this issue, see Bakeman & Adamson, 1984; Tomasello, 1995a). Nevertheless, despite limitations in the operationalization of this phenomenon, joint engagement remains an important indicator of infants' ability to coordinate and share attention to objects with social partners.

Given the amount of discussion concerning the role of joint engagement in the development of everything from language to theory of mind, there have been surprisingly few investigations of extended periods of joint engagement in the first year of life. The first was Trevarthen and Hubley's (1978) descriptive study of the early intersubjective development of one infant. The infant, Tracey, was observed in a laboratory 32 times during her first year of life. Tracey was seated in an infant seat, her mother was instructed to play with and talk to her, and the ensuing interactions were filmed. In her first 6 months, Tracey showed interest in both objects and her mother, but she showed no evidence of coordinating the two. Between 6 and 8 months, Tracey glanced occasionally to her mother's eyes during object play, and she watched her mother carefully during a game in which she made her mother move in synchrony with her own actions on an object. Between 8 and 9 months of age, Tracey began to exchange smiles with her mother while playing with blocks, and, at 10 months, Tracey began for the first time to look to her mother's face concerning the object, for example, when receiving it or when something entertaining was done to it. The more recent findings of Saxon, Frick, and Colombo (1997) also suggest 8–9 months as a key age in the emergence of joint engagement.

A larger and more systematic investigation into the developmental course of joint engagement was conducted by Bakeman and Adamson (1984). These researchers followed the joint-engagement skills of 28 infants longitudinally at 3-month intervals between the ages of 6 and 18 months. Mothers were asked to play with their infants—at home with a standard set of toys—as they might if they had a few minutes to devote to a spontaneous play period. This play was videotaped for 10 minutes. Infants' engagement states were coded as *Unengaged, Onlooking* (infant observing mother's activity without participating), *Persons* (infant engaging in face-to-face interaction with mother), *Objects* (infant playing only with object), *Passive Joint* (infant and mother playing together with the same object but infant showing no awareness of mother's participation or even presence), or *Coordinated Joint* (infant actively coordinating visual attention to both object and mother, i.e., joint engagement).

Bakeman and Adamson found that the frequency of occurrence of joint engagement, the percentage of time spent in joint engagement, and the mean duration of joint-engagement episodes all increased with age. Thus, whereas only about a third of 6- and 9-month-olds were observed at least once in coordinated joint engagement with their mother, 68% of 12-month-olds, 89% of 15-month-olds, and all the 18-month-olds engaged in joint engagement at least once (Adamson & Bakeman, 1985). Similarly, the mean percentage of time that infants spent in joint engagement increased significantly with age: time in joint engagement tripled between 12 and 15 months and then more than doubled again between 15 and 18 months (still, for infants of all ages, this percentage was relatively low, ranging only from 2% to 27%). The mean duration of joint-engagement episodes also increased significantly with age. The joint-engagement episodes of 18-month-olds were over three times longer on average than those of 12-month-olds. (For a study of joint engagement from 18 to 24 months of age, see Rocissano & Yatchmink, 1984.)

These findings indicate a relatively long period of time between the age at which infants first are capable of joint engagement and the age at which extended bouts of joint engagement become a significant part of their interactions with adults. Only a third of the 9-month-olds engaged in joint engagement at all (and then only for 2%, on average, of the total play period); 15- and 18-month-olds were the first to spend more than 10% of the session engaged in coordinated joint engagement, and it was not until 18 months that each infant was observed in coordinated joint engagement at least once. On the one hand, these low frequencies suggest the possibility that the earliest manifestations of joint engagement may not reflect a deep understanding of others as intentional beings. For example, infants' looks to mothers during object play could conceivably be conditioned responses to their mothers' smiles, contingent vocalizations, and other expressions of pleasure and interest (Moore & Corkum, 1994), or, similarly, infants might simply be checking for mother's presence, as is commonly described in the literature on infant attachment, which again would indicate something other than a monitoring of adult intentional relations to the world (Baldwin & Moses, 1996). On the other hand, however, it is also possible that infants are capable of triadic intersubjective interactions even earlier than 9 months of age but that some other factor, such as the ability to coordinate attention to multiple items or motor limitations, constrains them from showing this capacity with any frequency until relatively late in infancy (Trevarthen, 1979b).

Limitations of the existing studies of joint engagement preclude any definitive conclusions regarding the age of emergence of truly coordinated attention to objects and adults. For example, Rutter and Durkin (1987) reported that 9–36-month-old infants looked most to their mothers while mothers were vocalizing, and mothers in Bakeman and Adamson's (1984) study were later found to vocalize at a rate of over 16 utterances per minute (Smith, Adamson, & Bakeman, 1988)—which might suggest that infants were looking to their mothers only in response to something they said. Insofar as current results do depict the true state of affairs, however, we may conclude that infants first begin to engage in extended episodes of joint engagement with others at around 9 months of age but that such episodes do not occur frequently until 15–18 months of age or later. It should also be stressed that, to a much greater degree than the more individual measures of infants' joint attentional skills, such as gaze following and gestures, the amount of joint engagement in which infants participate at all ages depends in large measure on the skills and motivations of their social partners (Bakeman & Adamson, 1984) and on contextual factors (Ross & Lollis, 1987).

Following Attention and Behavior

It is difficult to know what infants understand of their social partners as intentional agents when they are looking to them and engaging with them in these extended periods of joint engagement. But when infants begin to follow into the attention or behavior of others in certain specific ways, a much more compelling case can be made that they understand something about the other person as an intentional agent. In particular, infants may follow into the attention of others by following the direction of their visual gaze or manual pointing gesture to an outside object, and they may follow into the behavior of others by imitating their physical actions on an object. Again, our main concern here is to identify the age at which infants seem to engage in these behaviors in a way that indicates some understanding of the adult's psychological relation or attention to the outside world.

Gaze Following

Gaze following may be seen as simply "looking where someone else is looking" (Butterworth, 1991b, p. 223), but to be of interest in the current context it must involve the infant monitoring the adult's attention to some degree. Thus, for example, if a toy makes an unexpected noise that attracts the attention of both infant and adult, the infant's look to the toy is a result of the attention-compelling properties of the toy rather than a monitoring of adult attention. Nor should we include cases in which the infant learns over repeated exposure that, when the adult does something (e.g., turns her head), an interesting sight is to be found in a certain direction. If the gaze direction of the adult is learned as a discriminative cue whose connection to phenomena in the outside world is not understood (as, perhaps, the sound of the alarm clock signals that a look toward the door will soon yield perception of Mommy), then it is not really *attention* following at all.

Scaife and Bruner (1975) conducted the first systematic study of infants' ability to follow the gaze of other persons. Infants in this study were seated facing an adult. For each trial, after establishing eye contact with the infant, the adult shifted his direction of gaze, turning his head, to one of several locations in the room. No targets that infants could see were used; the experimenter simply fixated on concealed marks on the wall. Using a cross-sectional design, these researchers tested 24 infants in the age range of 2–14 months. Results indicated that 30% of 2–4-month-olds, 39% of 5–7-month-olds, 67% of 8–10-month-olds, and 100% of 11–14-month-olds followed the adult's line of regard on at least one of two trials. Furthermore, 80% of "negative trials" involved no response: when infants responded, they usually did not turn in the wrong direction. These results would appear to suggest that even infants as young as 2–4 months of age can follow others' direction of gaze.

The problem is that proper interpretation of these findings requires some accounting of the probability that the infant will match the direction of the adult's head turn simply by chance. Collis (1977) calculated the probability of a positive response in at least one of the two trials by chance in this experiment and discovered that only infants older than 8 months were responding at levels higher than chance. This conclusion accords with Scaife and Bruner's observation that infants in the older groups often were observed to engage in checking, or "looking away, looking back at the experimenter and then looking away again," as if they were "looking for something to look at" (p. 265).

Churcher and Scaife (1982) attempted to replicate these findings with infants from 3 to 8 months of age, looking also at point following. The problem here was that they reported only ages of first occurrences of these behaviors, not frequencies or percentages, so there is no way to compare the observed results with those to be expected by chance. They do mention, however, that the most common response at all the ages studied was a look to the experimenter's eyes or to the pointing hand, "in a word, the appearance of total incomprehension" (p. 120). Corkum and Moore (1995, study 2) conducted a much more systematic study of infant gaze following—using

9

the same general procedures as Scaife and Bruner (1975) but with more experimental controls—and found that it was not until around 10 months of age that infants reliably followed the direction of adult gaze. (But, for some findings suggesting an earlier age, at least for targets close at hand, see D'Entremont, Hains, & Muir, 1997.)

On the basis of these studies, then, it appears that 8–10 months is the earliest age at which infants may be said to be following the general gaze direction of others. Other studies have attempted to explore infants' ability to use adult gaze to locate a specific target when there are several possible candidates in the general line of regard. For example, in a longitudinal study in which infants were observed every 3 months between 6 and 18 months, Morissette, Ricard, and Gouin-Décarie (1995) found that the age at which infants first could locate the correct target of the experimenter's look varied according to the angle and distance of the target with regard to the infant. Thus, only at 15 months (i.e., at some point between 12 and 15 months) did infants first begin to respond correctly when targets were located near and at a narrow angle with respect to them; only beginning at around 18 months did they respond correctly when targets were positioned at greater distances and angles.

Butterworth and his colleagues also varied target locations, this time with respect to position in the infants' scan path and visual field. At 6 months of age, infants in these studies looked to the same side of the room as the adult but were unable to locate correctly the particular target the adult fixated when more than one target was present (Butterworth, 1991a; Butterworth & Jarrett, 1991). When targets were presented one at a time, however, 6-month-olds accurately localized targets in their visual field (Butterworth & Cochran, 1980; Butterworth & Jarrett, 1991). At 12 months of age, infants were just beginning to be able to respond correctly when the target was the second object along their scan path (Butterworth & Jarrett, 1991). They were, however, still unable to localize targets behind them, outside their visual fields (Butterworth & Cochran, 1980; Butterworth & Jarrett, 1991). Infants at 18 months of age responded correctly whether targets were first or second along their scan path, and they could also search behind themselves, but only when their visual field contained no distractor targets (Butterworth & Cochran, 1980; Butterworth & Jarrett, 1991).

These results suggest that it is only between 12 and 15 months of age that infants begin to use adult gaze direction in a precise way to locate specific targets when distractors are also present. Several other studies have attempted to determine more precisely the cue that infants are using when they follow the gaze direction of others, that is, whether they use adults' head or eye orientation. In tasks comparing infants' responses when the experimenters turned their head and eyes together to targets with their responses when the experimenters directed their eyes to the targets but their head remained fac-

ing forward, Corkum and Moore (1995), Lempers (1979), and Lempers, Flavell, and Flavell (1977) all found that only infants age 12 months and older
responded correctly when eyes and head were oriented in the same direction
and that infants at all ages (i.e., through 19 months) performed poorly when
eye and head direction diverged.

Although there are some inconsistencies due to differences in scoring
criteria, position of targets, cues, and task requirements, findings across the
studies of gaze following are relatively consistent in some respects. Infants
begin to follow adult gaze direction consistently at around 10 months of age,
and they begin to use gaze direction to locate specific targets more precisely
during the period between 12 and 15 months. The extent to which infants
can do these things without the use of head direction—using eye direction
only—is currently not resolved, but in any case it is certainly not until after
these other developments.

Point Following

Most of the studies of infants' comprehension of pointing gestures use
methodologies very similar to those used for gaze following. In general, no
studies have found that infants younger than 9 months of age show any evidence of comprehending the attentional significance of pointing. For instance, Butterworth and Grover (1988, 1990) reported that 6- and 9-month-
olds were just as likely to fixate their mother's pointing hand as they were to
fixate the target to which she was pointing. Again, situational factors, such
as the location of the target relative to the adult and infant, affect younger
infants' performance. Lempers (1979) found that 9-month-olds could correctly fixate only nearby targets located in the space between them and the
adult, not more distal targets. The form of the adult's points also has a strong
effect on younger infants' point following. Murphy and Messer (1977) reported that, when sitting beside their mothers, 9-month-olds followed points
only when mothers pointed sideways *away* from the infants to a target on
their side. Points directed forward and across the infant were not yet followed
at this age.

In contrast, by 12 months of age, most infants reliably fixate targets instead of their mother's hand (Butterworth & Grover, 1988, 1990). Infants at
this age are also capable of following points both to nearby and to distant
targets (Lempers, 1979). By 14 months of age, infants in Murphy and Messer's
(1977) study were able to follow points regardless of their form (i.e., forward
or away from or across the infant). However, Desrochers, Morissette, and Ricard (1995) and Morissette et al. (1995) did not find evidence of comprehension of pointing until 15 months of age. So, as in the case of gaze following,
the age at which infants are able to locate a specific target when other objects
are present in the immediate environment is 12–15 months. As additional

evidence that infants do indeed understand something of adult attention in these interactions—as opposed to simply using head turning or pointing as discriminative cues—some investigators have also pointed out that infants of this age often check with adults after the gaze or point following; that is, they follow the adult's gaze or point and then look back to the adult for some kind of confirmation. This behavior suggests that infants understand that the adult is looking at something and that they need to confirm that they have fixated the correct object. Infants were observed to engage in checking "often" between 8 and 14 months by Scaife and Bruner (1975, p. 265) and "sometimes" at 12.5 months by Butterworth and Cochran (1980, p. 262).

Thus, on the basis of the emergence of correct localization of targets, with some checking back with the adult, we can tentatively conclude that infants engage in true attention following (of gaze and points) during the age period between 12 and 15 months. With regard to comparing the two versions of attention following, several studies have found that point following tends to emerge before gaze following (e.g., Butterworth, 1991a; Lempers, 1979; Lempers et al., 1977; Morissette et al., 1995), although in some of these studies (those by Lempers and his colleagues) the positions and distances of the targets with respect to the infant and the adult differed for the gaze- and point-following tasks, making comparison difficult. More information is needed about additional infant behaviors, such as checking, in these two situations.

Imitative Learning

Imitation is not included among joint attentional behaviors in most theoretical analyses, perhaps because there are many types of imitation and social learning that do not require the coordination of intentions/attention to external objects. For example, human neonates reproduce some adult facial gestures within minutes after birth (e.g., Meltzoff & Moore, 1977, 1989; Reissland, 1988). Although there is some debate about the existence and nature of this skill (Anisfeld, 1991; Jones, 1996), for current purposes the crucial issue is that there are no outside objects involved; infant and adult are focused on one another directly in face-to-face interaction. The kind of imitation with which we are concerned here has to do with infants following into adult behavior on an outside object. This focus is necessary because only in these kinds of triadic situations is it possible to discern whether infants are actually monitoring the adult's intentions and attention toward something in the environment. Furthermore, the very best evidence that infants are monitoring something of the adult's psychological states toward the object is when they learn a *new* behavior toward it as a result of the observation, thus demonstrating an active adaptation to the adult's relation to the object. We call this *imitative learning*.

Many early studies of imitation of actions on objects lacked appropriate controls. For example, Pawlby (1977) observed eight infants in weekly, un-structured interactions with their mothers from age 4 months to approxi-mately 10 months. She found many instances of "imitation" of simple actions on objects, for example, shaking objects or banging them together. Infants' reproduction of mothers' actions increased almost tenfold between 4 and 10 months of age. The problem is that it is impossible in such cases to know whether infants were truly imitating their mothers. Pawlby includes no men-tion either of the spontaneous rate of the "imitated" actions (i.e., the rate at which infants performed those actions in the absence of a demonstration) or of the proportion of instances in which mothers attempted unsuccessfully to get their infants to imitate. Thus, the infants in this study might have been performing the only actions that those particular objects readily afforded, with older infants more capable of performing those actions than younger infants. This issue is also an issue for the studies of Piaget (1962) and other researchers, such as Masur and Ritz (1984), McCall, Eichorn, and Hogarty (1977), and Rodgon and Kurdek (1977), all of whom report imitation of fa-miliar actions on objects in the age range 7–10 months. In addition, in all these studies, the actions were extremely simple (e.g., dangling a ring on a string or hitting two blocks together), and therefore learning of a new behav-ior was very likely not involved in most cases.

To address these issues, other studies have included control groups of various types. For example, Abravanel, Levan-Goldschmidt, and Stevenson (1976) observed infants at 3-month intervals longitudinally from 6 to 18 months and also cross-sectionally from 6 to 15 months. They included a con-trol group of infants at each of the ages studied in the cross-sectional group in order to assess spontaneous production of the modeled actions. When only those actions that were produced more frequently by the modeling group than the control group were considered, a significant increase in infants' imi-tation scores (including partial imitations) was found to occur between 9 and 12 and between 12 and 15 months of age. Again in this study, however, the actions and objects used were mostly familiar to the infants, and there is therefore no clear evidence that the infants were actually learning a novel behavior.

Killen and Uzgiris (1981) and McCabe and Uzgiris (1983), on the other hand, demonstrated for 7–22-month-old infants a variety of actions that were novel in the sense that they were performed with conventionally inappropri-ate and "abstractly shaped" objects, for example, "drinking" from a toy car and "hugging" a piece of wood (for a discussion of the different types of novelty, see Meltzoff, 1988a). Both pairs of investigators reported that imita-tion of these actions increased with age, with very little imitation of this type until 12–16 months. McCall, Parke, and Kavanaugh (1977) created other kinds of novelty in that they demonstrated actions on objects that they themselves had created (and replaced the few actions that infants performed spontaneously in free play with alternate actions). Examples of target actions included rocking a semicircular block and making a rattle out of two cups and a small cube. Results indicated that 12-month-olds successfully imitated fewer than 30% of the simpler actions on objects and only 5% of the complex ones requiring two steps. Fifteen- and 18-month-olds showed somewhat higher levels (40%–60%) of imitation of the simpler actions, but even 18-month-olds imitated fewer than a quarter of the more complex actions. Abravanel and Gingold (1985) presented 12- and 18-month-olds with such things as a rag doll stuffed inside a transparent cylinder (the target action was pushing the doll out with a drumstick) and a xylophone (the action was removing one of the xylophone's keys and striking the other two keys with it). They found no effect of modeling for the 12-month-olds—the infants reproduced the target actions no more frequently than did same-aged infants in control groups who had seen no demonstration—but they did find an effect for the 18-month-olds.

Only a few studies of imitation have included additional controls to rule out forms of social learning other than imitation. For example, it may be that, when adults pick up and play with an object, infants are likely to follow suit, that is, to become more interested in manipulating that object as well. Stimulus enhancement of this type is well known to occur with a variety of animal species in social learning situations as well (for a review, see Zentall, 1996). The problem is that stimulus enhancement effects make it more likely that infants will actively manipulate objects, thus raising the baseline probability that they will perform the target action without paying any attention to the demonstration at all. A variation of stimulus enhancement is called *emulation learning* (Tomasello, 1990, 1994); in emulation learning, infants see in the adult demonstration some affordances of the object that they might not have discovered on their own and then want to reproduce them.[1] It is important to distinguish this interesting and important form of social learning from imitative learning because it is a process in which infants learn about objects instead of about the attention or behavior of other human beings. There is also the possibility in some cases that children may mimic an adult motor pattern without understanding its intentional significance, the way that a parrot mimics human speech; this process should also be distinguished from imitative learning (Tomasello, 1996a).

Only a few studies have included the control conditions necessary to demonstrate that infants are indeed reproducing a novel action by following

---

[1] Note that, if there is only one readily available behavioral means that may be used to exploit an affordance of an object for a given species, it may appear as though one individual is imitating another when in fact the attempt for both is simply to reproduce the affordance in the easiest manner.

into adult attention and behavior. First, Meltzoff (1988b) randomly assigned 9-month-olds to one of four groups: an imitation group, which received models, and three control groups that did not. The control groups included a baseline control group, in which infants were simply given the objects to play with; an "adult-touching" control group, in which the experimenter only passively held objects instead of modeling actions on them; and an "adult-manipulation" control group, in which the experimenter demonstrated the end results of the target actions using different means from those modeled for the imitation group. These last two controls were designed to address the possibility that any reproduction of the model could be due to stimulus enhancement and/or emulation as opposed to imitation. Results indicated that half the infants in the imitation group reproduced two or more of the three demonstrated actions; fewer than 20% of them imitated all three actions. One problem here is that the emulation-affordances explanation might still hold in some cases. For example, one of the modeled actions was pressing a button on a box to produce a beeping noise. Infants in the adult-manipulation condition were shown that the box could make a beeping noise, but they were not shown that the button on the box could be pressed. This information might be all that the infants in the imitation group tuned in to.

A stronger demonstration of imitative learning in infants was provided by Meltzoff (1988a). In this study, 14-month-olds were shown a number of actions on objects, one of which is of special interest here. The object was a box with a translucent panel on top that lit up when touched. The action demonstrated was bending forward at the waist and touching the forehead to the light panel. This task is especially interesting in the current context, not only because this action was convincingly demonstrated to be novel (over two dozen pilot subjects as well as the 24 control subjects in the study never once produced it), but also because there is clearly more than one behavioral means to produce the end result. Indeed, it might be supposed that the most straightforward way for the infants to depress and thereby to illuminate the light panel would be to touch it with their hand. Meltzoff found that two-thirds of the infants in the imitation group imitated the unusual head-touching action even though 1 week had elapsed between the demonstration and the infants' first opportunity to imitate. Although simple mimicry is possible in this situation (i.e., infants might have reproduced the adult's action with no understanding of its intended result), this seems unlikely given Meltzoff's report that infants "directly and confidently set about producing the target actions when given the test objects" (Meltzoff, 1988a, p. 473) and, after successful imitation, often looked up to the adult and smiled. Similar results were obtained by Tomasello, Savage-Rumbaugh, and Kruger (1993), who found that 18-month-olds, the youngest children studied, reproduced both means and end result on the majority of their "simple" tasks and a significant minority of their "complex" tasks, most of which had multiple possible means to the modeled end result.

Finally, two recent studies have tested more directly what infants understand about others' intentions using imitation paradigms. In the first, Meltzoff (1995) presented 18-month-old infants with two types of demonstrations (along with the control demonstrations from his previous studies—see above). Infants in the target demonstration group saw the adult perform actions on objects, much as in Meltzoff's previous studies. Infants in the intention demonstration group, however, saw the adult try but fail to achieve the end results of the target actions; for example, the adult tried to pull two parts of an object apart but never succeeded in separating them (infants in this group thus never saw the target actions performed). Meltzoff found that infants in both these groups reproduced the target actions equally well; that is, they appeared to understood what the adult intended to do and performed that action instead of mimicking the adult's actual surface behavior.

In the second study, infants' understanding of others' intentions was investigated from a different point of view. Whereas Meltzoff (1995) presented infants with demonstrations of unfulfilled intentions, Carpenter, Akhtar, and Tomasello (1998) studied infants' imitation of accidental and intentional actions. In this study, 14–18-month-old infants watched an adult perform some two-action sequences on objects that made interesting results occur. One action of the modeled sequences was marked vocally as intentional ("There!"), and one action was marked vocally as accidental ("Woops!")—with order systematically manipulated across sequences. Infants were then given a chance to make the result occur themselves. Overall, infants imitated almost twice as many of the adult's intentional actions as her accidental ones, indicating that they differentiated between the two types of actions and that they were able to reproduce, again, what the adult meant to do and not her actual surface behavior.

Reproducing adults' behavior is something infants do from a very early age. The primary issue of concern here is when they reproduce actions on objects in a way that allows us to be confident that they are tuning in to the adult's intentions and attention on outside entities. The first clear evidence of this is found at around 14 months of age, although the performance of some infants at 9 months of age is suggestive.

Summary

Attention following and imitation are not typically discussed as two instances of the same underlying phenomenon. But both involve the infant seeing the adult do something toward an outside entity and then attempting to follow into the adult's intentions and attention in the situation. It might be hypothesized that imitative learning is the more difficult of these skills because both gaze following and point following require only that the infant turn her head—something that she has been doing in orienting behaviors from soon after birth—whereas imitative learning requires the production of behaviors that are in most cases more complex and in all cases at least somewhat more novel. However, to our knowledge, no studies have examined these skills longitudinally in the same group of children to see if this is indeed the case.

Directing Attention and Behavior

Human infants demonstrate their understanding of adults as intentional agents, not only by following into their attention and behavior, but also by attempting to direct their attention and behavior to outside entities through acts of intentional communication. Under the broadest definition, even infants' earliest behavior is communicative in the sense that adults are able to interpret it and respond appropriately; for example, a newborn's cries may indicate to her mother that she is hungry or in pain, or an infant's reach toward an object may indicate to her father that she wishes to have that object. But intentional communication refers to those instances in which the infant "realizes *as he emits his signals* that they will serve a communicative purpose"; the signals are "aimed at the adult listener, [instead of] at the goal itself" (Bates, Benigni, Bretherton, Camaioni, & Volterra, 1979, p. 34). Given an infant signal of some kind (a ritualized behavior not physically effective in obtaining a goal by itself) that is produced intentionally (indicated by persistence, sometimes with alternating means, until the goal is reached), the main evidence that infants' behavior is intentionally communicative is that they direct their signals toward another person, alternating their gaze between that person and the goal. Such behavior indicates that infants understand the other person, not just as another physical object to be physically manipulated, but as a communicative partner who can perceive and respond to their signals.

Bates et al. (1975) observed two main purposes for which infants intentionally communicate with adults about outside entities. On the one hand, infants may desire an object or activity and therefore attempt to direct the adult's behavior to help obtain that goal; for example, the infant may reach to an object in a stylized manner (e.g., opening and closing hand), whine, and look to her mother. Because they request adult behavior, these are called *imperative gestures*. On the other hand, infants may simply desire that the adult attend to something in the environment, to share attention to it; for example, the infant may hold up an object to show it to an adult. Because they request adult attention, not behavior, these are called *declarative gestures*. Intentional communication for either of these purposes involves the infant's understanding that adults are psychological beings whose intentions and attention may be brought into line with their own intentions and attention. It should be noted that the best-known infant gesture—pointing—may serve either of these functions. The development of imperatives and declaratives will be discussed in turn.

Imperatives

Infants reach for objects and whine from a fairly early age, but, for these behaviors to be considered intentional communication, there must be some evidence that the infants are directing their reaching and whining to the adult whose behavior they wish to influence, not to the object itself. The problem is that infants may learn associatively that certain behaviors on their part reliably lead to certain results without any understanding of the role of the other person (Gómez, Sarriá, & Tamarit, 1993). A look to the other during the act of communication would, then, reflect only an expectation that the other was about to react—the way an infant might look to the ground expectantly as she dropped an object—not any understanding that the other person must perceive the signal and then decide what to do about it. It is for this reason that some researchers have insisted that the infant's looks to the communicative partner be directed at the face. On the assumption that infants will look to the parts of the adult that are relevant to achieving their goal, looks to the adult's hands or legs would indicate infants' understanding of the adult as an animate object who was about to move and do something, but a look to the face, which is not directly involved in moving the adult or achieving any physical goal, is a much better indication that the infant understands the adult as a psychological being.

Bates et al. (1975) were among the first to examine infants' intentionally communicative gestures in detail. For example, they observed an infant just under 10 months of age attempting to obtain a box that her mother was holding in her arms by pulling at her mother's arms, pushing her whole body against the floor, and approaching the box from different angles—without once looking up at the mother's face. By 11 or 12 months, however, this infant had begun to alternate her gaze between a desired object and the adult's face when requesting; at around 13 months, she began to include requestive pointing in these sequences. Interestingly, another infant at around 12 months did not always look at the adult during her initial command, but, if the listener failed to respond, she would look to the adult's face and issue a more insistent command. Similar results were obtained in further studies by Bates and her colleagues with larger samples. Bates et al. (1979), for example, found that requests increased steadily in terms of both frequency and ritualization during the period between 9 and 13 months, although this study included no measure of gaze direction (with the result that looks specifically to the face could not be determined). Likewise, Bretherton, McNew, and Beeghly-Smith (1981) determined by maternal report that, whereas 10½-month-olds only rarely requested objects by pointing or other ritualized motions or sounds, half to two-thirds of 13-month-olds did so.

Other researchers report similar findings. For example, Bruner (1977) reported that requestive pointing first emerged in one infant at the age of 13 months, and Bruner (1982) reported that gaze alternation during requests appeared in his subjects between 10 and 15 months of age. Similarly, in a longitudinal study of seven infants' requesting behavior, Sugarman (Sugarman, 1984; Sugarman-Bell, 1978) distinguished between "coordinated person-object orientation" and "object-oriented acts" (i.e., infant behaviors that were and were not intentionally communicative requests). She found that some infants first began to direct adults' behavior in coordinated person-object orientation at around 8–10 months of age but that only at 13–14 months did a substantial number of infants' interactions with mothers include such intentionally communicative behavior. Zinober and Martlew (1985) likewise found a large increase in the number of their two subjects' requestive gestures between 10 and 12 months.

Since all these studies involved infants in natural interactions with their mothers in a fairly restricted set of circumstances, it could be argued that perhaps infants were not seen in all the situations necessary for observing their full communicative competence. Harding and Golinkoff (1979), therefore, attempted to elicit vocal and gestural imperatives through the use of "frustration episodes." In these episodes, an attractive object was placed just out of reach of infants while their mothers, who had already shown infants that they could help obtain the object, ignored infants and pretended to read. Unfortunately for current purposes, results were reported, not in terms of age, but on the basis of infants' scores on a test of causal development. None of the infants at Piaget's stage 4 of causal development (mean age = 9.7 months) showed any intentionally communicative behavior. Just over 70% of infants at stage 5 (mean age = 11.6 months), on the other hand, produced at least two vocal and/or gestural imperatives during the frustration episodes. Similarly, Perucchini and Camaioni (1993) also used procedures designed to elicit imperatives. These researchers observed infants longitudinally at 11 and 14 months of age in two situations in which windup toys were activated for a few seconds by the experimenter but then left inactive. Nine of the 14 infants in this study pointed imperatively at the windup toys at 11 months, and all of them did so at 14 months—in apparent attempts to have the experimenter restart the toy (it is unclear whether these researchers required looks to the experimenter's face during pointing, however).

Declaratives

Infants use such declarative gestures as holding up and showing objects and pointing to objects in order to attract adults' attention to outside entities. The use of these gestures would thus seem to imply that the infant understands that adults have attentional states that they may be induced to change by means of communicative signals of various sorts. Declarative gestures also suggest that infants value sharing adults' attention simply for its own sake. For many researchers, therefore, declarative gestures are a much clearer indication that infants understand other persons as intentional agents than are imperative gestures (Camaioni, 1993; Tomasello, 1995a). It is thus interesting and important, in this regard, that there is very little evidence for declarative gestures either in nonhuman primates (Gómez et al., 1993) or in children with autism (Baron-Cohen, 1993).

For most infants, showing objects and pointing to objects both emerge in the age period between 10 and 13 months. With regard to showing (i.e., holding objects up toward the adult's face, typically with a bent arm to distinguish the gesture from one giving or offering an object), age of onset is consistent across a variety of studies. Bakeman and Adamson (1986), Bates et al. (1979), and Ross and Lollis (1987) found some infrequent showing beginning at 9 months of age; Bates et al. (1975) and Bruner (1977) observed the first showing in their subjects at 10 months; and two-thirds of mothers in Bretherton et al.'s (1981) study reported that their 10½-month-olds showed objects. The findings with regard to pointing are not quite as consistent, at least partly because even 3-month-old infants sometimes extend their index fingers toward people and objects (Bates et al., 1975; Hannan, 1987), thus making indications that they are using their gesture communicatively even more important. Gaze alternation between the object and the adult during pointing typically is considered an indication that infants are checking to see whether adults are paying attention to their communicative signal. The first instances of points at objects that are accompanied by such gaze alternation occur between 9 and 10½ months of age (Bretherton et al., 1981; Lempers, 1979; Leung & Rheingold, 1981; Murphy & Messer, 1977).

It should be noted that, whereas declarative showing and pointing (with gaze alternation) first appear at around 9–10 months of age, they do not occur with great frequency until 12–15 months of age (Bakeman & Adamson, 1986; Bretherton et al., 1981; Lempers, 1979; Lempers et al., 1977; Ross & Lollis, 1987). In addition, there are some indications that, at these younger ages, infants may not yet be fully coordinating their attention to both object and adult, despite the presence of some form of gaze alternation (Franco & Butterworth, 1996). With particular regard to pointing, infants appear to pass through a "peculiar transitional period" at the early ages in which they point to the object, "swing around and *point at the adult* with the same gesture, and return to look at the object and point toward it once again" (Bates et al., 1975, p. 217). This calls into question the interpretation that infants' gaze alternation serves to determine whether the adult perceives their gesture toward the object.

Also troubling is the finding that early declarative pointing may depend on the location of the object to which the infant is pointing. Zinober and Martlew (1985), for instance, found that gaze alternation during pointing to nearby objects appeared by 10 months, whereas in the case of distal objects it was not observed until 14 months. Likewise, in a longitudinal investigation of four infants' gaze alternation during pointing, Masur (1983) found that, whereas infants first pointed with gaze alternation at 9 months of age, they did not point to objects that were not in the possession of the mother until around 13 months of age. Finally, the temporal characteristics of the gaze alternation accompanying infants' points undergo change with age as well. At 12 months of age or younger, infants typically point to an object and then turn to look at the adult; at 14 months, they point and look to the adult at the same time; and, by 16 months, infants first look to the adult as if to see whether she is attending, only then pointing to the object (Desrochers et al., 1995; Franco & Butterworth, 1996).

These findings of quantitative and qualitative differences in the nature of early declarative pointing during the age period between 10 and 16 months suggest that infants are only gradually learning about how gestures achieve their communicative goals. Thus, it may happen that infants' early non-communicative pointing to objects evokes responses from adults, which they then come to expect. If caregivers reliably provide expressions of interest and attention following infants' pointing, they may learn to expect these reactions and turn to the adult following pointing in anticipation of them (Moore & Corkum, 1994). Such behaviors as checking with the adult before pointing are not easily explained in this manner, however, and therefore very likely reflect older infants' deeper understanding of adults' attention per se.

This is not to say that by 16 months infants understand all the subtleties involved in adult attention; they clearly do not. For example, Lempers et al. (1977) presented infants with a variety of objects and asked them to show the objects to adults. Whereas 12-month-olds did occasionally show the objects, they most often did so without regard for the orientation of the objects to the adults, even after extensive prompting. For example, when asked to show a picture, these infants did not hold the picture vertically and right side up to take account of the adult's perspective. They also attempted to show objects to adults whose hands were covering their eyes or who had their eyes closed. Eighteen-month-olds sometimes presented the picture in its appropriate orientation to the adult, but more often they did not. Half the 18-

month-olds removed the adult's hands from her eyes before attempting to show, but none responded correctly when the adult's eyes were closed. Povinelli and Eddy (1996) found that, even after their second birthdays, many children will gesture to adults whose eyes are closed. The overall point is that, by 16 months of age, infants seem to have a good understanding that the adult has intentional control over her attention, but they may not have mastered such subtleties as the particular organs with which adults attend or the angle from which they view things.

Only a few studies have investigated the sequencing of the emergence of imperative and declarative gestures, and the results are mixed. Perucchini and Camaioni (1993) found that imperative pointing generally preceded declarative pointing, but, because subjects were observed at only two time points (11 and 14 months), many displayed the two types of gestures for the first time at the same age (also, the experimental and coding procedures may have influenced these results).[2] Zinober and Martlew (1985) also found that, in general, instrumental (i.e., imperative) gestures preceded deictic (i.e., declarative) gestures in their two subjects, although, in this study, instrumental gestures included a wider range of gestures than those considered here and these researchers might also not have distinguished between imperative and declarative giving. When infants' points were considered separately, however, Zinober and Martlew found that deictic pointing preceded instrumental pointing. Bates et al. (1975) did not explicitly examine which type of gesture emerged first, although it appears that, in the Bates et al. (1979) study, declarative gestures emerged before imperative gestures.

Language

Most researchers place the emergence of infants' first words after the emergence of communicative gestures, that is, beginning around 12–13 months on average for Western, middle-class infants (e.g., Bates et al., 1979). Infants' first words are often nonreferential in the sense that they serve simply to mark an important social event (e.g., *bye-bye, thank you*). Referential words used to make reference to external objects or activities (e.g., *ball, up*) usually emerge a month or two later (Bates et al., 1979). There is very little evidence concerning whether imperative or declarative uses of referential words emerge earlier in development.

---

[2] For example, during Perucchini and Camaioni's (1993) declarative-inducing events, the experimenter alternated gaze between the infant and the event—e.g., moving butterflies—and thus infants might have been less likely to point out the event to her than if she had pretended not to see it. It also appears as though gaze alternation was required for the infants to be given credit for declarative but not imperative points.

Summary

Despite variations in experimental procedure, setting, coding, and scoring criteria across studies and skills, it may be concluded that, overall, infants' major social-cognitive skills all emerge largely within the age period between 9 and 15 months. Infants begin participating in episodes of joint attentional engagement with adults at around 9 months of age, but it is only at some point between 12 and 15 months that joint engagement becomes a relatively routine part of infant-adult interactions. Infants follow an adult's gaze and pointing at levels higher than would be expected by chance by 10 months of age, and they become capable of localizing with some accuracy the targets of adults' gaze and points even when several targets are present by 15 months of age (sometimes checking back with the adult). Although infants reproduce adults' behavior within minutes of birth, only at some point between 9 and 14 months do they begin to engage in truly imitative learning of novel actions on objects. Infants first produce intentionally communicative imperative and declarative gestures and vocalizations at around 10 months of age, with signs of the careful monitoring of the other's attention in the months that follow (along with the emergence of conventional language).

There are no studies in which the development of all these social-cognitive skills has been followed longitudinally together in the same children. There are, however, a few studies that have investigated more than one of these skills at a time. For example, several studies have investigated the relation between attention following, in the form of the comprehension of pointing, and attention and behavior directing, in the form of production of pointing. Desrochers et al. (1995), in a longitudinal study, and Lempers (1979), Lempers et al. (1977), and Leung and Rheingold (1981), in cross-sectional studies, all found that comprehension of pointing (attention following) tended to emerge on average slightly before production of communicative pointing, although no significant correlations were found between these two skills among infants. Desrochers et al. (1995) found significant correlations between each of these skills and later language.

Bates et al. (1979) investigated several of these social-cognitive skills—in particular, intentionally communicative gestures, words, and imitation (although the imitation tasks that Bates et al. used consisted of vocal and gestural imitation and were thus not imitative learning tasks because they were familiar actions and were not directed to outside objects)—together in a sample of 25 infants observed longitudinally four times between the ages of 9½ and 12½ months. They found that infants' scores on each of the intentionally communicative gesture measures were highly interrelated, that infants' scores on these measures (especially pointing) were good predictors of language development, and that infants' imitation scores predicted their scores on both gestures and language. Bates et al. (1979) also included tests of object-related skills. They found that object permanence and spatial relations in general were not highly correlated with communicative development or imitation. In addition, several other studies have investigated the connection between joint engagement and early language (for reviews, see Tomasello, 1988; and the next section).

In general, however, it is fair to say that very little is known about the interrelations among these skills within individual infants, either in terms of order of emergence or in terms of their possible intercorrelations. Because they all have been hypothesized to rest on the same underlying understanding, that is, the understanding that other people attend to things and behave intentionally toward them, one would expect the development of each of these skills to be related to the others. One hypothesis is that infants should be able to coordinate attention to an object and another person (i.e., show joint engagement) before they are able to follow into and direct others' attention and behavior because the former requires only checking with the adult (looking to the face) whereas the latter skills require following or directing the adult's attention to some specific outside entity. The sequencing of skills also should depend in part on various performance factors having to do with the response demands on infants in particular tasks; for example, it is very likely easier to look where someone is looking than to reproduce others' complex actions on objects. A major goal of the current study, therefore, was to provide a more comprehensive look at the ontogeny of these various skills of early social cognition—sharing attention, following of attention and behavior, and directing of attention and behavior—and how they relate to one another sequentially and within infants.

JOINT ENGAGEMENT AND EARLY LANGUAGE

Owing mainly to the theoretical and empirical work of Bruner, a number of researchers interested in how young children begin to acquire language during the second year of life have also investigated processes of joint attention. The focus of these researchers has been almost exclusively on the interacting adult-child dyad and how the dyad establishes and maintains relatively extended episodes of joint engagement. The basic idea is that joint-engagement interactions are based on social processes more basic than language and that they therefore make language acquisition possible by creating a shared referential framework within which the child may experientially ground the language used by adults. Said another way, if linguistic symbols are social conventions that gain their communicative significance by "agreement" among users, the child can acquire active use of a linguistic convention only if she enters into this agreement by participating in the kinds of social interactions (language games) that constitute that convention's communicative significance. Also important to the process are the specific ways in which adults introduce infants to new pieces of language within these interactions that may make it either easier or more difficult for children to acquire their conventional uses.

Brief History and Definition

Bruner (1975a, 1975b, 1977, 1983) laid out a way of thinking and talking about language acquisition, not in terms of the structures of formal linguistics, but rather in terms of processes of communication. The basic argument is that there is a continuity in the process by which children communicate with others prelinguistically and linguistically. At the root of this commonality are processes of joint attention. Infants learn to comprehend new pieces of language by following into the adult's attentional focus as she refers to various entities in the immediate environment. The kinds of situations in which this is most likely to occur are relatively routinized interactive sequences in which the infant has ample opportunity to comprehend the adult's behavioral and communicative intentions without the aid of language itself. When infants learn a new piece of language in such situations, they begin to use it with the same communicative purposes for which they used such prelinguistic forms of communication as deictic and other gestures.

Bruner's basic point about comprehension is that infants do not have adult-like linguistic skills to help them understand what is going on in a situation and that they must therefore have other ways of establishing a shared referential framework in their social interactions. New pieces of language are first comprehended in these kinds of interactions precisely because their functional significance is redundant with some aspect of the infant's already-established understanding of the situation. Bruner (1981, 1983) called these kinds of social interactions—including everything from diaper-changing routines to recurrent games with particular toys—*formats* for early language acquisition. These formats have three essential features: (*a*) a simple content, in that there are a small number of attentionally salient and simple elements whose interrelations may be easily understood by the infant; (*b*) a number of repetitions in the infant's experience so that she may abstract a task structure that has a predictable sequence, with perhaps some semipredictable variations; and (*c*) a clear role structure for the participants, most often reversible so that the infant may at first play a more passive role and then later a more active role. Bruner (1983) also stressed that many early formats have a playful affective tone as well, which not only motivates the infants but also allows them to "distance" themselves from the proceedings enough to consider their own role in the interaction. It should be noted that, although Bruner did not stress the fact, his theoretical position is open to the addendum that,

25

if infant and adult at some point are able to establish joint attentional interactions without the routinization deemed necessary at the earliest stages of development, this would still provide a shared referential framework conducive to the learning of new linguistic forms.

Because Bruner's account of the social interactional bases of early language was created to oppose the nativistic theories of language acquisition prevailing at the time—and so is often called the *social-pragmatic approach* to language acquisition—much of his focus was on the adult's role in structuring a situation for the child within which she could begin to enter into conventional linguistic communication, what eventually came to be called adult *scaffolding*. This constituted the essence of what Bruner (1983) referred to as the language-acquisition support system, or LASS, which served as a counterpoint to Chomsky's (1968) innate language-acquisition device, or LAD. But it is clear from Bruner's accounts that he was also aware of the contributions that the child was making to these interactions as her social-cognitive skills of following into and directing the adult's attention gradually developed, as outlined in the discussion above of joint attention as social cognition.

Joint-Engagement Episodes and Early Language

Bruner and his colleagues initiated two lines of investigation that illustrated this way of looking at early language acquisition, with some subsequent follow-ups by other investigators in each case. One line focused more on joint action in the prelinguistic period and the establishing of routines and mothers' language in them, and the other focused more on joint engagement and language use after the child had acquired some language skills. First, Ratner and Bruner (1978) tracked two infants' learning and practice of two versions of a hiding-finding game with their mothers from 5 to 9 months of age. In each case, over successive episodes the game became more routinized, but with some variations introduced periodically by the mother to keep the game lively. Over time, each infant became able to predict certain steps in the game, and even variations, and eventually became able to switch roles with the mother, actually hiding things from her. The mothers' language was also highly predictable, both in terms of content and in terms of timing in the game structure, again with some limited variations. Along these same lines, Bakeman and Adamson (1986) found that the vast majority of all conventionalized acts (mainly gestures and words) by both infants and their mothers were produced when they were jointly engaged with an object (both participants focusing on the same object; Bakeman & Adamson's, 1984, passive joint engagement and coordinated joint engagement). Similarly, although they did not analyze the social interactional situations in detail, Acredolo and Goodwyn (1988) reported that many of children's early symbolic gestures that are learned via imitation seem to arise and occur in particular places in well-practiced social routines.

The second line of research was initiated by Ninio and Bruner (1978), who tracked one child's establishment of a set of book-reading routines with his mother from 8 to 18 months of age. From the beginning of the study, there was a routinized nonlinguistic "dialogue" about the book-reading game between child and mother, with a clear turn-taking structure. Gradually over the months, the child became able to switch roles with the mother, doing such things as asking her to name pictures for him (pictures that previously she had asked him to name). Also, on many occasions, the child came to substitute newly learned pieces of language for the nonlinguistic gestures and vocalizations that had served as his turn in previous episodes, for example, naming a picture when previously he had pointed to it and vocalized (as the mother had done in previous episodes). Snow and Goldfield (1983) provided further support for these findings in their observations of another mother-infant dyad engaged in repeated episodes of a book-reading routine. Like Ninio and Bruner, they found that the child's language emerged most often in the most predictable parts of the routine interaction and, moreover, that at these junctures the infant often adopted precisely the language the mother had used in previous episodes of book reading.

Bruner's arguments, and these empirical investigations supporting them, are about what is *necessary* for an infant to break into the world of conventionalized communication known as language. Tomasello and Todd (1983) took the argument a step further by investigating the possibility that individual differences in the way that mother-child dyads established and maintained joint-engagement interactions might be related to various aspects of the child's early language development. Using an adaptation of Bakeman and Adamson's (1984) coding scheme for joint engagement, these investigators observed six mother-infant dyads at monthly intervals from the infant's 12th to 18th month. The main finding was a very high correlation between the amount of time that infants spent in joint engagement with their mothers during the six observation periods of the study and the size of the infants' vocabulary at the end of the study ($r = .84$). Several lines of evidence, including cross-lagged correlations, supported the hypothesis that it was the joint-engagement episodes that supported the infants' acquisition of words, not the other way around. Along similar lines, Smith et al. (1988) also found a positive correlation between the amount of time that infants spent in joint engagement with their mothers at 15 months and their vocabulary size at 18 months ($r = .46$).

A variation on this approach was reported by Tomasello, Mannle, and Kruger (1986), who investigated the relation between joint engagement and early language in triadic interactions among mothers and their twin infants—who are known to be significantly delayed in early language development (for a review, see Tomasello, Mannle, & Barton, 1989). The reasoning was that it would be very difficult for an adult to establish and maintain dyadic joint-engagement interactions with either child in this more complex and demanding interactional situation (see also Schaffer & Liddell, 1984) and that this might be related to the delay in language acquisition characteristic of twins. Using the same coding scheme as Tomasello and Todd (1983), the investigators observed the dyadic social interaction of 12 singleton children with their mothers and the triadic interactions of six twin pairs (12 children) with their mothers. The main finding with regard to joint engagement was that the twin infants spent only one-tenth of the time in dyadic joint engagement with their mothers that the singleton infants spent with their mothers (with the figure being closer to one-third when the triadic form of joint engagement including all three participants was included for the twins as well). Most important, positive correlations were found between the time spent in joint engagement at 15 months of age and vocabulary size at both 15 and 21 months of age for both singletons and twins analyzed separately as well as for the sample as a whole ($r = .73$ and .74 for 15 and 21 months, respectively).

It should be pointed out that there is one important difference—previously alluded to—between Bruner's notion of a language-acquisition format and the operationalization of joint engagement used in these studies of individual differences. In these studies, the joint-engagement interaction may or may not have been a routine that the mother and infant had established over time. The dyads (and triads) were presented with a novel set of toys, and any interactions in which they came to share attention to one or more of those toys with others were counted as joint-engagement episodes. Presumably, in the months preceding these studies, mothers and their children had developed some generalized procedures for interacting with objects and toys that they then applied in the experimental situation, but this was not explicitly investigated. The important point is that both routine interactions with particular objects and more generic types of joint-engagement episodes that are established more spontaneously are both important for scaffolding the infants' early linguistic interaction and learning. The reason is that both serve to provide a delimited, well-defined, and socially shared referential context independent of language, to which any novel language may be assumed to refer.

Adult Directing and Following into Infant Attention

Nonlinguistically based episodes of joint engagement may play an important, perhaps even a necessary, role in children's early language development, but they are obviously not the whole story. Children also must experience the actual linguistic symbols that they are to learn. It turns out that joint attentional processes are an important aspect of this process as well, in some fairly specific ways.

A consistent finding in the literature on early word learning is that young children who have mothers who interact with them in a directive interpersonal style—what Nelson (1973) called a "social-regulative style"—have smaller early vocabularies than other children, especially with respect to object names. Using a number of different operationalizations of maternal directiveness and children's language, this negative relation has been found by Nelson (1973), who looked at all maternal utterances in imperative syntactic form; by Akhtar, Dunham, and Dunham (1991) and Della Corte, Benedict, and Klein (1983), who looked at all maternal utterances with a prescriptive pragmatic function; and even by Harris, Jones, Brookes, and Grant (1986), Tomasello et al. (1986), and Tomasello and Todd (1983), who all used nonverbal measures of maternal directiveness.

Nelson (1981) reviewed earlier studies that had found this same negative relation and identified a number of different hypotheses that might explain it. Her preferred hypothesis was that young children are learning from their mothers the functional significance of language. Children who hear language used more for referential functions will learn many object names to serve this same function (so-called referential children), whereas children who hear language used regulatively and directively will be led to learn a few more general purpose terms (e.g., *gimme* for all objects) to regulate and direct the behavior of others (so-called expressive children).

Tomasello (1988) and Tomasello and Farrar (1986a), on the other hand, hypothesized that the key factor in this negative relation was joint attention, albeit on a more micro level than in classical investigations of relatively extended episodes of joint engagement. These investigators argued that, when an adult uses an unknown piece of language in an attempt to direct the young child's attention to something new, to comprehend the communicative significance of that new language the child must shift her current attention and attempt to determine the adult's focus. On the other hand, when the adult uses an unknown piece of language in an attempt to follow into the child's current focus of attention, the child need not switch her attention at all. In this case, coordination of attention between adult and child depends on the adult's ability to determine the child's current focus of attention, which is arguably more sophisticated than the child's ability to determine the adult's focus of attention. It should be noted that, in theory, this effect should hold whether or not the child is engaged in any kind of extended episode of joint engagement; however, it may be that, in extended episodes of joint engagement, the infant may be more aware of, or more motivated toward, the goal of coordinating attention with the adult.

Support for this interpretation was provided in two studies by Tomasello and Farrar (1986a). In the first study, 24 children were videotaped at 15 and

21 months of age in naturalistic interactions with their mothers. Episodes of joint engagement were identified using a modified version of the Bakeman and Adamson (1984) coding scheme, and, in a second coding pass, features of mothers' and children's language were transcribed and coded. It was found, first, that both mothers and children spoke more and carried out longer conversations inside than outside joint-engagement episodes. Most important to current concerns, it was also found that mothers who followed into their children's already-established focus of attention as they spoke to them inside these joint-engagement episodes at 15 months of age had children with larger vocabularies at 21 months of age ($r = .62$). On the other hand, mothers who more often used their language in an attempt to direct their children's attention anew in these episodes had children with smaller vocabularies at 21 months ($r = -.46$).

The second study attempted to provide experimental support for this correlational finding—which might conceivably be due to any number of factors, including an influence of the child's language on the mother's use of language. An adult experimenter attempted to teach a novel word to 10 17-month-old children in one of two ways. In the "follow-in" condition, the adult used the new word to indicate an object on which the child's attention was already focused. In the "direct" condition, the adult used the new word in an attempt to direct the child's attention to an object on which she was *not* currently focused. A subsequent comprehension test found that the children were better at comprehending the novel word if they had experienced it in the follow-in condition, thus providing support for the correlational finding. Asking this same question, Dunham, Dunham, and Curwin (1993) used a larger sample of 18-month-old children and added a number of other control conditions and analyses. They also found that adult models that followed into the child's already-established attentional focus on an object facilitated children's word learning relative to models that were used in an attempt to direct the child's attention to something new.[3]

Akhtar et al. (1991) provided a very important refinement of the hypothesis that young children's word learning is facilitated when an adult uses new language in an attempt to follow into, rather than to direct, their attentional focus. In a study of naturally occurring conversations between mothers and their 13-month-old children, these investigators distinguished between two different kinds of directives in adult speech to children. That is, in a situation in which an adult and a child are playing with a ball, the adult might do one

---

[3] Vibbert and Bornstein (1989) and Smith et al. (1988) found positive relations between mothers' attempts to draw their children's attention to objects and early language, but in neither of these studies did investigators distinguish cases in which children were already focused on the object from cases in which they were not.

of two things that could be considered directive. On the one hand, the adult might attempt to direct the child's attention to some new object or toy (called *lead prescriptives,* e.g., "Now let's play with the truck"). On the other hand, the adult might stay focused on the ball but direct the child's attention to some new aspect of that object (called *follow prescriptives,* e.g., "It has stripes"). The former case is analogous to a change of conversational topic, whereas the latter is analogous to simply making a novel comment on an established topic.

What Akhtar et al. found was that mothers' use of lead prescriptives at 13 months of age was negatively related to children's productive vocabulary size 9 months later at 22 months of age ($r = -.33$), whereas mothers' use of follow prescriptives was positively related to vocabulary size at this same age ($r = .78$). This refinement demonstrates that the directives that are negatively related to children's language development are mainly those that force them to focus on an entirely new entity, as was the case in both the Tomasello and Farrar (1986a) and the Dunham et al. (1993) experimental studies. It may also account for the positive findings that mothers' "encouragement of attention" is sometimes positively related to children's language development (Ruddy & Bornstein, 1982; Tamis-LeMonda & Bornstein, 1989; Vibbert & Bornstein, 1989), as this may often occur within the boundaries of a shared topic. In all, it is clear that utterances that in some sense follow into the child's already-established focus of attention make the task of learning a new word more manageable for nascent language learners.

It must be emphasized that, as children get older, there may be less of an advantage for linguistic models closely tailored to their current attention and interests. Indeed, in subsequent experiments on word learning, Baldwin (1991, 1993a, 1993b) has found that, under some circumstances, young children can switch their attention to the adult's focus to learn a new word from as young as 19 months of age (and they never assign a label to a referent simply because they are looking at it when the adult utters a novel label). In a series of studies, Tomasello and his colleagues found the same thing for children in the age period between 18 and 24 months (e.g., Akhtar, Carpenter, & Tomasello, 1996; Akhtar & Tomasello, 1996; Tomasello & Akhtar, 1995; Tomasello & Barton, 1994; for a review, see Tomasello, in press). The likely scenario is that children are able to follow adult attention in some limited situations from the beginning of language development; it is just that initially they are not very skilled at this when the task is to determine the precise referent that the adult intends when using a novel piece of language in a directive manner, perhaps especially in more difficult language-learning situations (e.g., with multiple potential referents in the immediate context). As development proceeds, they become more skilled at following adult attention to novel referents in a wider variety of situations.

Summary

There have been some questions about Bruner's hypothesis of language scaffolding following ethnographic reports of the way children learn language in other cultures (e.g., Scheffelin & Ochs, 1986). The basic observation is that even children who are not introduced to language in the heavily adult-scaffolded games and rituals characteristic of many Western middle-class families—which include a large amount of speech following into children's current focus of interest and attention—acquire complete language competence nonetheless. But in none of these reports are systematic data reported in which the language development of very young children is quantified developmentally. It may very well be that, whereas older children do not need these kinds of social interactions and language models, younger children do if they are going to begin acquiring language in the months immediately following their first birthdays. No correlational studies comparable to those reported above—in which adult-child joint engagement is correlated with children's language—have been conducted with children from these cultures.

A central question in all this research is thus whether individual differences in the ways that mothers and infants participate in joint engagement are associated with individual differences in the children's very earliest communicative skills. All the correlational studies of this relation concern children's outcome at 18 months of age or older (and the experimental studies concern children 17 months of age and older). By this age, many Western, middle-class children have had "the naming insight" and have begun acquiring new words at a rapid rate (the vocabulary burst). The question thus remains whether joint engagement and adult linguistic models sensitive to the child's focus of attention are an important aspect of children's earliest communicative skills in their most fragile phases near the first birthday—including both gestural communication and language comprehension, which have never been correlated with joint engagement. It is not known whether joint attentional interaction—both in the sense of nonlinguistic joint engagement and in the sense of adult models that follow into the infant's already-established attentional focus—is an important part of the process for children this young.

THE CURRENT STUDY

Although we know much more about children's early social cognition and joint attention than we did just a decade ago, there are still very few studies of any of these skills from a longitudinal point of view. More important, there are virtually no studies of any kind aimed at relating all these skills to one another, and to the subsequent emergence of language, developmentally. The goals of the current studies are thus three:

1. to establish a developmental trajectory for each of several important skills of early social cognition and joint attention, especially joint engagement, gaze and point following, imitative learning, imperative and declarative gestures, and language;

2. to investigate the developmental interrelations among these different skills in early ontogeny, both in the sense of an ontogenetic sequence and in the sense of the intercorrelations of these skills within children; and

3. to investigate whether joint engagement and maternal language (i.e., language used to follow in or direct child attention) predict in a quantitative fashion children's very earliest skills of gestural and linguistic communication.

After a description of the methods of the studies in Chapter II, we pursue the first two of these goals in Chapter III and the third in Chapter IV. In Chapter V, we conclude with a discussion of children's early skills of social cognition and the ways in which children use these skills to participate in the cultural and communicative activities into which they are born.

II. METHOD

PARTICIPANTS

Twenty-four mother-infant dyads participated in the study from infant age 9 through 15 months. There were 12 male and 12 female infants; 14 were firstborns, and 10 were later borns. Dyads were from middle- and upper-middle-class families (22 Caucasian, 2 African American) living in the Atlanta metropolitan area. Twenty-two of the infants were born full term, that is, no more than 2 weeks early. The remaining two infants were born early (one was born 16 days early, and the other was born 1 month early), but, according to their mothers, neither of these infants had any major complications at birth or any subsequent developmental delays. Eight of the infants attended day-care facilities on a full-time basis, and 16 were cared for primarily at home by their mothers.

Most of the participants were recruited by telephone from the Emory University Psychology Department's child participants file, which consisted of a list of names of children whose parents had volunteered to participate in studies of child development in general. The remaining participants were recruited by letter from a nearby day-care center and a child-parent play group. Mothers were contacted by telephone 2–3 weeks before their infants' 9-month birthday. Each agreed to bring her infant to the Psychology Department once per month from 9 to 15 months within a week of the infant's monthly birthday, for a total of seven visits. Parents gave written consent for their infant's participation. Compensation for participation included a T-shirt, a book, and a copy of the videotape of each session.

All 24 dyads attended each of the seven sessions. For 15 of the 168 sessions, infants were seen slightly later than 1 week after their monthly birthday owing to scheduling problems (mean for these late sessions = 10.1 days after the birthday, range = 8–16 days). In addition, on two occasions, sessions had to be terminated and rescheduled owing to the fussiness of the infant. In both these cases, infants were seen again within a week of the terminated

TABLE 1

MEAN DIFFERENCE SCORE FOR NUMBER OF DAYS INFANTS WERE SEEN BEFORE $(-)$ OR AFTER $(+)$
THEIR MONTHLY BIRTHDAYS FOR EACH SESSION AND THE RANGES OF THESE SCORES

	MONTH						
	9	10	11	12	13	14	15
Mean difference score	3.0	2.0	1.5	1.5	2.0	2.0	1.7
Range	-5 to 11	-3 to 10	-5 to 8	-7 to 14	-7 to 12	-5 to 16	-6 to 10

session. Table 1 presents the mean age difference score from the monthly
birthday and the range of these scores for each time point.

Mothers also were asked to return written follow-up measures (described
below) at infant ages 18 and 24 months. Twenty mothers responded at 18
months (11 male and 9 female children), and 15 mothers responded at 24
months (7 male and 8 female children).

GENERAL PROCEDURE

Each of the seven monthly visits was conducted in a 10 $\times$ 12-foot playroom at the Department of Psychology, which was decorated with child-
friendly posters and stuffed animals (see Figure 1). Sessions lasted approximately 1 hour and were videotaped using a stationary videocamera.

The general procedure for each session was as follows. At the beginning
of each session, infants were videotaped for 10 minutes while playing with
their mother and a standard set of toys. After this free-play period, two female
experimenters (E1 and E2) entered the room, and E1 played with the infant
for a few minutes until the infant appeared to have warmed to her. At this
point, E1 began to conduct a series of structured tasks with the infant that
lasted roughly 30–60 minutes, during which time mothers completed a vocabulary checklist (see below). The session ended with follow-up questions concerning the vocabulary checklist and the scheduling of the next month's visit.

There were thus two main parts to each session, corresponding to each
of the two studies (although the chronological order is reversed). For Study
1, infants' social-cognitive skills were assessed during the structured tasks; this
is called the *experimental* part of the session. For Study 2, infants' and mothers'
skills of joint engagement, and mothers' language to infants during these
interactions, were assessed from the initial free-play part of the session. Information about infants' communicative gestures and language was collected for
this second study as well, by means of a vocabulary checklist filled out by
mothers. Detailed observational and coding procedures and information

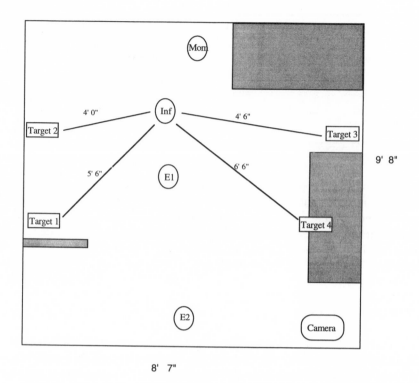

Figure 1.—The testing room, with approximate measurements. All targets were between 2 and 4 feet off the floor.

about interobserver reliability for the measures for each of the studies are reported below, in turn.

STUDY 1: STRUCTURED TESTS OF SOCIAL COGNITION

Observational and Coding Procedures

Following the free-play period, while mothers were completing the vocabulary checklist, E1 administered the series of social-cognitive tasks to the infant. During this part of the session, E1 and the infant sat on the floor facing each other, E2 sat on a chair behind E1 and coded the infant's behavior, and the mother sat on a chair near the infant filling out the vocabulary checklist and/or watching the session. At times, mothers were asked to sit on the floor with their infants to help keep them focused on the tasks. Mothers were asked not to practice the tasks with their infants at home and were asked to refrain from giving infants any assistance during testing. Children's performance on the tasks was coded live by E2 (criteria are given below), and videotapes were used to resolve any questions about what had happened during periods in which E2 was unable to code confidently for some reason (e.g., blocked vision, infant's rapid behaviors).

To deal with some of the problems of repeated measurements over months, some care was taken to vary the objects and props used to administer the tasks—but without having the objects confounded with age across children. Toward that end, infants were divided into three groups corresponding roughly to the time of their first visit (i.e., the first eight infants seen were in the first group, the second eight were in the second group, and the third eight were in the third group). There were three sets of objects or props for each task. A different set was used for each group of infants at a given age, and then each group proceeded on to the other two sets in the 2 succeeding months—with recycling after 3 months. For example, one group of infants saw one set of attention-following targets at 9, 12, and 15 months, one set at 10 and 13 months, and one set at 11 and 14 months. The other groups saw different sets at those same monthly intervals. More detail about exactly which objects and props were varied for each test is provided in the detailed descriptions of the tasks given below. The ordering of the tasks themselves during any given session for a given child was determined randomly prior to that session, with the exception that two tests of the same general type (e.g., point and gaze following) were never administered consecutively. After infants had succeeded on a task during three consecutive monthly sessions, that task typically was not administered during subsequent sessions (but was assumed to be mastered).

The different tasks were grouped together theoretically on three hierarchical levels. The first, most specific level was that of the individual tasks, for example, the gaze-following task. The second was the skill level at which highly similar tasks were grouped (e.g., the skill of imitative learning comprised the imitation of instrumental actions task and the imitation of arbitrary actions task). The third level corresponded to the groupings under which the literature was reviewed in the introduction: sharing attention, following attention and behavior, and directing attention and behavior. What this meant specifically was the following. First, there was only one sharing-attention skill and task, and that was joint engagement. Second, the following-attention and -behavior skills (with their constituent tasks in parentheses) were attention following (gaze-following task, point-following task) and imitative learning (imitation of instrumental actions task, imitation of arbitrary actions task). The directing-attention and -behavior skills were communicative gestures (imperative task, declarative task) and referential language (first referential word). There was thus a total of eight social-cognitive tasks grouped into five skills within the three overall categories. In addition, infants were presented with two obstacle tasks—one involving a physical obstacle and one involving a social obstacle—to determine whether they treated physical and social obstacles differently. Finally, infants were also presented with two object-related tasks—object permanence and spatial relations—to see whether these tasks correlated with the social-cognitive tasks to the same extent that the social-cognitive tasks intercorrelated among themselves.

The main dependent measure for all the tasks and skills in Study 1 was age of emergence (9, 10, 11, 12, 13, 14, or 15 months), that is, the age at which an infant was first able successfully to perform a particular task or skill (regardless of performance at subsequent months). Each task had its own set of criteria for passage, criteria that were based on previous research (see below). In all cases, criteria such as gaze alternation, correct responding to two sides of the room, and expectant looks were used to distinguish task behaviors that required social understanding from those that did not. In order for a *skill* to be scored as having emerged, at least one good observation of the skill was required from one or more of its constituent tasks. In a few cases, individual infants did not meet the criteria for emergence of a given task or skill during the period between 9 and 15 months. In those cases, infants were credited with emergence of the task or skill at 16 months.[4]

Measures

The eight social-cognitive tasks (comprising five skills) and their specific procedures of administration and scoring are outlined below. They are grouped according to their overall theoretical grouping as well as the skill that they are measuring. In all cases, a child was considered to have a skill at a given month if she passed any of the tasks measuring that skill. After the main social-cognitive tasks have been described, the obstacle tasks and object-related tasks will then be described.

Sharing Attention

Skill of joint engagement.—Unlike the other four social-cognitive skills, joint engagement is the only skill and task in the overall category of sharing attention. It is important to note that, to keep this task comparable to the others, joint engagement was measured when the child was interacting with the experimenters during the experimental part of the session (joint engage-

---

[4] This happened relatively rarely—for 92% of the infants, all the skills but referential language emerged during the course of the study—and results of the analyses that did not use this scoring procedure were similar to results of those that did. The numbers of infants who did not meet the criteria for emergence of each skill during the period between 9 and 15 months are reported in Chapter III.

ment with the mother during the free-play period will be a key measure for Study 2 only):

1. *Joint-engagement task.*—E2 coded videotapes of this part of the sessions for infants' first instance of joint engagement with one of the two experimenters. Joint engagement was coded when infants looked from an object to the experimenter's face and back to the same object, thus coordinating attention to both the adult and the object. The episode had to last at least 3 seconds total, and episodes in which the infant's look to the adult's face was clearly in response to some adult behavior (e.g., language) were not counted. The age of emergence (AOE) of joint engagement was thus considered to be the age of the infant's first episode of joint engagement with an experimenter.

Following Attention and Behavior

Skill of attention following.—For the attention-following tasks, four targets, stuffed animals, were placed around the room. Two hung from the wall on one side of the room, and two rested on a chair and a shelf on the other side of the room (see Figure 1). Sets of targets were rotated across months as described above, and the particular target used for each trial was randomized. There were two trials for each of the tasks, one to a target on the left side and one to a target on the right side of the room:

2. *Gaze-following task.*—E1 and the infant sat facing each other. The infant was given a relatively uninteresting toy with which to play. At some point when the infant was looking down at the toy, E1 called the infant by name, waited for eye contact, and then with an excited facial expression and vocalization (a gasp) looked at the assigned target (i.e., turned her head to fixate the target object for a few seconds). E1 alternated her gaze between the infant's eyes and the target several times, maintaining the excited expression and completely turning her head each time. E1 then waited a few seconds before going on to the next task to allow for delayed responding.

3. *Point-following task.*—The procedure for the point-following task was identical to that for the gaze-following task, with the addition that E1 pointed to the target with her right hand while alternating her gaze between the infant's eyes and the target.

For both the gaze-following and point-following tasks, E1's gazing and pointing continued either until infants fixated a target or, if their gaze did not leave E1, until E2, who was watching the infant's face, determined that the infant had clearly seen several of E1's head turns or points. Infants were scored as having passed a given trial if they correctly localized the target object (as opposed to merely looking to the correct side of the room or the like). In addition, E2 recorded any instances of checking (i.e., gaze alternation on the part of the infant between the object and E1's face or pointing hand). The AOE of gaze following was the age at which infants first passed both gaze-following trials; the AOE of point following was the age at which infants first passed both point-following trials; and the AOE of attention following as a skill was the age at which infants passed either of the two tasks.

Skill of imitative learning.—The imitation tasks used specially created boxes, each of which had at least two actions that could be performed on it and an exciting end result that occurred if the target action was performed (e.g., colored lights, a colorful spinning wheel, etc.). The two tasks were imitation of instrumental actions and imitation of arbitrary actions. These differed only in the boxes used and the actions modeled. A complete list of the modeled actions is included in the Appendix, and illustrations of the boxes are presented in Figure 2. For both imitative-learning tasks, children were shown a different action at each month. All actions were pilot tested to ensure that infants at each age were capable of performing them. The actions were designed to be of comparable difficulty; however, in case they were not, the actions were counterbalanced across ages so that each action was modeled for an equal number of children at each age. To keep infants' interest and motivation levels high, and to further minimize carryover effects, end results and the appearance of boxes were varied according to the schedule described above so that a given infant saw different-looking boxes and end results from month to month (with equal representation of boxes and end results at any given age)—recycling after each 3-month period.

The general procedure was as follows. A box was brought out, and infants were encouraged to play with it alone for 1–2 minutes. If they performed the to-be-modeled action spontaneously, one of several alternate actions was substituted. E1 then caught the infant's attention and proceeded to model the target action, sharing vocally and facially in infants' excitement when the end result occurred. Models were repeated two more times, and then E1 oriented the box toward the infant, if necessary, and encouraged the infant to respond without naming the action (e.g., "Can you do that?"). Infants were given approximately 1 minute to respond. If they correctly reproduced the modeled action, the end result was activated. This sequence was then repeated once more during a second trial, for a total of six models and two response periods:

4. *Imitation of instrumental action task.*—Instrumental actions were actions on objects such as opening a hinge or compressing a spring. The objects for the instrumental actions (e.g., the hinge) were mounted on small wooden squares and attached to the top of a 30 × 30 × 16-centimeter wooden box. In order to reduce the likelihood of infants re-

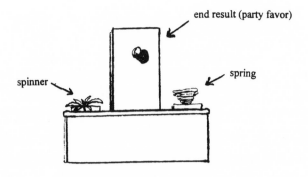

end result (party favor)

spinner

spring

Instrumental Actions Box

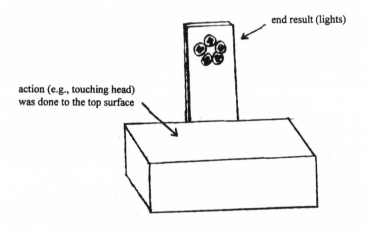

end result (lights)

action (e.g., touching head)
was done to the top surface

Arbitrary Actions Box

FIGURE 2.—The imitative learning boxes. Figure is not to scale

producing the modeled action because there was nothing else to do on the box, there were two objects on each box, although only one was used in the model.

5. *Imitation of arbitrary action task.*—Arbitrary actions included bodily movements such as patting or touching the head to the surface of a $30 \times 46 \times 16$-centimeter wooden box. The surface was in all cases completely flat, with no objects attached.

In previous studies of imitation, it has been difficult to differentiate between mimicking and imitative learning. That is, if infants reproduced the behavior of the model without any understanding that it was a means to an end (i.e., mimicked it), they achieved the end result just the same. Imitative learning, as opposed to mimicking, requires that the infant reproduce the adult's behavior and goal, that is, for example, bend down and touch the top of the box with the head with the intention of activating the light. This study included a way of distinguishing between mimicking and imitative learning and thus assessing the intentional understanding of the infants. Following any response by infants, activation of the end result was delayed for about a second. Infants' attention was coded during this second to see whether they looked expectantly to the end result. If infants were just mimicking E1 (i.e., reproducing the topography of the modeled action without understanding its goal), one would not expect them to look expectantly to the end result. If instead infants were engaging in imitative reproduction of a goal-directed action, they should look expectantly to the end result following their action. To be considered to have passed the current tasks, infants had to have both performed the appropriate action and looked expectantly to the end result. The AOE of the two imitative-learning tasks was thus the age at which they met these criteria for the task, and the AOE of the imitative-learning skill in general was the age at which they passed either of the two tasks.

Directing Attention and Behavior

Infants can attempt to direct the attention and behavior of adults in at least three different ways: using declarative gestures to direct attention (such as showing, giving, and some forms of pointing), using imperative gestures to direct behavior (such as reaching and pointing with whining), and language. We recorded any of these as they occurred during the experimental part of the session, but we also had elicitation procedures aimed at the two gestural communication behaviors (varying the objects involved across months, as described above).

Skill of Communicative Gestures.—As in the case of joint engagement, it is important to point out that, to keep these measures comparable with the others, only gestures used during the experimental part of the session were counted for this measure:

6. *Declarative gestures task.*—To elicit the production of declarative gestures such as showing and pointing, two situations were presented in which infants were likely to want to obtain the attention of the adults. In these situations, the infant first was given a relatively uninteresting toy with which to play. A few seconds after the infant started playing with the toy, E2 surreptitiously either (*a*) made a stuffed animal dance around in midair (by pulling it from a string using a pulley on the ceiling) or (*b*) made a puppet move around from behind a partition. Both the stuffed animal and the puppet moved behind E1's back, in front of but out of reach of the infants. E1, E2, and the infant's mother pretended not to notice.

7. *Imperative gestures task.*—To elicit the production of imperatives, two situations were presented in which infants were likely to want some action by an adult. After achieving eye contact with the infant, E1 either (*a*) placed an attractive toy inside a transparent container and locked the container or (*b*) activated a small windup toy for several seconds. E1 then handed the locked container or the motionless windup toy to the infant.

Following Perucchini and Camaioni (1993), adults first reacted to any infant behavior to the objects or the adult (e.g., pointing or reaching) with a comment and/or the name of the object (e.g., "Yes, that's Grover"). If behavior to the adults or the object continued, the adults responded by giving the object to the infant (or, in the case of the imperative-eliciting test involving the windup toy, operating the toy). This two-step response by the adults was designed to help identify the communicative intent, whether declarative or imperative, of any infant behavior to the adults or the object. Infants' responses were coded as *imperatives, declaratives,* or *no response* according to a modified version of Perucchini and Camaioni's (1993) coding scheme. *Imperatives* were behaviors in which the infant reached for or pointed to the object while alternating gaze between the object and an adult's face or, in the cases of the locked container and windup toy, gave the object to an adult and looked to the adult's face. These gestures usually were accompanied by grunts or whines and persisted when the adult simply made a verbal comment. *Declaratives* were behaviors in which the infant pointed at, showed, or gave the object to an adult, alternating gaze between the object and the adult's face, typically vocalizing as if to comment on the object. This behavior ceased after the adult commented. *Other responses* also were recorded.

Although particular situations were designed to elicit the different types of gestures, either type of gesture could potentially be scored for any of the eliciting situations. In addition, any spontaneous productions of intentionally

43

communicative gestures during this experimental portion of the session were noted on code sheets by E2. These gestures were later watched on videotape by E1 and determined to be imperative or declarative, using the criteria described above. Most important, if infants were satisfied by the adult's attention, the gesture was coded as declarative; if infants' gestures persisted when the object was not given immediately, the gesture was coded as imperative. Likewise, if infants' vocalizations were interested or inquisitive, the gesture was coded as declarative; if they were demanding or frustrated, the gesture was coded as imperative. Any ambiguous cases were discussed with E2 until a consensus was reached. In all cases, only gestures that were accompanied by gaze alternation between the object and the adult's face were counted as intentionally communicative gestures. The AOE of each individual gesture was the age at which infants first produced that gesture while meeting all the above criteria, with the AOE of the gestural communication skill the age at which they produced any gesture meeting the criteria.

Skill of language.—There is only one task to characterize this skill, the use of referential words. To keep this measure comparable with the others, only language used during the experimental part of the session was counted for this measure:

8. *Referential language.*—Any spontaneous productions of words during the experimental part of the session were noted. Words were then classified as referential (i.e., used for concrete objects or actions) or non-referential (i.e., function words and social words such as prepositions, articles, and greetings) by E2 using criteria from Nelson (1973). Only referential words were counted. The AOE of referential language was considered to be the age at which infants first produced a referential word during this part of the session with experimenters.

Obstacle Tasks

The purpose of these tasks was to assess children's reactions to physical and social obstacles, in particular whether they treated these different categories of obstacles differently. Thus, if children understand something about human beings as intentional agents, they should do something such as look to the face of the experimenter when she thwarted their goal-directed action, whereas they should use physical means to overcome physical obstacles:

9. *Physical obstacle task.*—In this task, an attractive toy was placed on the floor in front of the infant, and an obstacle, an open, transparent plastic box, was positioned upside down over the toy in such a way that the infant could see the toy but could not obtain it without moving the box. Infants were given approximately 1 minute to respond, and the test was repeated once later if infants did not succeed the first time. Obstacle

removal accompanied by gaze to the goal toy was required to pass this test. The AOE of this task was the age at which an infant first moved the obstacle while focused on the toy.

10. *Social obstacle task.*—This task consisted of two subtasks: the blocking and teasing tasks. These followed the general protocol of Phillips, Baron-Cohen, and Rutter (1992). In the blocking task, E1 gave the infant a small toy and, once the infant was engaged with it, suddenly covered the infant's hands with her own for 5 seconds. In the teasing task, E1 offered the infant an object, and then, as soon as the infant reached for it, E1 withdrew it and held it out of reach for 5 seconds. For both these tasks, the infant's direction of gaze was coded during the 5-second response period. Looks to E1's hands during this period were taken to indicate a lack of differentiation between physical and social obstacles, whereas looks to E1's face were taken to indicate a differentiation. The AOE of this task was the age at which infants looked to E1's face in either of these frustration episodes.

Object-Related Tasks

Two tests of infants' object-related skills, object permanence and spatial relations, were administered for comparisons with the social-cognitive skills. The object-related skills were expected to be unrelated to the social-cognitive skills:

11. *Object permanence task.*—A series of object permanence tests was taken with some modifications from Uzgiris and Hunt (1975, tests 4, 12, and 14). All involved hiding a small toy under one or more opaque screens. The procedure was as follows: E1 administered the easiest test (test 4) at the 9-month session. If the infant responded correctly (i.e., removed the screen and obtained the toy) and then repeated the correct response in a second trial, E1 proceeded to the next test (test 12), and so on. Infants were scored as passing a given test if they found the toy twice (under different screens, if applicable) during a single session. If an infant did not pass a test during a given session, the test was terminated, and the infant was given the preceding test first during the following session. The AOE of object permanence was considered to be the age at which infants first were able to find an object following one invisible displacement with two screens alternated (test 12). In this test, E1 placed a small toy under one of two screens using a cup; the empty cup was then placed in the middle of the two screens. This test was chosen as a criterion because it was the most advanced test that all infants passed during the period between 9 and 15 months.

12. *Spatial relations task.*—One of Uzgiris and Hunt's spatial relations tasks was also administered (test 6, which utilized the relation container-contained). Infants were presented with a large plastic cup and

some wooden blocks and given a few minutes to play with them. If they did not place at least one of the blocks in the cup during this time, E1 gave them a hint by inconspicuously putting a few blocks in the cup and then giving the cup back to the infants. The AOE of this skill was considered to be the age at which infants first placed two or more blocks in the container and removed two or more blocks from the container without a hint from E1.

A Final Methodological Note

Infants' mothers were present throughout the entire session. Infants occasionally participated in joint engagement with their mother, gestured or spoke to her, followed her gaze, imitated her actions, etc. Infants likewise occasionally followed the experimenter's gaze and imitated her actions outside the attention-following and imitative-learning tests. Such behaviors to infants' mothers and behaviors performed outside their respective tests were included in final analyses for only three skills: joint engagement, communicative gestures, and referential language. The reasoning was as follows. Whereas joint engagement, gestures, and words took the same form and could meet the same criteria no matter when and to whom they were produced, possible instances of attention following and imitative learning that occurred outside the experimental tests could not meet the criteria devised for those tests (e.g., no spontaneous act of imitation could meet all the criteria devised for the experimental tests in which the type of action, the novelty, the number of models, the end result, etc. were carefully controlled). This coding procedure enabled a comparison of all the skills on a comparable basis; that is, all measures included all instances of a behavior during the experimental portion of the session that met specific sets of criteria.

Reliability

Infants' behavior in each of these structured tests was coded live by E2; this coding was supplemented by a viewing of the videotapes when necessary. A trained research assistant who was blind to the hypotheses of the study coded 34 (20%) of the sessions independently for the purpose of assessing reliability. The research assistant coded 27 of the sessions live from behind a one-way mirror and seven of the sessions from the videotapes. At least three sessions at each time point, and at least one session for each infant at some time point, were coded for reliability. All three of the 9- and 10-month and one of the 11-month reliability sessions were coded from videotapes; two of the 11-month and all the 12–15-month reliability sessions (ranging from four to nine sessions) were coded live. Reliability was assessed in a slightly different way for two measures, joint engagement and referential language. For joint

TABLE 2

RELIABILITY: PERCENTAGE AGREEMENT AND COHEN'S KAPPAS
FOR EACH OF THE SOCIAL-COGNITIVE AND OBJECT-RELATED TASKS
FROM STUDY 1

	Percentage Agreement	Cohen's Kappa
Attention following:		
Gaze following	90	.76
Point following	97	.94
Imitative learning:		
Instrumental actions	100	1.00
Arbitrary actions	100	1.00
Communicative gestures:		
Proximal declaratives	97	.87
Distal declaratives	97	.94
Imperatives	90	.77
Obstacle tasks:		
Social obstacle	98	.96
Physcial obstacle	94	.65
Object-related tasks:		
Object permanence	96	.91
Spatial relations	96	.92

engagement, reliability for identification of joint-engagement episodes had already been assessed for these infants during the 10-minute play periods with mother (see next section). Agreement between E2 and the research assistant for this coding was 97%; Cohen's kappa was .75. For referential language, words of any type during sessions were infrequent for most infants. When they occurred, E1, E2, and infants' mothers discussed them and came to an agreement as to whether they should be counted.

Percentage agreement for each of the other tests separately (i.e., all but joint engagement and referential language, and breaking down communicative gestures into their different types—see Chapter III) ranged from 90% to 100%, with a mean percentage agreement of 96.1%. Cohen's kappas for these measures ranged from .65 (for the physical obstacle task; the next lowest was .76) to 1.00, with a mean kappa of .89. Table 2 presents the percentage agreement and Cohen's kappas for each of the measures used.

STUDY 2: JOINT ENGAGEMENT AND COMMUNICATION

Joint Engagement with Mother

The skills of mother-infant dyads to engage in periods of coordinated joint engagement were assessed during the 10-minute free-play period at the beginning of each visit.

47

Observational Procedure

At the beginning of each session, the mother and infant were seated on the floor of the playroom with one of four toy sets. Mothers were told that they should play with their infant "as you normally do at home" and that our interest was in how their infant "plays with the toys and with you." They were also instructed to try to keep their infant from venturing out of the videocamera's range. The experimenters left the mother and infant alone in the room to play until roughly 10–12 minutes had elapsed.

Four similar but nonidentical sets of toys were used for these play periods. The toys were selected for qualities that would serve to maximize infant and parent interest while promoting shared activities. Each set included each of the following types of items: bucket, shovel, blocks, ball, doll or animal, stacking cups, small figurines, toy with wheels, picture book, and small rolling objects. A given infant played successively across months with the four different toy sets—to avoid the boredom associated with having the same toys available at every monthly session. There was a recycling of toy sets for a given child after the first 4 months (although on a few occasions infants were mistakenly given a set out of its designated sequence—to no discernible effect). Different infants began the sequence with different toy sets so that a given set was not associated with any particular monthly session.

Coding Procedure

A primary coder coded the first 10 minutes of videotaped play periods second by second, beginning at the time the experimenters left the room and ending after a total of 600 seconds of time (10 minutes) was spent on-screen. As they became more mobile with age, infants spent an increasing amount of time off-screen over the course of the study, ranging from an average of 1.3 seconds off-screen at 9 months to 89.1 seconds at 15 months.

Coding procedures replicated in all important respects those used for the "coordinated joint engagement" category in Bakeman and Adamson's (1984) coding scheme. The infant's coordination of attention was evinced by alternation of gaze from an object to the mother's face and immediately back to the object. Infants also could start a joint-engagement episode with a verbalization (i.e., an intelligible word) to the mother about an object (without necessarily looking to the mother's face). The mother's attention to a shared object was evinced by her touching the object, continually gazing at the object, and/or talking about the object. For example, an infant might push a car toward her mother, look up to her mother's face, and then look back to the car while the mother watches and comments, "You're pushing it."

Joint-engagement episodes continued until either the infant or the mother shifted her attention away from the shared object for 3 or more seconds. Infants typically ended episodes by shifting their attention to a new object, but sometimes they would continue playing with the object for an extended period, during which they no longer acknowledged the mother's attention. Therefore, episodes were terminated if 10 seconds elapsed without either another look toward the mother, a communicative gesture, or an intentional vocalization directed to the mother.

Reliability

A second coder, who was blind to the specific hypotheses of the study, independently coded 28 (17%) of the play periods for joint-engagement episodes. Four complete sessions at each of the seven time points were randomly selected for reliability coding to ensure that each infant was coded at least once but not more than twice. Overall agreement on time spent in joint engagement, as assessed on a second-by-second basis, was 97%. A Cohen's kappa of .75 indicated that a "good to excellent" level of agreement was achieved (Bakeman & Gottman, 1986).

Gestures and Language

For purposes of this study, which was more concerned with the quantitative aspects of communicative competence than was Study 1, measures of infants' communicative abilities were obtained via maternal report.

Observational and Coding Procedures

Mothers completed the MacArthur Communicative Development Inventory (CDI) Infant Form (Fenson et al., 1993) at each monthly session (the Toddler Form was used for the follow-up procedure through the mail at 18 and 24 months). The CDI Infant Form consists of a written list of gestures, words, and actions that have been found to characterize the communicative skills of many English-speaking infants between 8 and 16 months of age. The instrument has been found to be both highly valid and reliable in a number of ways. Specific information on the internal and external validity of the CDI (both Infant and Toddler Forms) can be found in Fenson et al. (1993).

The First Communicative Gestures section (pt. II, sec. A) of this form lists 12 intentionally communicative gestures that can be marked as used "not yet," "sometimes," or "often." These communicative gestures include *point, give, wave,* and so forth. The Vocabulary Checklist (pt. I, sec. D) lists 396 words that are separated into 19 semantic categories. Each word can be marked "understands" for comprehension or "understands and says" for production or can be left blank. For comprehension of language, mothers were instructed to include only those words that they felt their infant would understand and respond to on only hearing the word (i.e., in the absence of other behavioral or contextual cues). For production of language, mothers were instructed to include only words that were used to refer to more than one example of a class of objects, on more than one occasion, and in more than one context. Thus, in the current study, mothers were instructed about the communicative intent, context, and use of their infant's gestures and comprehension and production of language to make these measures as stringent as other measures used (i.e., in all cases, we tried to select only those manifestations of a skill in which infants clearly understood something of the social significance of what they were doing). As such, the current procedures may have produced more conservative estimates of these measures than the original MacArthur procedures (see Tomasello & Mervis, 1994).

Mothers used the same CDI booklet each month, indicating new gestures and words acquired. After each session, E2 wrote the month of the visit next to each new mark, thus providing a cumulative record of the number of gestures and words acquired each month throughout the study. Words and gestures indicated on the booklet were tallied after each session. Occasionally, E2 would herself mark (and initial) a word in the booklet on the basis of her discussions with the mother.

In addition, another version of the MacArthur CDI, the Toddler Form, designed for assessing vocabulary and grammatical development of children aged 16–30 months, was mailed to the parents for follow-up production measures at ages 18 and 24 months. Only the 680-word checklist for production was included in the mailing. Both versions of the CDI include several sections that were not relevant to this study (e.g., noncommunicative gestures and actions, understanding phrases, grammar); these sections were not analyzed. The Toddler Forms were sent to mothers with the same instructions concerning referential use of new words and were to be filled out within 2 weeks before or after their child turned 18 and 24 months of age.

Maternal Language

Coding Procedure

Transcriptions were made of each mother's utterances during the 10-minute play periods for the 9-, 12-, and 15-month sessions only. Utterances were coded for their relation to the infant's focus of attention utilizing the same "follow" or "lead" classification of utterances used in Akhtar et al. (1991; see also Tomasello & Farrar, 1986a; and Tomasello & Todd, 1983).

A primary coder used videotapes and transcripts of the play sessions to code utterances as either following into the infant's attention (*follow*), leading the infant's attention away (*lead*), or *other*, using the following definitions:

Follow.—Statements or commands that contained a reference to an object that the infant was holding and/or looking at or that were related to the infant's ongoing activity with an object (e.g., "Put the red block on top," said while the mother and infant are engaged in stacking blocks and the infant is holding a red block, or, "You did it!" when the infant places the block on the tower).

Lead.—Statements or commands that referred to something other than the object of the infant's interest (e.g., while the mother and infant are engaged in stacking blocks and the infant is holding a red block, the mother directs her infant's attention to a new activity with, "Put the ball in the bucket," or, "Let's look at the book now").

Other.—All other utterances that were not considered statements, requests, or commands (e.g., utterances used in social play ["peeka-boo"], conventional social expressions ["thank you"], or imitations of the infant's speech).

Reliability

To assess interobserver reliability, a second coder independently coded a random sample of 20% of the play period transcripts from each of the three age points. Overall agreement was 89%, and a mean Cohen's kappa of .83 was obtained, indicating an excellent level of agreement on this coding scheme.

III. RESULTS OF STUDY 1:
STRUCTURED TESTS OF SOCIAL COGNITION

Results are presented in two sections, corresponding to the two main objectives of this study. One objective of the study was to investigate the developmental progression of each of the target social-cognitive skills individually. The first set of analyses thus compares the responses of infants at each age to each of the tasks. A second objective of the study was to explore the developmental relations among the different skills. In the second set of analyses, we thus (*a*) determine the relative order of emergence of the skills and (*b*) investigate intercorrelations among individual infants' scores on each of the measures.

INDIVIDUAL MEASURES

Using criteria specified in Chapter II above, the age of emergence (AOE) of each task and skill was identified for each infant. Descriptive statistics and descriptions of developmental progressions are presented below for each of the social-cognitive and other tasks and skills. In addition, age effects are investigated for each measure that is presented in the figures, using Cochran Q and McNemar tests. Results of Cochran Q tests for each skill across the 7 months were significant for all skills ($p < .0001$), so only results from the McNemar tests that identify significant differences between two ages are reported below (all significant results for sequential pairs of months are reported, but only the more interesting of the results for nonsequential pairs are reported).

Joint Engagement

All 24 infants engaged in at least one joint-engagement episode with one of the two experimenters at age 9 months. The mean, median, and mode AOE of *joint-engagement episode with the experimenter* were thus 9.0 months.

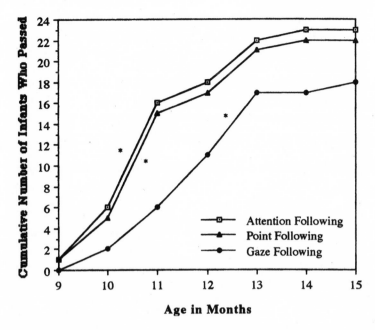

FIGURE 3.—Cumulative number of infants passing attention following and its component tasks for each time point (* $p < .05$).

Attention Following

The attention-following skill had two tasks: gaze following and point following. To eliminate the possibility of chance responding or bias toward one side of the room, following points and gaze twice—to targets on each side of the room—was required as a criterion for emergence of each of these skills.[5] Figure 3 shows the AOE curves for attention following and for point following and gaze following individually.

Gaze-Following Task

The mean AOE of *gaze following* to both sides of the room was 13.0 months (SD = 2.1), the median was 13 months, and the modes were 13 and

[5] A comparison was made of infants' rates of following points and gaze to targets on the left (the infants' right, and the side of the room slightly closer to infants and E1) and the right sides of the room. Infants responded differently depending on the direction of E1's points and gaze. The average age at which infants first followed E1's points was earlier when she pointed to the left side of the room (mean AOE = 9.6 months) than when she pointed to the right (mean AOE = 11.6 months; $t[23] = 5.3$, $p < .001$). Similar results were obtained for gaze following: the average age at which infants first followed E1's gaze was earlier when she looked to the left (mean AOE = 10.7 months) than when she looked to the right (mean AOE = 12.5 months; $t[23] = 4.1$, $p < .001$).

16 months. The number of infants passing this test steadily increased until 13 months, at which point the curve leveled off. There was a significant age effect between 12 and 13 months (McNemar, $p < .05$). Of the 18 infants who passed this test during the period between 9 and 15 months, 17 did so between 10 and 13 months; individual AOEs were relatively evenly distributed throughout this age range.

Point-Following Task

The mean AOE of *point following* (following points to both sides of the room) was 11.7 months (SD = 1.8), and the median and mode were both 11 months. The number of infants passing this test increased dramatically until 11 months, at which point the curve began to level off (see Figure 3). There was a significant increase in the number of infants passing point following for the first time between 10 and 11 months (McNemar, $p < .01$). Of the 22 infants who followed both points in a single session, 14 did so for the first time at 10 or 11 months.

The AOE of attention following as a skill was considered to be the age at which infants first passed either both gaze-following tests or both point-following tests during the same session (i.e., followed E1's gaze or points to both sides of the room). The mean AOE of *attention following* was 11.5 months (SD = 1.6), and the median and mode were both 11 months.[6] The distribution of individual AOEs matched almost exactly the distribution of point following. There was a significant age effect between 10 and 11 months (McNemar, $p < .01$) for this skill. The earliest nonsequential age effect for attention following (and for point and gaze following separately) was between 9 and 11 months (McNemar, $p < .05$). One infant never followed either E1's gaze or her points to both sides of the room in the same session.

Checking (i.e., gaze alternation between the object and E1's face or pointing hand after following her head turn or point, as if to ascertain that the correct target was fixated) has been taken as evidence that infants understand the purpose of adults' head turns and points. Checking in this study was infrequent at every age: only three obvious instances were recorded, one each at 13, 14, and 15 months, for different infants. This finding likely was a result of two factors: the obvious targets we used (as opposed to the invisible targets used by some other studies) and the fact that the experimenters and

[6] We also conducted an additional set of analyses in which infants were given credit for passing these tasks if they either localized the correct target or just looked to the correct side of the room. The same pattern of results was obtained using this criterion: the mean AOE of gaze following was 11.5 months (only one infant did not pass by 15 months), the mean AOE of point following was 9.9 months, and the mean AOE of attention following was 9.8 months.

the infants' mothers usually reacted with praise after infants fixated the correct target. Therefore, infants could be relatively certain that they were correct and thus had no need to check.

There was another indication that infants were attempting to follow into and share the experimenter's focus of attention, however. Eight infants (only one of whom was one of those who checked) pointed to the target after following E1's gaze to it. These infants and three others also imitated E1's points to targets, but the fact that infants often pointed to targets following E1's *gaze* (i.e., head turn alone), where there was no possibility of imitation, suggests that these infants knew that they were sharing a focus of attention with the adult. This production of pointing after gaze following began for one infant at 10 months, for two infants at 12 months, for four infants at 13 months, and for one infant at 14 months.

Imitative Learning

Figure 4 shows the AOE curves for imitative learning (i.e., following behavior) and for imitation of instrumental actions and imitation of arbitrary actions individually.

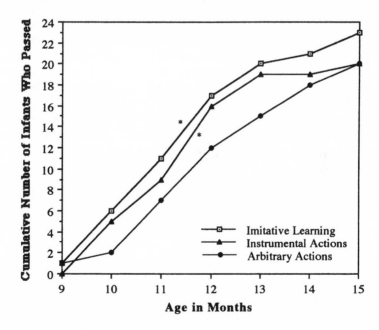

FIGURE 4.—Cumulative number of infants passing imitative learning and its component tasks for each time point (* $p < .05$).

Instrumental Actions

The mean AOE of *imitation of instrumental actions* was 12.3 months (SD = 2.1), and the median and mode were both 12 months. There was a significant age effect between 11 and 12 months (McNemar, $p < .05$). No infants imitated an instrumental action at 9 months; most did so for the first time between 10 and 13 months. Four infants did not pass imitation of instrumental actions during the period between 9 and 15 months.

Arbitrary Actions

The mean AOE of *imitation of arbitrary actions* was 12.9 months (SD = 2.1), the median was 12.5 months, and the modes were 11 and 12 months. There were no significant age effects. One infant passed this test for the first time at 9 months, and one did so at 10 months; 16 infants passed this test between 11 and 14 months. Four infants did not pass imitation of arbitrary actions during the period between 9 and 15 months (only one of these infants also did not pass imitation of instrumental actions).

Because it could be argued that requiring an expectant look to the end result following the infant's response was too strict a criterion for the AOE of imitative learning, analyses also were conducted using as the criterion for the AOE only the successful reproduction of E1's model, regardless of whether there was an expectant look. When this more generous criterion was used, the mean AOE was 10.6 months (SD = 1.5) for instrumental actions and 12.5 months (SD = 2.1) for arbitrary actions.

The AOE of imitative learning as a skill was considered to be the age at which the infant first passed one or both of the imitative learning tests using the stricter criterion (i.e., requiring an expectant look to the end result). The mean AOE of *imitative learning* was 11.9 months (SD = 1.8), and the median and mode were both 12 months. The distribution of individual AOEs for imitative learning as a general measure roughly matched the distribution of AOEs for imitation of instrumental actions. There was a significant age effect between 11 and 12 months (McNemar, $p < .05$). The earliest nonsequential age effect for imitative learning (and for imitation of instrumental and arbitrary actions separately) was between 9 and 11 months (McNemar, $p < .05$). One infant never imitated either an instrumental action or an arbitrary action during the course of the study.

Communicative Gestures

Communicative gestures included shows, points, and gives. We also coded infants' reaches. However, it was difficult at times to distinguish between infants' reaches and points (some infants' reaches turned into points, and vice versa; some infants also reached with a very slightly extended index

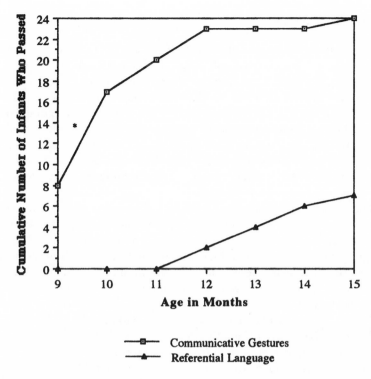

FIGURE 5.—Cumulative number of infants producing communicative gestures and referential language for each time point (* $p < .05$).

finger). For the purposes of analyses, reaches are thus encompassed by points; that is, points were defined as an extension of the arm toward an object, with or without the extension of the index finger. All gestures required gaze alternation between an object and the adult's face. Figure 5 shows the AOE curves for communicative gestures as a general measure and referential language.

On average, the earliest communicative gestures to emerge were *shows*. The mean AOE of shows was 10.7 months (SD = 1.7). Twenty-three of the 24 infants produced a show by 12 months; one infant never produced a show. On average, the next communicative gestures to emerge were *gives,* although the individual AOEs for this gesture were relatively evenly distributed throughout the entire period between 9 and 15 months (and one infant never produced a give). The mean AOE of gives was 12.1 months (SD = 2.1). The next communicative gestures to emerge, on average, were communicative *points*. The mean AOE of this gesture was 12.3 months (SD = 1.9). All the 21 infants who produced a point during the sessions first did so between 10 and 14 months; three infants never produced a point.

Declarative Gestures

Declarative gestures serve to direct others' attention. However, some declarative gestures are more complex than others. For example, when infants show objects to adults, they bring the objects into the adult's focus of attention and are thus sharing with adults rather than directing their attention elsewhere (the same applies to declarative gives). When infants point declaratively to objects, however, it is usually to direct adults to turn to look at distant objects. We thus will consider these two types of declarative gestures—proximal declaratives (sharing attention with others, i.e., shows and declarative gives) and distal declaratives (directing others' attention, i.e., declarative points)—separately in some analyses.

The mean AOE of *declarative gestures as a group* was 10.3 months (SD = 1.6), and the median and mode were both 10 months. The distribution of AOEs for this measure roughly matched that of shows, the earliest communicative gesture to emerge, on average. The mean AOEs of each of the declarative gestures individually were as follows (the numbers of infants who never produced the gesture are given in parentheses): shows, 10.7 months (one infant); declarative gives, 13.3 months (nine infants); and declarative points, 12.6 months (four infants). There was a significant age effect for declarative gestures between 9 and 10 months (McNemar, $p < .01$). One infant never produced a declarative gesture during the sessions.

The mean AOE of *proximal declarative gestures* was 10.5 months (SD = 1.6), the median was 10 months, and the mode was 9 months. There was a significant age effect between 9 and 10 months (McNemar, $p < .05$). The mean AOE of *distal declarative gestures* was 12.6 months (SD = 2.0),[7] and the median and mode were both 12 months. There was a significant age effect between 11 and 12 months (McNemar, $p < .05$). The earliest nonsequential age effect for declarative gestures (and for proximal and distal declarative gestures separately) was between 9 and 11 months (McNemar, $p < .05$).

Imperative Gestures

Imperative gestures serve to direct others' behavior and intentions. The mean AOE of *imperative gestures* was 12.7 months (SD = 1.6), and the median and mode were both 13 months. The mean AOEs for each of the imperative gestures (with the numbers of infants who never produced the gesture in parentheses) were as follows: imperative gives, 13.4 months (three infants); and imperative points, 14.0 months (nine infants). There was a significant age effect between 12 and 13 months (McNemar, $p < .01$). The earliest nonsequential age effect for imperative gestures was between 9 and 12 months

---

[7] Note that this is a full 2 months later than proximal declarative gestures.

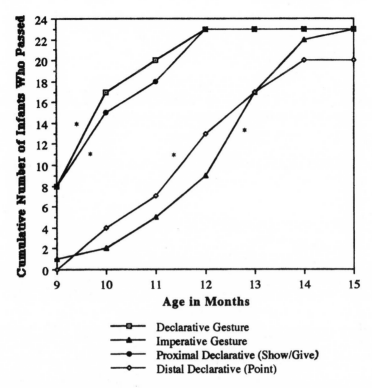

FIGURE 6.—Cumulative number of infants producing the different types of communicative gestures for each time point (* p < .05).

(McNemar, p < .01). One infant never produced an imperative gesture. Figure 6 shows the AOE curves for declarative and imperative gestures and for proximal and distal declarative gestures.

The mean AOE of *communicative gestures* as a group, that is, the age at which infants first produced any communicative gesture, was 10.3 months (SD = 1.4). The median and mode were both 10 months. The curve for this measure increased sharply between 9 and 10 months, then more gradually between 10 and 12 months, at which point it leveled off. There was a significant age effect between 9 and 10 months (McNemar, p < .01). All infants were observed to produce at least one communicative gesture during the course of the study.

Language

The majority of the infants (17 of the 24) did not produce a referential word during their visits. No infant produced a referential word during the

9–11-month sessions; two infants first did so at 12, at 13, and at 14 months; and one did so at 15 months (see Figure 5 above). The mean AOE of this skill was thus somewhat later than 15 months (when 16 months was used as the AOE for infants who did not produce a word during the period between 9 and 15 months, as above, the mean AOE of *referential language* was 15.2 months, SD = 1.4). There were no significant age effects between sequential pairs of months; the earliest nonsequential age effect for referential language was between 9 and 14 months (McNemar, $p < .05$). Seven infants who did not produce referential words in the laboratory were reported on the Mac-Arthur CDI (see Study 2) to have done so at home (one at 11 months, two at 12 months, one at 13 months, two at 14 months, and one at 15 months).

Obstacle Tasks

Social Obstacle

The social obstacle task had two parts: blocking and teasing. In each case, the infant had to look to the adult's face when their play with an object was blocked in some way. Figure 7 shows the AOE curves for the blocking and teasing tasks. The mean AOE of checking the adult's face during the *blocking*

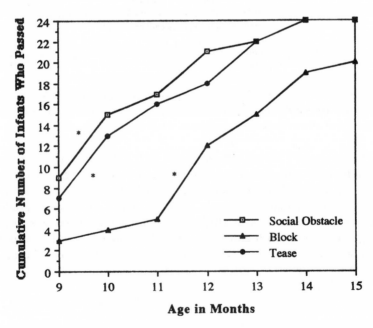

FIGURE 7.—Cumulative number of infants passing social obstacle and its component tasks for each time point (* $p < .05$).

test was 12.8 months (SD = 2.2), the median was 12.5 months, and the mode was 12 months. There was a significant age effect between 11 and 12 months for this skill (McNemar, $p < .05$), which emerged for most of the infants between 11 and 14 months. Four infants never looked to the experimenter's face following the blocking of their hands. The mean AOE of checking the adult's face during the *teasing* test was 10.8 months (SD = 1.7), the median was 10 months, and the mode was 9 months. There was a significant age effect between 9 and 10 months for this skill (McNemar, $p < .05$). This skill emerged for just over half the infants at 9 or 10 months. All infants looked to the experimenter's face following the tease during at least one session.[8] The AOE of passing the *social obstacle* task as a whole was 10.5 months (SD = 1.6), the median was 10 months, and the mode was 9 months. There was a significant age effect between 9 and 10 months for this skill (McNemar, $p < .05$). The earliest nonsequential age effect for the skill (and for teasing separately) was between 9 and 11 months (McNemar, $p < .01$); the earliest nonsequential age effect for blocking was between 9 and 12 months (McNemar, $p < .01$). All infants exhibited this skill at least once during the course of the study.

Physical Obstacle

A third obstacle task was the physical obstacle task. The mean AOE for the *physical obstacle* measure was 9.2 months (SD = 0.5), and the median and mode were both 9 months. There were no significant age effects for this skill. Twenty-one of the 24 infants passed this test at 9 months.

Object-Related Tasks

Two object-related tasks, spatial relations and a measure of object permanence, were included as a nonsocial comparison to the social-cognitive measures. Figure 8 shows the AOE curves for the object-related skills.

Object Permanence

The mean AOE for our *object permanence* measure was 12.3 months (SD = 1.2), the median was 12 months, and the modes were 12 and 13 months. There were significant age effects between 10 and 11 months, 11

---

[8] Phillips et al. (1992) made a distinction between looking to the adult's face during the teasing (ambiguous) and the giving (unambiguous) portions of this test. In the present study, infants rarely looked to the experimenter's face immediately after her give (over half the infants never did this at any of their visits, and the others did it only occasionally).

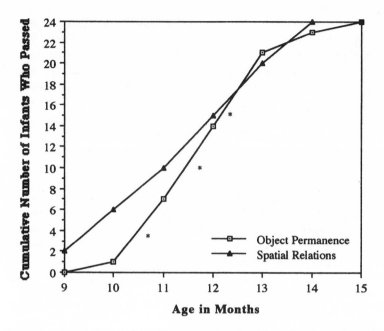

FIGURE 8.—Cumulative number of infants passing the object-related tests for each time point (* $p < .05$).

and 12 months, and 12 and 13 months; the earliest nonsequential age effect was between 9 and 11 months (McNemar, $p < .05$). Most infants passed this test between 11 and 13 months.

Spatial Relations

The mean AOE of *spatial relations* was 11.8 months (SD = 1.6), the median was 12 months, and the modes were 12 and 13 months. There were no significant sequential age effects; the earliest nonsequential age effect was between 9 and 11 months (McNemar, $p < .01$). Individual AOEs for this skill were relatively evenly distributed throughout the period between 9 and 14 months. All infants passed this test by 14 months.

Gender and Birth-Order Differences

Mean AOEs for male and female infants were compared for each measure. The mean AOEs for males and females were significantly different for only one measure: imitation of arbitrary actions. Females (mean AOE = 12.0 months) passed the imitation of arbitrary actions test significantly earlier on average than did males (mean AOE = 13.8 months; $t[22]$ = 2.27, $p <$ .05). There were no significant differences in mean AOEs for any skills between first- and later-born infants.

DEVELOPMENTAL INTERRELATIONS

Order of Emergence

As can be seen in Figure 9, the five main social-cognitive skills emerged in the following order, on average: joint engagement (mean AOE = 9.0 months), communicative gestures (mean AOE = 10.3 months), attention following (mean AOE = 11.5 months), imitative learning (mean AOE = 11.9 months), and referential language (after 15 months). The following set of analyses investigated the sequencing of emergence of the skills for individual infants. The order of emergence of the skills was identified for each infant,

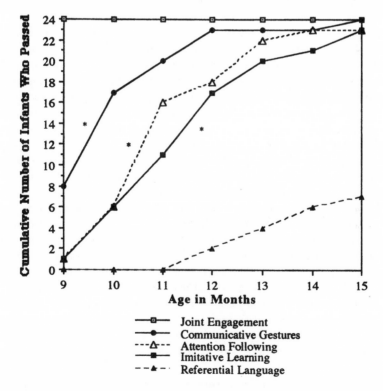

FIGURE 9.—Cumulative number of infants passing each of the main social-cognitive skills for each time point (* $p <$ .05).

and the different patterns of emergence were counted and statistically analyzed.

A reliable pattern of emergence was found both for the social-cognitive skills and for most of the tasks within each skill. Results are presented below, first, for the patterns of emergence of all five of the main social-cognitive skills as a group. Other theoretically interesting groupings of the social-cognitive skills and tasks are then examined, and an analysis of the age range in which the skills emerged is presented.

Order of Emergence of the Five Social-Cognitive Skills

Individual infants' patterns of emergence for the five social-cognitive skills (i.e., joint engagement, attention following, imitative learning, communicative gestures, and referential language) were determined. Because in many cases two or more skills emerged in the same month for individual infants, patterns of emergence in this analysis included skills that emerged *before or in the same month as* other skills.

Figure 10 shows the most common pattern of emergence for the five main social-cognitive skills as a group, along with the number of infants who displayed this pattern. The pattern was joint engagement → communicative gestures → attention following → imitative learning → referential language. Fifteen (62.5%) of the 24 infants each showed this pattern. This percentage is significantly different from the percentage that would be expected by chance (2%; binomial test, $p < .0001$).[9] Figure 10 also shows the numbers of infants who displayed each pair, triplet, and quadruplet ordering within the main pattern. As mentioned above, this analysis included patterns in which skills emerged before or during the same month as others. Another analysis was performed as a check to make sure that this did not artificially inflate the number of infants fitting the pattern. For seven of the infants, each of the five major skills emerged in a different month. When the ordering analysis was conducted using the patterns of these infants only, thus restricting the ordering procedure to skills that came *before,* not before or in the same month as, others, a similar percentage (four of seven, or 57%) of infants showed the same pattern of emergence. This percentage is also different from what would be expected by chance (1%; binomial test $p < .0001$).

In order to test statistically the scalability of this sequence of skills, a Guttman (1950) scalogram analysis was conducted on all 24 infants. This type of analysis tests the extent to which a particular order of emergence is reproducible in the sample; in sequences that are highly scalable, later-emerging skills

---

[9] This number was calculated by dividing the number of different ways an infant could display this pattern given the "before or in the same month as" rule (792) by the total number of different patterns possible given that rule (32,768).

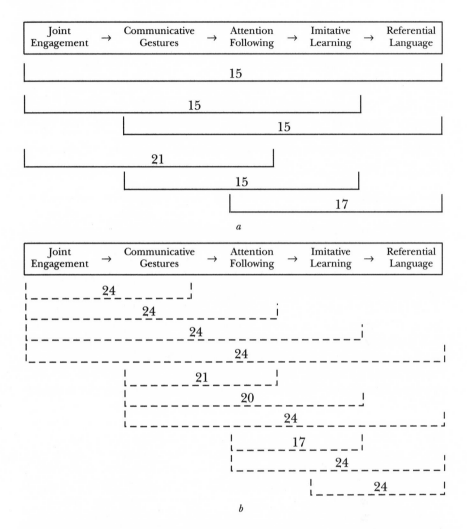

FIGURE 10.—The most common pattern of emergence of the main social-cognitive skills, with the numbers of infants displaying the pattern and its component patterns. *a*, Fifteen (62.5%) of the 24 infants fit this entire pattern of emergence. Fifteen (62.5%) infants also fit each of the two possible ordered quadruplets within the entire pattern. Fifteen (62.5%) to 21 (87.5%) infants fit each of the possible ordered triplets within the entire pattern. *b*, Here, the lines beneath the pattern connect *pairs* of abilities (and do *not* include any abilities in the middle, unlike in Figure 10*a*). Seventeen (70.8%) to 24 (100%) of the infants fit each of the possible ordered pairs within the entire pattern.

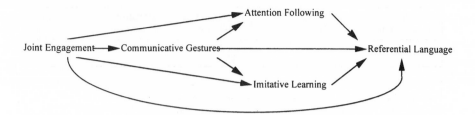

FIGURE 11.—Results of the ordering-theoretic-method analysis. Lines represent prerequisite relations; the directions of the arrows show the order of emergence of each pair.

appear only in individuals who have already acquired earlier-emerging skills.[10] Infants' pass/fail scores for each of the main social-cognitive skills at the 12-month time point, midway between 9 and 15 months, were used; skills were ordered according to the number of infants passing each one at 12 months. This resulted in the pattern of emergence specified above. Results indicated that this pattern was highly scalable: the coefficient of reproducibility (Rep) was 0.98. Green's (1956) index of consistency, a more conservative measure that takes chance into account, also indicated high scalability ($I = 0.73$). Inspection of the resulting array of infants' scores indicated that, of the 24 infants, only three did not fit the pattern perfectly at this age, with the only difference being that all three passed imitative learning before attention following. Thus, for example, if an infant had produced a referential word at 12 months, he or she had also displayed all the other main social-cognitive skills by that time.

Whereas scalogram analyses involve the entire sequence of skills, another type of analysis, Bart and Airasian's (1974) ordering-theoretic method, identifies prerequisite relations between pairs of skills (i.e., pairs of skills that always emerge in the same order). Figure 11 presents a representation of the results of this analysis, which also was conducted using infants' scores at the 12-month time point. Again, results were consistent with the same pattern of emergence: joint engagement → communicative gestures → attention following → imitative learning → referential language. With a tolerance level of zero, prerequisite relations were found between all pairs of skills except one. The attention-following and imitative-learning pair was the only pair found not to have a prerequisite relation; that is, not all infants passed attention following before imitative learning (or vice versa).

The pattern joint engagement → communicative gestures → attention following → imitative learning → referential language was thus highly reli-

[10] It should be noted that this analysis and the following analyses are conducted at one time point (12 months) and thus avoid any problems that may be associated with counting instances in which a skill appeared before or in the same month as (as opposed to simply before) another, as in the initial pattern analysis reported above.

able, both overall and at the midway point of this age range. There were some infants whose overall patterns of emergence were different from this pattern, however. The majority of the infants who did not fit the pattern differed only in the ordering of attention following and imitative learning: five infants had the pattern joint engagement → communicative gestures → imitative learning → attention following → referential language. These two patterns together thus accounted for 20 of the 24 infants (83%). In the patterns of the remaining infants, only the three middle skills varied.

The Place of Object-Related Skills

In order to determine whether object-related skills fit into the above pattern of social-cognitive skills, spatial relations and the object permanence measure were added into the scalogram analyses. With these additions, the Guttman's coefficient of reproducibility (*Rep*) was 0.92; the more conservative Green's (1956) index of consistency, which takes chance into account, indicated that this group of items was *not* scalable ($I = 0.44$). The ordering-theoretic method also was conducted with the social-cognitive and object-related skills together. Results of this analysis also tended to support the independence of the object-related skills with respect to the social-cognitive ones. For the most part, spatial relations and the object permanence measure had prerequisite relations only with the social-cognitive skills at each end of the social-cognitive developmental scale. Joint engagement and communicative gestures emerged before both spatial relations and the object permanence measure, and the latter two skills emerged before referential language for all infants, with the exception of one infant for whom the object permanence measure emerged before communicative gestures. There were no prerequisite relations between spatial relations and attention following or imitative learning, or between the object permanence measure and attention following or imitative learning, or between spatial relations and the object permanence measure.

Other Patterns of Emergence

Patterns of emergence also appeared on the level of the individual tasks within the main skills. Within attention following, point following emerged before or in the same month as gaze following for 22 of the 24 infants (before for 13 infants); this ordering (i.e., point following → gaze following for 13 infants and gaze following → point following for 2 infants) was statistically significant (Sign test, $p < .05$). Within imitative learning, imitation of instrumental actions emerged before or in the same month as imitation of arbitrary actions for 17 infants (before for 12 infants); this ordering (i.e., imitation of instrumental actions → imitation of arbitrary actions for 12 infants and the reverse order for seven infants) was not statistically significant. Within communicative gestures, declarative gestures emerged before or in the same month as imperative gestures for 23 infants (before for 21 infants); this ordering (i.e., declaratives → imperatives for 21 infants and the reverse order for one infant) was statistically significant (Sign test, $p < .05$). Proximal declarative gestures emerged before or in the same month as distal declarative gestures for 21 infants (before for 18 infants); this ordering (i.e., proximal → distal for 18 infants and the reverse order for three infants) was statistically significant (Sign test, $p < .05$).

Patterns of emergence of other theoretically interesting combinations of the social-cognitive skills were also investigated. First, the physical obstacle task can be taken to be a measure of the infant's expression of his or her own intentionality in the sense of differentiating means and ends (Piaget, 1952). We thus investigated whether infants displayed their own clearly intentional behavior, as measured by the physical obstacle task, before they showed some understanding of others' intentions, as measured by the social-cognitive tasks—as was hypothesized by Tomasello (1995a). Infants' own intentionality emerged before or in the same month as joint engagement for 21 of the 24 infants, before or in the same month as communicative gestures for 23 of the 24 infants, and before or in the same month as all the other skills (including the social obstacle task) for all 24 infants.

Second, an analysis investigating the order of emergence of the comprehension and production of communicative gestures was conducted. Point following was used as a measure of comprehension of communicative gestures, and infants' production of any communicative gesture was used as a measure of production of communicative gestures. Production of communicative gestures emerged before or in the same month as comprehension of communicative gestures for 21 infants (before for 16 infants); this ordering (production before comprehension for 16 infants and the reverse ordering for three infants) was statistically significant (Sign test, $p < .05$). When comprehension and production of communicative points alone were considered (i.e., infants' declarative or imperative points were used as a measure of production of communicative points), comprehension tended to precede production, although this ordering was not statistically significant: 16 infants followed the experimenter's points before or in the same month as they pointed themselves for the first time (before for 13 infants), whereas eight children pointed themselves before following the experimenter's points.

Third, the social-cognitive tasks were grouped according to their function as indicated by the large-scale categories described previously (with some minor modifications). Thus, we looked at individual tasks and their AOEs within the three broad categories of sharing, following, and directing. Crossed with these was the distinction of attention versus behavior, yielding a 3 × 2 matrix, as seen in Figure 12. The second two broad categories are perfectly straightforward: they involve following into others' attention or behavior and directing others' attention or behavior, as described previously.

The first category, sharing attention, suggested two modifications in order accurately to reflect what we observed across tasks. First, the distinction between proximal and distal gestures seemed important. When infants held up objects to show them to the adults, the behavior was not really directive in the same sense as when they pointed to distal entities. Whereas in pointing to distal entities the infants directed the adult to some object outside their ongoing interaction, requiring the adult to change her direction of attention, showing objects to adults always took place within the ongoing social interaction and did not require the adult to change her direction of attention at all. Indeed, when infants held up objects to show them to adults, they seemed to expect that the adult was already looking as they did not alternate gaze between adult and object as they often did in distal pointing; they simply looked up at the adult's face and held up the object simultaneously. For these reasons, we decided to group proximal gestures (mostly showing) with joint engagement in the sharing attention category—as simply a more active version of sharing attention with an adult about an object with which they were already interacting in most cases.

The second modification involved the social obstacle task. Like joint engagement and proximal gestures, the key infant behavior in this task was a look to the adult's face. It could thus be seen as a kind of "checking" on the adult: *Someone interrupted my play, and I need to look to her face to see what is going on.* From this perspective, joint engagement may be seen as checking on the adult as well: *Something interesting happened with this object, and I need to check to see if my partner appreciates it also.* In any case, for purposes of this exploratory analysis, we decided to regard the social obstacle task as a kind of "checking adult behavior" and therefore to include it under the newly named category *sharing/checking attention and behavior* (whereas joint engagement was regarded as sharing/checking adult *attention* because it occurred in the absence of overt adult behavior). This then makes for a ninth task to be included in this analysis (note that referential language was not used because, from a functional point of view, it was redundant with gestures—although it could be included in Figure 12 without necessitating any changes). The nine tasks falling into the six categories are thus the following:

Sharing/checking attention.—Joint engagement, proximal declarative gestures (shows).
Sharing/checking behavior.—Social obstacle.
Following attention.—Gaze following, point following.
Following behavior.—Imitation of instrumental actions, imitation of arbitrary actions.

Directing attention.—Distal declarative gestures (points).
Directing behavior.—Imperative gestures.

Figure 12 shows the time line for the emergence of these tasks using this grouping. An analysis using the first task to emerge in each of the three groups for each infant, collapsing across attention and behavior, found that most infants progressed from sharing to following to directing. Twenty of the 24 infants followed this pattern (the other four infants directed for the first time before following for the first time). For most of the infants, this pattern held both for attention separately (19 infants shared attention before following attention and followed attention before directing it) and for behavior separately (13 infants checked behavior before following behavior and followed behavior before directing it). The pattern of attention before behavior held within each functional grouping as well: in general, infants shared/checked others' attention before their behavior, followed others' attention before their behavior, and directed others' attention before their behavior.

Age of Emergence Ranges

The preceding set of analyses described the order in which the social-cognitive and other skills emerged. It did not address the specific timing of the emergence of the skills, however. In the next set of analyses, we investigated how tightly the main social-cognitive skills clustered together in time by examining the periods of time in which these skills emerged. Joint engagement was excluded from these analyses because this skill had emerged for all infants by the beginning of the study; referential language was excluded because this skill had not emerged for the majority (17 of 24) of infants by 15 months. In the first analysis, the time in which it took infants to show all three of the remaining social-cognitive skills (i.e., communicative gestures, attention following, and imitative learning) was examined by counting the number of months it took each infant to show all three skills in any order for the first time. One infant showed all three skills for the first time in the same month. The three skills emerged in 2 months or less for six infants (25%), in 3 months or less for 14 infants (58%), in 4 months or less for 19

FIGURE 12.—Time line for sharing/checking, following, and directing other's attention and behavior. Ages given within the grid are mean ages. Numbers beneath the grid are the numbers of infants for whom the two skills or sets of skills emerged in the given order. For example, all 24 infants shared/checked before or in the same month as following. For 17 infants, attention following emerged before or in the same month as imitative learning. Twenty of the 24 infants followed the entire pattern of sharing, then following, then directing. ([a] Joint engagement → proximal declarative gestures: 24; joint engagement → social obstacle: 24; social obstacle → proximal declarative gestures: 15.)

	Share/Check (9–10 months)		Follow (11 months)	Direct (12 months)
Attention	Joint engagement (9.0 months)	Proximal declarative gestures (10.5 months)	Gaze following and/or point following (11.5 months)	Distal declarative gestures (12.6 months)
Behavior	Social obstacle (10.5 months)		Imitation of instrumental and/or arbitrary actions (11.9 months)	Imperative gestures (12.7 months)

a

24   17   20   15

infants (79%), in 5 months or less for 21 infants (88%), and in 6 months or less for 23 infants (96%).

The second analysis investigated the actual age, as opposed to the time period, by which all three of these skills first emerged (in effect, this analysis includes four skills, as joint engagement emerged by 9 months for all infants). All these skills emerged by age 10 months for two infants (8%), by 11 months for 8 infants (33%), by 12 months for 14 infants (58%), by 13 months for 18 infants (75%), by 14 months for 20 infants (83%), and by 15 months for 22 infants (92%).

Summary

There was a common pattern of emergence for the five main social-cognitive skills. Almost two-thirds of the infants followed the same pattern of emergence: joint engagement → communicative gestures → attention following → imitative learning → referential language. Most of the infants who did not fit this pattern differed only in the ordering of attention following and imitative learning (for a total of 20 of 24 infants). For over half the infants, the three middle skills (communicative gestures, attention following, and imitative learning) emerged in 3 months or less; for almost 80% of the infants, they emerged in 4 months or less. Nonsocial, object-related skills (i.e., spatial relations and the object permanence measure) did not fit into the above pattern, instead emerging relatively inconsistently with respect to the social-cognitive skills. Most infants progressed from sharing/checking others' attention and then behavior, to following into others' attention and then behavior, to directing others' attention and then behavior.

Correlations

In order to investigate the relations among the skills further, the AOEs of each skill were correlated using Pearson product-moment correlations (one tailed since we predicted positive correlations) to determine whether infants who demonstrated one skill earlier also performed others earlier. Cross-lagged correlation analyses using infants' scores (i.e., pass or fail) on each of the skills at each age were also conducted.

AOE Correlations

Correlations among the main social-cognitive skills are listed in Table 3 (joint engagement could not be correlated with the other skills because it had emerged for all infants by 9 months, at the beginning of the study). The AOE of communicative gestures was significantly positively correlated with

TABLE 3

CORRELATIONS MATRIX FOR THE MAIN SOCIAL-COGNITIVE SKILLS

	Communicative Gestures	Attention Following	Imitative Learning	Referential Language
Communicative gestures	. . .	.46*	.30[a]	.46*
Attention following		. . .	.33[b]	.36*
Imitative learning			. . .	.31[c]
Referential language				. . .

NOTE.—Joint engagement could not be correlated with the other skills because it had emerged for all infants by 9 months.

[a] $p < .08$, but the correlation between imitative learning and distal declarative gestures was significant ($r = .43$, $p < .05$).

[b] $p < .06$, but the correlation between imitative learning and point following was significant ($r = .38$, $p < .05$).

[c] $p < .08$, but the correlation between referential language and imitation of arbitrary actions was significant ($r = .39$, $p < .05$).

* $p < .05$.

both the AOE of attention following ($r = .46$) and the AOE of referential language ($r = .46$), and attention following was significantly positively correlated with referential language ($r = .36$, $p < .05$). The remaining three correlations approached significance. When the main social-cognitive skills were broken down into their component tasks, however, for each pair of skills significant correlations were found between one of the skills and a component of the other skill. That is, whereas the correlation between imitative learning and communicative gestures only approached significance ($r = .30$, $p < .08$), the correlation between imitative learning and distal declarative gestures was significant ($r = .43$, $p < .05$). Likewise, the correlation between imitative learning and attention following only approached significance ($r = .33$, $p < .06$), but there was a significant correlation between imitative learning and point following ($r = .38$, $p < .05$). The correlation between imitative learning and referential language also only approached significance ($r = .31$, $p < .08$), but there was a significant correlation between imitation of arbitrary actions and referential language ($r = .39$, $p < .05$).

To examine whether the significant correlations were due to the two skills in each pair emerging at the same age or emerging at different ages in a predictable order, paired, two-tailed t tests were conducted for each of the main social-cognitive skill correlations. For most pairs of skills, significant differences (all at the level of $p < .001$) were found between the AOEs of each skill: communicative gestures and attention following ($t[23] = 3.80$); communicative gestures and referential language ($t[23] = 16.65$); attention following and referential language ($t[23] = 10.97$); imitative learning and communicative gestures ($t[23] = 4.13$); and imitative learning and referential language ($t[23] = 8.58$, all p's $< .001$). These pairs of skills thus emerged at different ages in a predictable order. There was no significant difference between the AOEs of imitative learning and attention following, on the other

TABLE 4

CORRELATION MATRIX FOR THE OBJECT-RELATED AND THE
SOCIAL-COGNITIVE SKILLS

	Spatial Relations	Object Permanence
Communicative gestures	.41*	.09
Attention following	.13	.15
Imitative learning	.46*	.44*
Referential language	.32	.28

*$p < .05$.

hand ($t[23] = 1.05$, $p > .30$), or between the AOEs of imitative learning and point following ($t[23] = 0.41$, $p > .68$). This finding is consistent with the ordering and mean AOE results presented above, which indicated that these skills emerged at the same age.

There were some significant correlations between object-related and social-cognitive skills (see Table 4). Spatial relations was significantly positively correlated with communicative gestures ($r = .41$), and both spatial relations ($r = .46$) and the object permanence measure ($r = .44$) were correlated with imitative learning of actions on objects. The two object-related skills, spatial relations and the object permanence measure, were also correlated with each other ($r = .37$, $p < .05$).

AOE correlations were also investigated at the different levels used in the ordering analyses. First, correlations between various components of the main social-cognitive skills were examined. Within attention following, gaze following and point following were not significantly correlated ($r = .22$, $p = .15$). Within imitative learning, imitation of instrumental actions and imitation of arbitrary actions were significantly positively correlated ($r = .58$, $p < .001$). Within communicative gestures, the AOE of infants' first declarative gesture was significantly correlated with the AOE of their first imperative gesture ($r = .44$, $p < .05$), and the correlation between proximal and distal declarative gestures ($r = .30$) approached significance ($p < .08$). Of all the different types of communicative gestures, only proximal declarative gestures were significantly correlated with referential language ($r = .40$, $p < .05$). In addition, the correlation between comprehension and production of communicative gestures, that is, the correlation between point following and production of any communicative gesture, was significant ($r = .43$, $p < .05$).

Cross-Lagged Correlations

Figure 13 shows representations of results of the cross-lagged correlation analyses for selected pairs of the main social-cognitive skills. Phi correlations

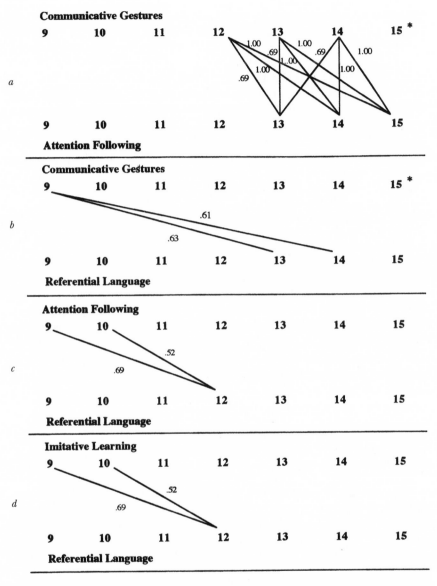

FIGURE 13.—Cross-lagged correlations for the selected social-cognitive skills at each month. Lines represent significant correlations between months ($p < .005$). (* All infants had produced a communicative gesture by 15 months, so no correlations are given for this month.)

were used on infants' pass/fail scores at each month; because of the large number of correlations, a significance level of .005 was used. All significant correlations were positive. There were significant correlations between several pairs of different skills. For instance, communicative gestures at 12, 13, and 14 months were correlated with attention following at 13, 14, and 15 months in both directions (e.g., communicative gestures at 13 months were correlated with attention following at 14 months, and attention following at 13 months was correlated with communicative gestures at 14 months; see Figure 13*a*). Early communicative gestures, attention following, and imitative learning were all correlated with referential language at later months (see Figure 13*b–d*). There were no significant correlations between communicative gestures and imitative learning or between attention following and imitative learning at individual months.

Summary

There were several significant correlations between the AOEs of the main social-cognitive skills: attention following, communicative gestures, and referential language were all intercorrelated. There were also several significant correlations between individual tasks and abilities at the skill level, with the AOEs of all pairs of the social-cognitive skills or their components being interrelated. A few correlations were found between the object-related skills and some of the social-cognitive skills. Finally, cross-lagged correlations showed that infants' pass/fail scores on the social-cognitive skills at individual sessions were also often intercorrelated.

DISCUSSION

The age of emergence and developmental progression of the individual measures of this study were overall very similar to those found in other studies in which similar measurement procedures were used. Thus, all 24 infants in the study were observed to engage in at least one brief episode of joint engagement with an adult at 9 months of age, which accords with the original age posited by Trevarthen and Hubley (1978). Although Bakeman and Adamson (1984) found that fewer than half their 9-month-olds engaged in coordinated joint attention, their time sample was only 10 minutes, whereas ours, for purposes of this measure, was approximately 1 hour. We also found that most of the infants checked the adult's face when something in an interaction went wrong (during the blocking and teasing tasks) between 10 and 11 months of age, in general accordance with Phillips et al. (1992), who found that basically all their 9–18-month-olds behaved in this way. Infants in our study thus shared or checked adults' attention or behavior in one of these two ways, mostly both, by 9 months of age.

With regard to following attention, previous research has found that, although infants follow the gaze of others in a general way between 8 and 10 months of age (Scaife & Bruner, 1975), it is not until 12–15 months of age that they are able to localize specific targets (Butterworth & Cochran, 1980; Butterworth & Jarrett, 1991). Our findings of an average age of emergence of 13 months for gaze following accords with this previous research. Our findings that infants' ability to follow pointing gestures to targets emerged roughly 1 month earlier is also in accord with previous research (e.g., Butterworth & Grover, 1988, 1990). In our sample, infants passed one or the other of these attention-following tasks, on average, at 11.5 months of age. With regard to following behavior, Meltzoff (1988a, 1988b) established a developmental window for imitative learning of actions on objects—ruling out simpler forms of social learning such as stimulus enhancement and emulation learning—at 9–14 months of age. Our finding that infants engaged in imitative learning of both instrumental and arbitrary acts mostly between 12 and 13 months of age fits comfortably within this window. Somewhat surprisingly, we did not find a statistically significant advantage for the imitative learning of instrumental over arbitrary acts. In our sample, infants passed one or the other of these imitative learning tasks, on average, at 11.9 months of age.

Communicative gestures are not a homogeneous set, and thus we found that showing objects emerged on average between 10 and 11 months, whereas pointing—for either imperative or declarative purposes—emerged between 12 and 13 months. These ages are in general accord with previous research (e.g., Bates et al., 1979; Bretherton et al., 1981). We found no evidence of imperatives before declaratives (as reported by, e.g., Perucchini & Camaioni, 1993), and this is therefore an issue for future research. Indeed, we found that, on average, infants produced proximal declaratives (mostly shows) before imperatives and that they produced declarative points before imperative points. The average age at which infants in our study first produced a clearly communicative gesture of one of these types (usually shows) was 10.3 months. In terms of language production during the session, our sample was a bit late relative to many samples, with an average age of emergence of sometime after 15 months of age. This is likely due to our relatively strict definition of language production as requiring the flexible use of referential words.

Our findings thus strongly support the generally held view that the period from 9 to 12 months of age represents a crucially important age in the emergence of infants' skills of social cognition. Over half our infants displayed *all* the main social-cognitive skills that we measured, with the exception of production of referential language, by 12 months of age. It is noteworthy that these results were obtained even though for each and every task we required certain key accompaniments to the infants' behavior (e.g., gaze alternation, expectant looks, following gaze to both sides) that seemed to indicate more than just a behavior learned by rote, that is, accompaniments that seemed to require the infant to take account of the adult's intentions or attention. Although the validity of any one of the tasks could be criticized, and thus its age of emergence called into question, it is hard to imagine that all the tasks have fatal flaws—which would have to be of a different nature for different tasks—allowing them to be passed in ways that do not require the understanding of others as intentional agents. We will return to this point in Chapter V below. We thus believe that the current results provide very strong support for the hypothesis that 9–12 months is the critical age period, at least for American, middle-class infants, in the emergence of their initial skills in understanding the intentions and attention of other persons.

The most novel and interesting findings of the current study concerned the developmental interrelations among these various measures of early social cognition and communication. The most common order of emergence of the five major social-cognitive and communicative skills measured was joint engagement → communicative gestures → attention following → imitative learning → referential language. This was true for the group on average and on the level of individual infants as well, as almost two-thirds of the infants followed this exact pattern of emergence. When attention following and imitative learning are allowed to alternate (given that they both involve following into the attention/behavior of others), 20 of the 24 infants followed the pattern. These quantitative patterns are somewhat generous in that they count "ties" among the age of emergence as consistent with the pattern, but more rigorous statistical analyses (scalogram and order-theoretic analyses) confirmed that these patterns were indeed strongly characteristic of the sample.

When we descend to the task level, we still find very consistent ordering patterns. Given our bifurcation of the declarative gestures into proximal declaratives (mostly shows), which emerged very early, and distal declaratives (mostly points), which emerged two months later, and our interpretation of the social obstacle task as a task of checking adult behavior, a very interesting pattern emerged. Twenty of 24 infants engaged in sharing/checking attention and behavior, then following into attention and behavior, then directing attention and behavior. That is, during the period between 9 and 11 months, infants looked up to adults in periods of joint engagement, looked up to them in the social obstacle task, and looked up to them as they also held objects up for them to see. During the period between 11 and 12 months, they actively followed the trajectory of the adults' pointing and gazing, and they followed into the adults' behavior on objects by imitating it (with an expectation that it would lead to the same goal). Finally, during the period between 12 and 13 months, infants began attempting to redirect the adult's attention to some specific location outside the local space around them and to request various adult behavior imperatively, using distal gestures such as pointing (and, somewhat later, referential words).

This ordering of skills and tasks held even though the task demands involved across tasks were made to be as comparable as possible, both in the sense of information-processing demands and in the sense that we required in each case some indication that the infant understood something of the adult's intentions or attention in the task. Somewhat different measurement operations were used for different skills as we attempted to adapt to their different natures (e.g., some skills were measured throughout the session, whereas others could be displayed only in their structured tasks). However, skills that were measured throughout the session did not all emerge earlier than those measured in the structured tasks (i.e., referential language emerged last), and reliable orderings were found for skills and tasks that were measured in the same ways (e.g., joint engagement emerged before communicative gestures, point following emerged before gaze following, and individual communicative gestures emerged in a predictable order).

In addition, our results for the individual skills accorded quite well with the findings of other studies, which sometimes used different measurement operations (see above), and thus this is not a likely explanation for the ordering pattern that we observed. Nor would motoric difficulty seem to be an adequate explanation for the observed order of emergence. For example, motorically speaking, gestures would seem to be more difficult than attention following (simply turning the head), yet communicative gestures emerged before attention following for all but three of the 24 infants. Indeed, when expectant looks to the end result were not required as criteria for passing an imitative learning test, even imitative learning, clearly the most motorically challenging of the tasks, emerged on average before attention following and only slightly after communicative gestures. It is also noteworthy that the two object-related skills measured—object permanence and spatial relations— did not fit into this sequence in a consistent way across infants, providing some indication that all these skills are interrelated in ways that go beyond general maturational timetables applying to all ontogenetic sequences equally. In all, to our knowledge, the current study provides the most explicit and detailed account available to date of the developmental ordering involved in these different social-cognitive skills. Its theoretical significance will be discussed in Chapter V below.

Also of importance are the correlations among the tasks. All the social-cognitive and communicative skills intercorrelated positively, although in some cases only at moderate levels and only when individual tasks were considered. Significant positive correlations were found between the ages of emergence of each pair of the main social-cognitive skills or one of their constituent tasks (with the exception of joint engagement, which had emerged for all infants by 9 months, at the beginning of the study). It is perhaps of special interest that we found a correlation between the ages of emergence of imitative learning and distal declarative gestures (not proximal gestures), which makes sense because distal declarative gestures (i.e., points) are conventional and thus probably are learned or at least refined through imitation—which is probably not true of proximal gestures such as shows. Also, the correlation between the ages of emergence of referential language and imitation of arbitrary actions (but not imitation of instrumental actions) makes sense because, in order to learn to use referential words, infants must be able to imitate sounds only arbitrarily connected to their referents. Finally, the correlation between imitative learning and point following (but not gaze following) makes sense because both imitative learning and point following involve infants following the other's intention that they do something, whereas with gaze following, at least in infants' natural environments, this intention is less obvious. There were also several significant cross-lagged correlations between different skills at different ages, mostly involving one or another of the social-cognitive skills (especially communicative gestures, attention following, and imitative learning) predicting the age of emergence of referential language. Contrary to our expectation, there was no correlation between the emergence of point following and gaze following.

In truth, we expected that there would be higher correlations than there were among these various skills, on the basis of the hypothesis that they are all manifestations of infants' emerging understanding of others as intentional agents (Tomasello, 1995a). However, the problem was that these skills emerged in such a rapid manner for most infants (for almost 60% of the infants in 3 months or less and for almost 80% of the infants in 4 months or less) that there was very little variability for the correlations to work with. Obviously, a more finely grained approach—for example, sampling infants' behavior every week—would be required to establish correlations that accounted for large portions of the variance in skills that emerged in such close developmental synchrony. Overall, then, given that our measurement interval was 1 full month, and given that infants acquired the skills in relatively rapid succession, with the result that there was relatively little variability in ages of emergence, it is in some ways amazing that we obtained the correlations that we did.

The fact that each of our two object-related tasks (the object permanence measure and spatial relations) was positively correlated with imitative learning, and that spatial relations was positively correlated with communicative gestures, should temper our interpretation of these correlational findings in terms of a single underlying social-cognitive skill. It may be of interest to note that the social-cognitive skills involved in these correlations also involve objects: imitative learning involved manipulating the physical apparatus, and the age of emergence of communicative gestures was due almost totally to shows, which involved holding up objects to adults. This might suggest that object manipulation is an important factor in the social-cognitive skills that correlated with the object-related skills. And, of course, it opens the possibility that underlying all the skills that we measured is the maturing of some very general information-processing ability or the like. Again, the theoretical implications of these correlational findings will be discussed in Chapter V below.

We have made some fairly broad claims about the skills that we investigated in this study, but of course we, as most other investigators, used Western, middle-class infants as participants. It is not known whether the ordering patterns and interrelations that we have found would hold for infants raised in other cultural environments. In addition, it is important to note that the social-cognitive skills measured in this study are almost uniformly impaired in children with autism, whereas object-related skills are spared in these children. Similarly, our nearest primate relatives, the apes, also seem to have more human-like skills in the domain of object manipulation and knowledge than in the social-cognitive domain. These populations may therefore provide further evidence for some internal consistency among the most basic social-cognitive skills, along with a distinction between these skills and the object-related skills.

IV. RESULTS OF STUDY 2:
JOINT ENGAGEMENT AND COMMUNICATION

The main objective of Study 1 was to document the order of emergence and interrelations of a number of infant skills of social cognition expressed essentially individually. The main objective of Study 2 was to investigate infants' skills of social interaction with their mothers, in the form of relatively extended periods of joint attentional engagement, and how these skills relate to the emergence of infants' communicative skills. Whereas, in Study 1, the age of emergence was the outcome of interest for all infant skills, in Study 2, a more quantitative approach was taken—relating such things as the amount of time infants spent in joint engagement with their mothers and the actual number of words in their vocabularies. Also of interest were the way in which mothers used language in these interactions (either to follow into or to redirect their child's attention) and the ways in which this related to children's early vocabularies. The main feature distinguishing the current study from other studies investigating these same relations is the focus on very young children just beginning to communicate in conventional ways. We were able to study children this young by focusing on preverbal gestures and language comprehension as measures of their communicative competence (whereas other studies have focused on language production, which emerges only some months later).

Results are presented in two sections. In the first section, we focus on the development of mother-infant joint attentional engagement, maternal language, and communicative skills as individual measures. In the second section, we explore the various interrelations among these three sets of interactive phenomena.

INDIVIDUAL MEASURES

Each of the main variables—joint attentional engagement, communication, and maternal language—are described below. Means and standard errors of the mean are presented in the figures. Where applicable, age effects were tested with repeated-measures analysis of variance (ANOVA). When age effects were significant, they were tested for significant linear, quadratic, and cubic trends in order to evaluate the form of the effects. In order to obtain a greater understanding of the developmental patterns, significant age effects were examined with Helmhert comparisons (Abacus Concepts, 1989). This test compares the mean of an individual time point to the weighted mean of the remaining time points at older ages.

Joint Engagement

Recall that, for this study, the joint-engagement measures were obtained from the 10-minute free-play period at the beginning of infants' visits and measured infants' abilities to engage in relatively extended periods of joint engagement with their mothers. It is important to note that, in the previous major longitudinal study of this phenomenon, Bakeman and Adamson (1984) observed children only at 3-month intervals (6, 9, 12, 15, and 18 months). The current descriptive information will therefore serve to fill in the monthly gaps in that analysis.

Time in Joint Engagement

In the current sample of infants, the average time that mother-infant dyads spent in joint engagement gradually increased each month, rising from an average of 13 seconds (range 0–56, SD = 16.3) at 9 months to an average of 44 seconds (range 0–123, SD = 35.7) at 15 months. The dyads thus spent significantly more time in joint engagement with age ($F[6, 23] = 4.71$, $p <$ .001). Figure 14 illustrates this increase in mean time in joint engagement and its significant linear trend ($F[1, 23] = 26.8$, $p < .001$). This age effect resulted mostly from the increase in joint-engagement time between 9 and 12 months (Helmhert comparison at 9 months, $F[1, 23] = 11.17$, $p < .01$; at 10 months, $F[1, 23] = 8.84$, $p < .01$; and at 11 months, $F[1, 23] = 4.59$, $p < .05$). Between 12 and 15 months, joint-engagement time stabilized, showing no significant increases on a monthly basis.

Number of Joint-Engagement Episodes

The number of joint-engagement episodes also increased with age ($F[6, 23] = 4.06$, $p < .001$), from an average of 1.6 episodes (range 0–8, SD = 2.1) at 9 months to 4.3 episodes (range 0–13, SD = 3.2) at 15 months. Figure 15 illustrates this increase and the significant linear trend to this age effect ($F[6, 23] = 20.5$, $p < .001$). Like joint-engagement time, the frequency of

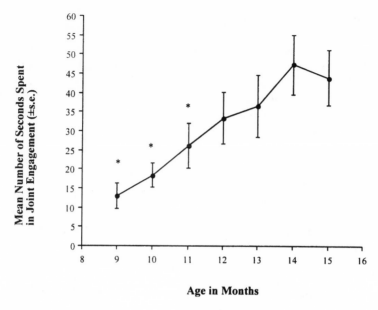

FIGURE 14.—Mean time spent in joint engagement in seconds at each time point (vertical lines are standard errors of the mean) (* $p < .05$).

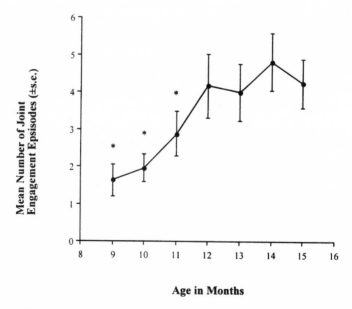

FIGURE 15.—Mean number of joint-engagement episodes at each time point (vertical lines are standard errors of the mean) (* $p < .05$).

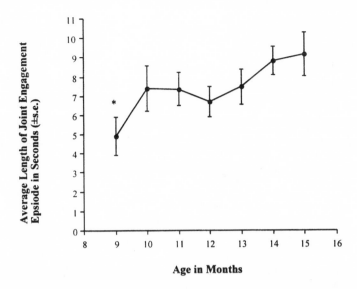

FIGURE 16.—Average duration of joint-engagement episodes in seconds at each time point (vertical lines are standard errors of the mean) (* $p < .05$).

episodes increased significantly between month 9 and month 12 (Helmhert comparison at 9 months, $F[1, 23] = 9.56$, $p < .01$; at 10 months, $F[1, 23] = 9.39$, $p < .01$; at 11 months, $F[1, 23] = 4.36$, $p < .05$) and leveled off between 12 and 15 months.

Durations of Joint-Engagement Episodes

The average duration of joint-engagement episodes also increased significantly with age ($F[6, 23] = 2.24$, $p < .05$), with a mean duration at 9 months of 4.89 seconds (range 0–17, SD = 4.8) and a mean duration at 15 months of 9.17 seconds (range 0–20.5, SD = 5.6). Figure 16 illustrates the significant linear trend ($F[1, 23] = 10.06$, $p < .01$). However, further comparisons revealed that this effect resulted mainly from a large increase in episode duration between 9 and 10 months (Helmhert comparison at 9 months, $F[1, 23] = 8.14$, $p < .01$). After this initial increase, mean durations were similar from 10 through 15 months, ranging between 6.7 and 9.2 seconds.

Individual Patterns of Joint Engagement

All these measures of joint attentional engagement reflect mean values for the entire group of 24 infants. However, there were large individual differences among mother-infant dyads in these measures at any given month as

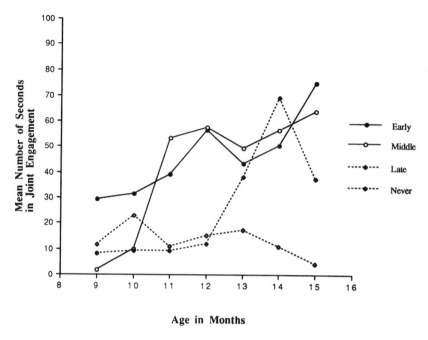

FIGURE 17.—Mean joint-engagement time of the early, middle, late, and never joint-engagement groups.

well as large intraindividual differences within dyads across months. We thus felt it necessary to look more closely at ontogenetic patterns of joint attentional engagement to see whether there were some identifiable profiles into which dyads could be grouped.

To this end, we plotted separately each dyad's time in joint engagement across months. The dyads fell quite naturally into four groups: early, middle, late, and never (see Figure 17). The six dyads in the early group began the study at 9 or 10 months with significant amounts of joint engagement (operationalized as approximately 30 seconds or more in one session—established post hoc in a way that maximally discriminated groups) and then increased to and maintained high levels of joint engagement (between 40 and 70 seconds) across the remaining months. The five dyads in the middle group began spending significant amounts of time in joint engagement at 11 or 12 months (with very little during months 9 and 10), and a high level was maintained throughout the rest of the study. The seven dyads in the late group had essentially no time in joint engagement until month 13 or 14, at which point their mean time increased sharply to high levels for the rest of the study. The fourth group of six dyads never showed an increase in their joint-engagement time, never engaging in significant amounts of joint engage-

TABLE 5

CORRELATION MATRIX FOR TIME SPENT IN JOINT ENGAGEMENT AT EACH TIME POINT

JOINT ENGAGEMENT	JOINT ENGAGEMENT						
	9	10	11	12	13	14	15
9 months	...	.10	.21	.25	−.03	−.01	.11
10 months		...	−.05	−.11	.04	−.26	−.19
11 months			...	.23	.14	.25	.50*
12 months				...	.15	.01	.42*
13 months					...	.20	.19
14 months						...	.25
15 months							...

* $p < .05$, two tailed.

ment; each dyad in this group had only 1 month in which they spent 30 seconds or more in joint engagement, with none of the remaining months (before or after this 1 high month) reaching this level. It is very interesting to note that the first three groups all look very similar (50-70 seconds of joint engagement) during the period between 14 and 15 months; it is the age at which they begin to increase their time in joint engagement that differs.

Although the majority of infants increased their time in joint engagement with age, most had fluctuations in their monthly values of joint engagement, sometimes dropping to zero or very small amounts of joint engagement for one session. Combined with the staggered onset times of emergence, these fluctuations were enough to produce instability in the amounts of time in joint engagement from month to month. Table 5 reports the correlations between joint-engagement time at different months. There were no significant correlations between consecutive monthly values of joint engagement, although time in joint engagement at 11 and 12 months was correlated with time in joint engagement at 15 months.

Other Variables

Potential effects of gender, birth order, and toy set used in the play session were analyzed for all three of the joint-engagement measures with repeated-measures ANOVAs. The only significant finding was that later-born infants spent more time in joint engagement per session ($M = 39.2$ seconds) than firstborn infants ($M = 25.7$ seconds, $F[1, 22] = 5.13$, $p < .05$).

Comparison with Previous Data

Figure 18 displays the current group's average amount of joint-engagement time across months converted to percentages and compared

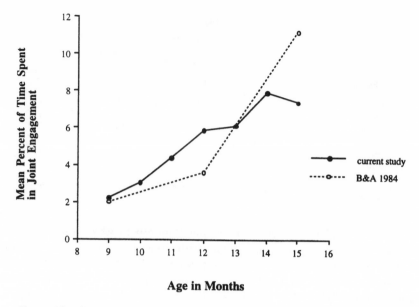

FIGURE 18.—Comparison of mean percentage of time spent in joint engagement in the current study with that in Bakeman and Adamson (1984).

with the corresponding data from the Bakeman and Adamson (1984) sample. Both studies found a significant increase in joint-engagement time with age, but the patterns were a bit different. As can be seen in Figure 18, the values at 9 months are nearly identical for the two samples, but then the current dyads show a steady monthly increase thereafter, in contrast to the Bakeman and Adamson sample, which shows no large increase in joint engagement until the 12–15-month time point. The current study's pattern of increase leveled off at 14–15 months, which would not be expected given Bakeman and Adamson's findings of a continued rise until 18 months of age. The current sample's value at 15 months (slightly, although not statistically, lower than 14 months) thus represents something of an aberration.

Summary

These analyses demonstrate that dyads in the current sample spent more time in joint engagement with age, mainly by increasing the frequency of joint-engagement episodes of similar durations. The significant rise in average joint-engagement time during the period between 9 and 12 months resulted in large part from more infants participating in joint engagement for significant amounts of time for the first time. Infants began participating in significant amounts of joint engagement in either the early, the middle, or the late months of the study, or not at all in some cases. There were no significant intercorrelations among consecutive monthly measurements of joint-engagement time, reflecting a fundamental instability in this measure at the level of individual months. This presumably reflects the fact that an individual infant's social-cognitive skills are only one of the variables affecting this measure, with other, more transient variables affecting time in joint engagement as well.

Maternal Language

Mothers' utterances to infants during the 9-, 12-, and 15-month play sessions were coded as utterances that attempted to follow into the infant's focus of attention (*follow*), as utterances that attempted to redirect the infant's attention (*lead*), or as *other* utterances. A repeated-measures ANOVA showed that the frequency of all maternal utterances did not increase significantly over time ($M = 34.0$ utterances at 9 months; $M = 39.4$ at 12 months; and $M = 41.0$ at 15 months). Likewise, no significant difference was found between the number of following ($M = 41.6$) and the number of leading ($M = 34.7$) utterances across the 3 months, and there was no interaction between month and utterance type.

Maternal Language Intercorrelations

Table 6 shows the intercorrelations among following and leading statements over time. The number of following statements at 9 months correlated significantly with the number of following statements at 12 and 15 months. The same was true for leading statements, indicating that mothers were fairly

TABLE 6

CORRELATION MATRIX OF MATERNAL LANGUAGE TYPES

	FOLLOW			LEAD		
	9	12	15	9	12	15
Follow:						
9 months	...	.50*	.62**	.56**	.41*	.37
12 months		...	.34	.16	.40*	.32
15 months			...	.42*	.14	.30
Lead:						
9 months				...	.52**	.56**
12 months					...	.29
15 months						...

* $p < .05$, two tailed.
** $p < .01$, two tailed.

consistent in their amount of both types of language over time. There were also some correlations between following and leading, reflecting the fact that these values are based on frequency of utterances, not proportions (i.e., mothers who talked a lot had high values of both).

Other Variables

Repeated-measures ANOVAs showed no significant effects of gender, birth order, or toy set on amounts of either following or leading maternal utterances at 9, 12, or 15 months.

Infant Communication Measures

Communication measures in this study were maternal reports of infants' communicative gestures and comprehension and production of language using the MacArthur CDI Infant Form.

Gestures

Figure 19a displays the mean number of different types of gestures recorded at each monthly age on the CDI (which includes 12 possible gestures). The use of communicative gestures clearly increased over time for the current sample. Infants averaged about two gestures (range 0–7, SD = 1.7) at 9 months and steadily increased to over eight gestures (range 3–12, SD = 2.1) at 15 months. There was a highly significant age effect ($F[6, 23] = 74.99$, $p < .001$), with both significant linear ($F[1, 23] = 440.27$, $p < .001$) and significant quadratic ($F[1, 23] = 8.03$, $p < .01$) trends. The curvilinear nature of these data seems to reflect the restricted range of the gesture measure at the high end.

Comprehension of Words

The average number of words comprehended by infants (as reported by mothers on the CDI) increased with age in a predictable manner (see Figure 19b). This increase was significant ($F[6, 23] = 47.13$, $p < .001$) and had significant linear ($F[1, 23] = 271.52$, $p < .001$) and quadratic ($F[1, 23] = 11.07$,

---

FIGURE 19.—a, Mean number of gestures produced at each time point. b, Mean number of words comprehended at each time point. c, Mean number of words produced at each time point (from the CDI). (Vertical lines are standard errors of the mean.)

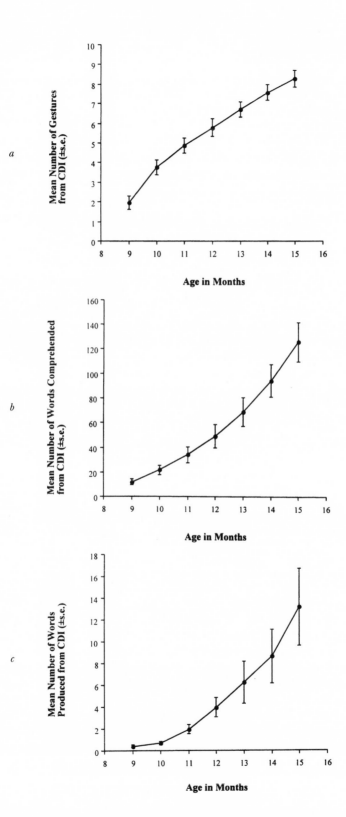

$p < .01$) trends. All infants followed a similar pattern of incremental increases each month, although these increases differed in magnitude. Thus, at any given age, their scores had a wide range; for example, at 9 months, the range was 0–42 words comprehended, and, by 15 months, the scores ranged from 6 to 281 words comprehended. The quadratic trend in this case seems to reflect a positively accelerating curve as infants begin comprehending words at different ages and then proceed at an ever more rapid rate over the course of the period between 9 and 15 months.

Production of Words

Figure 19c displays the mean number of words that infants produced at each age (as reported on the CDI). Mean production between 9 and 15 months increased significantly with age ($F[6, 23] = 11.02$, $p < .001$). This effect had significant linear ($F[1, 23] = 61.35$, $p < .001$) and quadratic ($F[1, 23] = 4.52$, $p < .05$) trends. Mean production at 9 months was 0.42 words, which was a product of nine infants whose scores ranged between one and two words and 15 infants who produced no words. By 15 months, all infants had at least one word in their productive vocabularies, with a range of 1–84 words. Again, the quadratic trend seems to reflect a positively accelerating curve as more infants begin to produce words at each age and at an ever more rapid rate within infants over the course of the study.

Production was also measured at 18 and 24 months by means of mailing CDI Toddler Forms to mothers. Twenty mothers responded at 18 months ($M = 67.6$ words, range 3–210 words), and 15 mothers responded at 24 months ($M = 194.6$ words, range 10–559 words). A repeated-measures AN-OVA indicated that neither group of responders at these two ages differed significantly from the nonresponders on their production scores during the period between 9 and 15 months.

Individual Patterns of Communication

It is important to note that, unlike the joint-engagement measures, for the communication measures all infants showed similar accumulating curves; they just began at different times. This simply reflects the cumulative nature of these measures as both mothers and researchers assume that children's gestural and linguistic repertoires are ever increasing over age (whereas joint engagement during a specified 10-minute period may fluctuate for children over time).

The three communication measures were quite stable over time. Correlations between consecutive monthly values for gestures ranged from $r = .77$ to $r = .94$, with a mean r of .85. Correlations between consecutive monthly values for comprehension ranged from $r = .70$ to $r = .98$, with a mean r of .92. Correlations between consecutive monthly values for production ranged from $r = .39$ to $r = .99$, with a mean r of .79.

Finally, intercorrelations among the three communication measures were calculated for the final age point of 15 months. Number of gestures produced and number of words comprehended were significantly correlated ($r = .43$, $p < .05$), but number of words produced did not correlate with either number of gestures produced ($r = .21$) or number of words comprehended ($r = .20$).

Other Variables

Repeated-measures ANOVAs found no significant differences for gender or birth order on any of the three communication measures.

Comparison to MacArthur Norms

The communication measures of the current sample compared to the MacArthur Infant Form norming study (Fenson et al., 1993) in the following ways. The absolute values for gestures were not directly comparable because the MacArthur analyses grouped several subscales that were not measured in the current study. However, the gesture curve of the current study closely resembles that of the MacArthur's total gestures. The comprehension and production scores for each infant in the current study at 15 months were ranked by the MacArthur fitted percentile scores (which are also broken down by gender). The average percentile rank for the current group's comprehension was 46 and ranged between the 5th and the 99th percentiles. For production, the current infants averaged at the 35th percentile and ranged between the 5th and the 99th percentiles. At 18 and 24 months, the current group's production reported on the CDI Toddler Form ranked at the 35th and 31st percentiles, respectively, both ranging between the 5th and the 90th percentile ranks of the CDI norming study. The relatively low production values in the current study may have resulted from our slight change of procedure (discussed above), in which mothers were encouraged to report only words that their infant used in a relatively flexible manner.

Summary

Infants in the current study gradually acquired means of communication over the course of the study, with the number of gestures produced and words comprehended and produced rising steadily over the period between 9 and 15 months. The infants looked very similar in their gesture production and word comprehension to the MacArthur norming sample, whereas they were slightly below average in their production of words (perhaps owing to the more stringent criteria used for flexible word production in the current study).

DEVELOPMENTAL INTERRELATIONS

Our main interest in this study was in how joint attentional engagement and maternal language predict infants' very earliest communication skills. In all analyses, the measure of joint attentional engagement used was time in joint engagement, and the measure of maternal language used was number of utterances that followed into the infant's already-established attentional focus (termed *maternal following;* in some cases, correlations with *maternal leading* utterances were also computed for comparative purposes). Results are organized by the three communication skills investigated: gestures, comprehension of words, and production of words.

For each of the three communication measures, we look first at how joint engagement and then maternal language correlate with communication skills on a month-by-month basis. In all cases, we use Pearson product-moment correlations, two tailed, with 22 degrees of freedom. For the joint-engagement measure, we also look at how the four different styles of joint engagement that characterized the dyads (i.e., early, middle, late, and never) relate to communication skills.

We then take a multivariate approach to predicting the communication skills, using multiple regression analyses to assess the predictive values of joint engagement and maternal following taken together and taken individually controlling for the other. To keep the number of equations manageable, the following procedure was followed. First, the outcome ages for each of the communication measures were established as 9, 12, and 15 months only (the first, middle, and last months of the study). Second, the same was done for the predictor variables, but with a slight modification. In the case of joint engagement, because the measure was unstable over time, we decided to represent its values at 9, 12, and 15 months for a given dyad as the amount of time that that dyad spent in joint engagement during all the months accumulated up to that month. Thus, 9 months is simply the amount of time at 9 months; 12 months is the amount of time at 9, 10, 11, and 12 months added together; and 15 months is the total amount of time a dyad spent in joint engagement added across all seven monthly data points.[11] To provide com-

---

[11] Note that, since all dyads had values at all months, this procedure is statistically equivalent to dividing each dyad's value by the number of months involved to derive an average monthly value.

parability, the same was done for the maternal following measure, although it should be recalled that this measure was taken only at 9, 12, and 15 months. It is important to note in this regard that the communication measures were already cumulative (a noncumulative measure of productive vocabulary, e.g., would be the number of new words acquired since the previous month, which is seldom done). Third and finally, predictions of outcome variables were made for age points concurrent with and older than the predictor variables, but not for prior age points (e.g., Joint Engagement 12 was used to predict gestures at 12 and 15 months but not at 9 months).

Thus, for each of the three outcome measures (gestures, word comprehension, and word production), six regression equations were run, three of the form

Joint Engagement 9 + Maternal Following 9 → outcome at 9, 12, and 15 months,

two of the form

Joint Engagement 12 + Maternal Following 12 → outcome at 12 and 15 months,

and one of the form

Joint Engagement 15 + Maternal Following 15 → outcome at 15 months.

The intercorrelations between the predictor variables at these different times are presented in Table 7. There were no significant correlations between joint engagement and maternal following at any of the time points tested, and, in fact, none of these correlations exceed .20. Correlations within each variable at the three time points were quite strong, as would be expected (thus corroborating that making joint engagement a cumulative variable helped considerably in stabilizing the measure).

TABLE 7

INTERCORRELATIONS BETWEEN THE PREDICTOR VARIABLES JOINT ENGAGEMENT AND MATERNAL FOLLOWING

	JOINT ENGAGEMENT			MATERNAL FOLLOWING		
	9	12	15	9	12	15
Joint engagement:						
9 months	⋯	.57**	.31	.02	.07	−.01
12 months		⋯	.75***	.05	.12	.17
15 months			⋯	−.01	.15	.20
Maternal following:						
9 months				⋯	.86***	.86***
12 months					⋯	.94***
15 months						⋯

** $p < .01$, two tailed.
*** $p < .001$, two tailed.

Gestures

Correlations with Joint Engagement

Time spent in joint engagement at 9, 11, 12, and 15 months was significantly, positively correlated with gestures at various ages between 10 and 13 months (see Table 8). Although the correlations were scattered across the time points, 80% of the significant correlations occurred between early joint engagement (9–12 months) and early gestures (10–13 months), with correlations in both chronological directions. Also note that the correlations between joint engagement at 9 months and gestures at 9, 10, and 13 months approached significance (i.e., are .34 or greater, $p < .10$, two tailed). This matrix shows a pattern of relatedness between joint engagement between 9 and 12 months and communicative gestures almost totally at early ages.

As an additional way of assessing month-by-month relatedness of joint engagement and gestures, we also used the four different styles of joint engagement. Figure 20 illustrates the gesture production of the four groups (i.e., early, middle, late, and never) across the 7 months of the study. Because of the small numbers of participants in each of the groups, for purposes of statistical analysis we collapsed the groups into two: the earlier emergence group comprising the early and middle groups ($N = 11$) and the later emergence group comprising the late and never groups ($N = 13$). A repeated-measures ANOVA was conducted on the two collapsed groups (earlier and later) to investigate differences in the groups' rate of gesture production. The overall effect of group approached significance ($F[1, 22] = 3.35$, $p = .08$). The gesture production of these groups began to diverge around 11 months, and the gesture production of the earlier group exceeded that of the later group at 12 months ($t[22] = 7.48$, $p < .05$) and at 13 months ($t[22] = 4.31$, $p < .05$). Significant differences were not found at 14 or 15 months, perhaps because of the ceiling imposed by the gesture measure (there was a maximum of 12).

TABLE 8

CORRELATION MATRIX FOR JOINT ENGAGEMENT AND GESTURE PRODUCTION AT EACH TIME POINT

JOINT ENGAGEMENT	GESTURE PRODUCTION						
	9	10	11	12	13	14	15
9 months	.35	.35	.46*	.45*	.35	.28	.18
10 months	−.31	−.21	−.11	−.12	−.09	−.05	.09
11 months	−.02	.12	.30	.62**	.54**	.39	.23
12 months	.37	.49*	.51*	.48*	.43*	.24	.32
13 months	−.28	.06	.02	.23	.18	.28	.36
14 months	−.19	−.12	−.03	.19	.12	.35	.27
15 months	.34	.33	.45*	.42*	.28	.16	.14

* $p < .05$, two tailed.
** $p < .01$, two tailed.

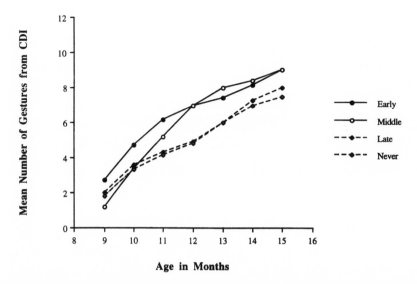

FIGURE 20.—Mean gesture production of the early, middle, late, and never joint-engagement groups at each time point.

Correlations with Maternal Following Language

There were no significant correlations between infants' use of communicative gestures and maternal following language. Two significant correlations were found between maternal leading language and gestures: there was a positive correlation ($r = .63$, $p < .01$, two tailed) between maternal leading language at 9 months and gestures at 9 months and a negative correlation ($r = -.48$, $p < .05$, two tailed) between maternal leading language at 12 months and gestures at 14 months. Thus, essentially no relation was found between maternal language and infants' gestures, and none should be expected since maternal language is not a direct source of information for infants learning to produce gestures.

Regressions

Six regression equations were calculated between the two predictor variables (joint engagement and maternal following) and the gesture measure in accordance with the analytic strategy outlined above (see Table 9). The only significant equation was found for the relations among the predictors at 12 months and the gestures at 12 months ($F[2, 21] = 10.56$, $p < .001$). Together, joint engagement and maternal following at 12 months accounted for about 45% of the variance in the number of gestures at that same age.

TABLE 9

| | GESTURE PRODUCTION | | | | | |
| | 9 Months | | 12 Months | | 15 Months | |
VARIABLE	β	t	β	t	β	t
Joint Engagement 9	N.S.		N.S.		N.S.	
Maternal Follow 9						
Joint Engagement 12	. . .		.71	4.55***	N.S.	
Maternal Follow 12			−.18	−1.16		
Joint Engagement 15	. . .		. . .		N.S.	
Maternal Follow 15						

*** $p < .001$, two tailed.

Furthermore, when Maternal Following 12 was controlled for statistically, Joint Engagement 12 was a significant and strong predictor of number of gestures ($\beta = .71$), but maternal following did not significantly predict gestures when joint engagement was held constant.

Summary

A significant positive relation was found between joint engagement and the production of gestures in the early months of the study (especially at 12 and 13 months of age). That is, the simple correlations showed a positive relation between joint engagement and gesture production at the earlier ages but not at the later ages. The regression analyses found a strong relation between joint engagement at 12 months and gestures at 12 months. In contrast, maternal following language had virtually no relation with gesture production at any age. Together, these analyses reveal a window of time from 9 to 12 months when joint engagement and gestures are related but when maternal language and gestures have basically no relation.

Comprehension of Words

Correlations with Joint Engagement

Time spent in joint engagement at 11, 12, and 13 months was significantly, positively correlated with word comprehension at various ages between 9 and 15 months (see Table 10), again in both chronological directions. All

TABLE 10

CORRELATION MATRIX FOR JOINT ENGAGEMENT AND WORD COMPREHENSION AT EACH TIME POINT

JOINT ENGAGEMENT	WORD COMPREHENSION						
	9	10	11	12	13	14	15
9 months	−.20	.05	.24	.27	.25	.21	.18
10 months	−.21	.09	.31	.39	.36	.34	.27
11 months	.14	.41*	.46*	.43*	.44*	.43*	.39
12 months	.53**	.45*	.31	.31	.45*	.52**	.58**
13 months	.17	.40*	.47*	.48*	.47*	.39	.27
14 months	.04	.15	.15	.13	.13	.16	.16
15 months	.10	.34	.26	.23	.24	.23	.26

* $p < .05$, two tailed.
** $p < .01$, two tailed.

14 of the significant correlations in this matrix occurred with joint engagement in this small window of time between 11 and 13 months. Note also that correlations between joint engagement at 10 months and word comprehension at 12, 13, and 14 months approached significance. Together these correlations show that joint engagement in the middle months (11, 12, 13) is related to word comprehension in the early, middle, and later months.

Figure 21 shows the word-comprehension levels of the four joint-engagement styles. As was done in the analysis of gestures, two groups were

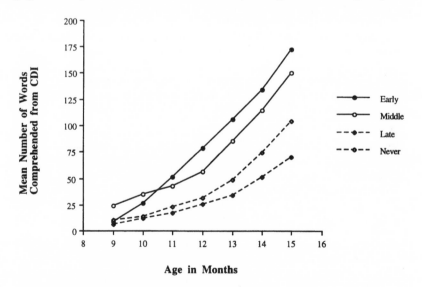

FIGURE 21.—Mean language comprehension of the early, middle, late, and never joint-engagement groups at each time point.

formed for purposes of statistical analysis: a group of earlier emergence and a group of later emergence dyads. A one-way ANOVA found that the earlier group comprehended significantly more words than did the later emergence group over the course of the study ($F[1, 22] = 10.12$, $p < .01$). A significant interaction between age and emergence group was also found ($F[6, 22] = 7.31$, $p < .0001$): the rate of increase in comprehension was high for the earlier emergence group throughout the study, while comprehension of the later emergence group did not begin to increase sharply until after 12 months of age. Thus, those infants who began participating in joint engagement at younger ages (i.e., by 12 months) understood more words at each age between 10 and 15 months than infants whose joint-engagement skills emerged later, sometime after 12 months of age (all 6 t tests, $p < .05$).

Correlations with Maternal Following Language

Many significant positive correlations can be seen between maternal following language and word comprehension in Table 11, predominantly between maternal following at 12 months and word comprehension at 11–15 months (with word comprehension at 15 months correlating with maternal following at all three time points). In contrast, maternal leading language did not correlate with word comprehension at any age. The simple correlations thus reveal a particularly strong relation between maternal following language at 12 months and word comprehension at the later ages.

Regressions

Table 12 displays the results from the six regression equations calculated between the predictor variables and word comprehension at 9, 12, and 15

TABLE 11

CORRELATION MATRIX FOR MATERNAL LANGUAGE AND WORD COMPREHENSION

MATERNAL LANGUAGE	WORD COMPREHENSION						
	9	10	11	12	13	14	15
Follow:							
9 months	.07	.27	.26	.28	.30	.35	.42*
12 months	−.18	.39	.56**	.60**	.53**	.51**	.44*
15 months	.44*	.41*	.29	.27	.30	.35	.45*
Lead:							
9 months	.01	.06	.02	.07	.10	.15	.22
12 months	−.10	.17	.25	.26	.23	.22	.22
15 months	−.06	−.01	.01	.04	.07	.12	.21

* $p < .05$, two tailed.
** $p < .01$, two tailed.

TABLE 12

SUMMARY OF REGRESSION ANALYSES FOR JOINT ENGAGEMENT AND MATERNAL FOLLOWING VARIABLES
PREDICTING WORD COMPREHENSION

	WORD COMPREHENSION					
	9 Months		12 Months		15 Months	
VARIABLE	β	t	β	t	β	t
Joint Engagement 9	N.S.		N.S.		N.S.	
Maternal Follow 9						
Joint Engagement 12	. . .		.54	3.62**	.61	4.52***
Maternal Follow 12			.45	3.05**	.43	3.13**
Joint Engagement 15	. . .		. . .		.49	3.20**
Maternal Follow 15					.44	2.85**

** $p < .01$, two tailed.
*** $p < .001$, two tailed.

months. Joint engagement and maternal following at 9 months did not predict word comprehension at any age. However, joint engagement and maternal following at both the 12- and the 15-month time points significantly predicted word comprehension at 12 and 15 months. First, joint engagement and maternal following at 12 months predicted word comprehension at 12 months ($F[2, 21] = 12.62$, $p < .001$, Adjusted $R^2 = .50$). Taken separately, Joint Engagement 12 and Maternal Following 12 were each significant predictors of comprehension, with beta weights of .54 and .45, respectively (for t values, see Table 12). Similarly, joint engagement and maternal following at 12 months predicted word comprehension at 15 months ($F[2, 21] = 16.94$, $p < .001$, Adjusted $R^2 = .58$). Taken separately, Joint Engagement 12 and Maternal Following 12 individually predicted word comprehension at 15 months, with beta weights of .61 and .43, respectively (for t values, see Table 12). Finally, joint engagement and maternal following at 15 months also predicted word comprehension at 15 months ($F[2, 21] = 11.43$, $p < .001$, Adjusted $R^2 = .48$). Taken separately, Joint Engagement 15 and Maternal Following 15 individually predicted word comprehension at 15 months, with beta weights of .49 and .44, respectively (for t values, see Table 12). In sum, both joint engagement and maternal following at both 12 and 15 months were significant predictors of word comprehension at those same and later age points.

Summary

Comprehension of words was greater between 10 and 15 months of age for infants whose joint-engagement skills had emerged by 12 months than for infants whose joint engagement emerged later. Simple correlations dem-

TABLE 13

Correlation Matrix for Joint Engagement and Word Production at Each Time Point

Joint Engagement	Word Production								
	9	10	11	12	13	14	15	18[a]	24[b]
9 months	−.36	−.01	−.01	−.01	.04	−.02	−.07	−.04	−.16
10 months	−.21	−.32	−.27	−.08	.01	.04	.02	−.16	−.11
11 months	.19	.09	−.19	−.16	−.11	−.12	−.18	.01	−.14
12 months	.19	.29	.18	−.02	−.12	−.14	−.16	−.02	−.14
13 months	.04	.31	−.02	.04	.00	.06	.09	.33	.29
14 months	.15	.16	−.04	.36	.41*	.43*	.52**	.63**	.56**
15 months	.09	.25	−.16	−.14	−.15	−.14	−.10	−.05	−.09

[a] $N = 20$.
[b] $N = 15$.
* $p < .05$, two tailed.
** $p < .01$, two tailed.

onstrated that both joint engagement and maternal following were signifi-cantly related to word comprehension, particularly during the middle months (11, 12, and 13 months). Regression analyses showed that each of these vari-ables independently was a strong predictor of word comprehension at both 12 and 15 months. Together, and by themselves, these two variables predicted over half the variance in infants' comprehension vocabularies.

Production of Words

Correlations with Joint Engagement

Table 13 illustrates that the only time at which joint engagement corre-lated with word production was at 14 months. That is, joint engagement at 14 months correlated positively and significantly with word production at 13, 14, 15, 18, and 24 months (and the correlation with production at 12 months approached significance). The correlations with production were especially strong at the later ages (i.e., 15, 18, and 24 months), and it therefore appears that a relation between joint engagement and later production may begin at around 14 months. This trend was not seen with joint engagement at 15 months, probably because of the less than expected amount of joint-engage-ment time that month.

Figure 22a shows the word-production levels of the four joint-engage-ment styles. Again, for purposes of statistical analysis, a group of earlier emer-gence and a group of later emergence dyads were formed. No significant difference was found between the earlier and the later groups in their amounts of word production. It can also be seen in Figure 22a that the word production of the late emergence group is numerically (although not statisti-

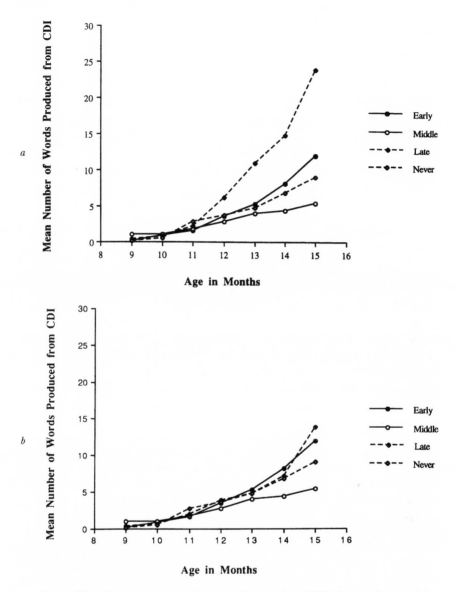

FIGURE 22.—Mean language production of the early, middle, late, and never joint-engagement groups at each time point. *a,* With outlier participant from the late group. *b,* Without outlier participant from the late group.

TABLE 14

CORRELATION MATRIX FOR MATERNAL LANGUAGE AND WORD PRODUCTION

MATERNAL LANGUAGE	WORD PRODUCTION								
	9	10	11	12	13	14	15	18[a]	24[b]
Follow:									
9 months	.27	−.10	.03	.31	.42*	.43*	.44*	.23	.36
12 months	−.08	−.03	−.24	.15	.30	.33	.36	.15	.24
15 months	−.03	−.11	.00	.22	.31	.30	.32	.19	.19
Lead:									
9 months	−.33	−.18	−.25	−.06	−.02	.04	.06	.02	−.18
12 months	−.21	−.17	−.53**	−.23	.01	.02	.07	.01	.03
15 months	−.11	−.14	−.03	.10	.00	.01	.07	.01	−.24

[a] $N = 20$.
[b] $N = 15$.
* $p < .05$, two tailed.
** $p < .01$, two tailed.

cally) higher than that of the other three groups. This is primarily the result of one infant in that group who had extremely high production scores between 12 and 15 months of age. For instance, this outlier infant's productive vocabulary at 15 months was 84 words, several times the amount of any other participant. Figure 22b presents the same data while excluding this outlier infant and better illustrates the similarity between the word production of the four groups.

Correlations with Maternal Following Language

Maternal following language at 9 months was significantly and positively correlated with production at 13, 14, and 15 months (see Table 14). One significant negative correlation was found between maternal leading language at 12 months and production at 11 months. Although not significant, the correlations between maternal leading language and production are all negative or less than .10, and the correlations between maternal following language and production in the period between 13 and 15 months are all positive and .30 or higher. Thus, there is apparently a much weaker relation between maternal following and word production than between maternal following and word comprehension, with the only reliable correlations being between a very early measure of maternal following and word production several months later.

Regressions

To predict word production at the 18- and 24-month time points in addition to the 9-, 12-, and 15-month time points, twelve equations were required

TABLE 15

SUMMARY OF REGRESSION ANALYSES FOR JOINT ENGAGEMENT AND MATERNAL FOLLOWING VARIABLES
PREDICTING WORD PRODUCTION

	WORD PRODUCTION								
	9 Months		12 Months		15 Months		18 Months[a]		24 Months[b]	
VARIABLE	β	t	β	t	β	t	β	t	β	t
Joint Engagement 9	N.S.		N.S.		N.S.		N.S.		N.S.	
Maternal Follow 9										
Joint Engagement 12	...		N.S.		−.26	−1.39	N.S.		N.S.	
Maternal Follow 12					.52	2.80**				
Joint Engagement 15	...		...		N.S.		N.S.		N.S.	
Maternal Follow 15										

[a] $N = 20$.
[b] $N = 15$.
** $p < .01$, two tailed.

(see Table 15). The only significant prediction was made by joint engagement and maternal following at 12 months for word production at 15 months ($F[2, 21] = 4.50$, $p < .05$, Adjusted $R^2 = .23$). When joint engagement was statistically controlled, Maternal Following 12 significantly predicted word production (ß = .52), but, when maternal following was controlled, Joint Engagement 12 did not significantly predict word production (ß = −.26; for t values, see Table 15).

Calibration of Joint-Engagement Analyses

The quantitative relation between joint engagement and word production was not as strong as had been predicted, so we explored the relation further in a subsequent analysis. We began by noting that the only significant correlations between joint engagement and word production occurred with the measure of joint engagement at 14 months, which was also the month with the greatest amount of joint engagement observed in the study. This suggested that word production may not correlate with joint engagement until a certain amount of time is spent in joint engagement (until the measure gets "off the floor" longitudinally). Coupled with the previous descriptions of individual styles of joint engagement, which showed that individuals reached criterion levels of joint engagement (i.e., 30 seconds) at different times throughout the study, this suggested an approach in which the relation is explored for individuals only after they attain a criterion amount of joint-engagement time.

Following this line of reasoning, the joint-engagement and word-production measures were "calibrated" for the age at which the joint-engagement criterion was met. That is, individual infants' joint-engagement and word-production measures were paired and set to a starting point defined by the month when joint-engagement time first totaled at least 30 seconds. The month that this criterion was met by an individual infant was denoted as *Joint Engagement 0,* and *Word Production 0* was then defined as word production for that infant at that same month. Thus, each infant's joint-engagement and word-production values were calibrated to the age at which a minimum amount of time was spent in joint engagement (instead of strictly by age, as in the previous analyses). These calibrated joint-engagement and word-production data were compared at three time points: at the month of joint-engagement criterion (Joint Engagement 0, Word Production 0), 1 month later (Joint Engagement 1, Word Production 1), and 2 months after the criterion month (Joint Engagement 2, Word Production 2). Cumulative values of joint-engagement time and word production were used.[12] Simple correlations were run with joint engagement and word production at these three time points. Because four infants met joint-engagement criterion at 14 or 15 months, they could not be included in all three time points. Therefore, all 24 infants were included at the first time point (Joint Engagement 0), 23 infants at the next time point (Joint Engagement 1), and 20 infants at the last time point (Joint Engagement 2).

Correlations with joint engagement.—Calibrating to joint-engagement criterion revealed significant positive correlations between joint engagement and word production at these three time points (see Table 16). The amount of time spent in joint engagement up through the month in which the criterion was met (Joint Engagement 0) was strongly related to word production at the same month ($r = .59$) and 1 month later ($r = .63$) (the correlation with word production 2 months later was .44, $p = .056$, two tailed). Joint-engagement time up to 1 month after criterion (Joint Engagement 1) approached a significant correlation with word production at the same time at Word Production 1 ($r = .40$, $p = .058$), and it related quite strongly with production 1 month later at Word Production 2 ($r = .66$). Joint engagement and word production 2 months after joint engagement reached criterion

[12] Values of joint engagement were cumulated from 9 months up to the month of joint-engagement criterion (and 1 and 2 months after for Joint Engagement 1 and Joint Engagement 2) and thus consisted of the total amount of joint engagement until the age when the criterion was met (or 1 or 2 months after). A second version of this analysis used joint-engagement values beginning at the month of criterion and cumulating over the next two time points. Because most subjects had low levels of joint engagement prior to their first criterion month, these two versions of the data produced nearly identical results, with only slight differences in the strengths of relations but not in the pattern of significant findings. The results of the first version, which cumulates across the entire study, are reported here.

TABLE 16

CORRELATION MATRIX FOR CALIBRATED JOINT ENAGAGEMENT AND WORD PRODUCTION

	WORD PRODUCTION		
JOINT ENGAGEMENT	Word Production 0[a]	Word Production 1[b]	Word Production 2[c]
Joint Engagement 0	.59**	.63**	.44
Joint Engagement 1	...	.40	.66**
Joint Engagement 2	...	...	.61**

[a] $N = 24$.
[b] $N = 23$.
[c] $N = 20$.
** $p < .01$, two tailed.

(Joint Engagement 2 and Word Production 2) were also strongly correlated at .61.

Thus, when joint engagement and word production are examined during the window of time in which joint-engagement time first reaches a minimum criterion, a strong, positive relation is found between these two variables.

Correlations with maternal following language.—Maternal following language measures were collected at only three time points and could not be calibrated in a similar manner to the monthly joint-engagement data; therefore, the total number of maternal following utterances across the entire study was used to represent maternal following (i.e., Maternal Following 15 from previous analyses) in similar analyses using the previously calibrated word-production data at time points Word Production 0, Word Production 1, and Word Production 2. No significant correlations existed between these measures ($r = .36$, .35, and $-.22$ at Word Production 0, Word Production 1, and Word Production 2, respectively).

Regressions.—To follow up on these new correlations, multiple regression analyses were repeated using these calibrated data. Thus, joint engagement at three time points (Joint Engagement 0, Joint Engagement 1, and Joint Engagement 2) and maternal following across all ages (Maternal Following 15) were used as predictors of word production at the same time points (Word Production 0, Word Production 1, and Word Production 2) in an identical manner to the previous regression equations with the original word-production measures.

Five of the six equations tested indicated significant predictive power. Joint Engagement 0 and Maternal Following 15 predicted word production at the first and second time points, Word Production 0 and Word Production 1, accounting for 47% and 50% of the variance, respectively (for Word Production 0, $F[2, 21] = 11.08$, $p < .001$; for Word Production 1, $F[2, 20] =$

TABLE 17

Summary of Regression Analyses for Calibrated Joint Engagement and Maternal
Following Variables Predicting Word Production

	Word Production					
	Word Production 0[a]		Word Production 1[b]		Word Production 2[c]	
Variable	β	t	β	t	β	t
Joint Engagement 0	.63	4.09***	.65	4.30***	N.S.	
Maternal Follow 15	.42	2.71*	.38	2.53*		
Joint Engagement 1		...	.48	2.60*	.66	3.42**
Maternal Follow 15			.43	2.35*	.01	.03
Joint Engagement 2		...		...	.59	2.97**
Maternal Follow 15					−.06	−.29

[a] $N = 24$.
[b] $N = 23$.
[c] $N = 20$.
* $p < .05$, two tailed.
** $p < .01$, two tailed.
*** $p < .001$, two tailed.

11.91, $p < .001$). Table 17 shows that the individual relations between these predictor variables and production outcomes were similar at both time points: Joint Engagement 0 significantly predicted word production at Word Production 0 and Word Production 1, with beta weights of .63 and .65, respectively, when Maternal Following 15 was held constant. Maternal Following 15 also had unique, significant predictive value with beta weights of .42 and .38, respectively, when Joint Engagement 0 was held constant.

Likewise, Joint Engagement 1 and Maternal Following 15 together were significant predictors of concurrent and later production (at Word Production 1 and Word Production 2), accounting for 28% of the variance at Word Production 1 ($F[2, 20] = 5.19$, $p < .05$) and 37% of the variance at Word Production 2 ($F[2, 17] = 6.60$, $p < .01$). Individually, joint engagement and maternal following were each significant predictors of production at Word Production 1, with similar beta weights of .48 and .43, respectively. In contrast, only Joint Engagement 1 was significantly correlated with word production at Word Production 2 (ß = .66), with Maternal Following 15 having virtually no relation to Word Production 2 values (ß = .01) at this later age. Finally, at the last time point, Joint Engagement 2 and Maternal Following 15 together were significant predictors of word production at the same month, Word Production 2 ($F[2, 17] = 5.09$, $p < .05$). Again, Joint Engagement 2 was a significant predictor of production at Word Production 2 (ß = .59), whereas Maternal Following 15 was not (ß = −.06).

Summary

The amount of time that mother-infant dyads spent in joint engagement was only weakly related to infants' production of words when these two measures were correlated on a month-by-month basis. In contrast, when joint engagement and word production were calibrated in terms of a criterion level of joint engagement, a consistently strong relation was revealed between these two variables. Several strong correlations were found between joint engagement and concurrent and later word production. Regression analyses confirmed this strong relation, finding that joint engagement at each time point was a significant predictor of word production at each time point. Factoring out this relation with joint engagement, maternal following language was also shown to be a significant predictor of word production at the 1st and 2d month after joint engagement met criterion but not 2 months after. Together these results suggest that a relation between joint engagement and word production does not begin until a significant amount of time is spent in joint engagement. Maternal following language relates positively to production at earlier ages but not at later ages, suggesting infants' lesser reliance on this maternal adjustment with age.

Correlations with the Social-Cognitive Measures from Study 1

The social-cognitive skills investigated in Study 1 might be supposed to have some relation to infants' communicative skills, and, indeed, in that study, the age of emergence of a number of these skills related quite strongly with the age of emergence of infants' first referential word—as reported there. There is less reason to suspect, however, that the social-cognitive measures from Study 1 should relate strongly to infants' communication skills as assessed quantitatively in terms of number of words and the like. Our reasoning follows closely the reasoning of Tomasello and Farrar (1986b) with regard to the relation between object permanence and children's early vocabulary.

Briefly, many studies in the 1970s investigated whether children who attained object permanence at an earlier age had larger vocabularies of object labels at some later age, investigations based on the reasonable assumption that, to name objects, the child should have a stable conception of them. However, a number of studies found that there was basically no relation between age of object permanence attainment (of whatever stage) and vocabulary size (for a review, see Corrigan, 1979). The point is that several subsequent studies showed that there was a relation between the age of emergence of certain object permanence skills and certain types of words (e.g., Gopnik, 1984; Tomasello & Farrar, 1986b); it is just that the relation did not extend to quantitative parameters involving the actual number of words learned. The overall conclusion is that, whereas certain cognitive skills are prerequisite to being able to learn words, the major determinants of the number of words learned are other things, presumably social factors having to do with the nature of the language spoken to the child, how that language is integrated with the ongoing interaction, and so forth.

In the current case, the reasoning was that, whereas such things as attention following and imitative learning are very likely prerequisites of word learning and should therefore be related to infants' ability to acquire words, there is no reason to suspect that the age of emergence of these skills for a given infant should be related in a systematic way to the number of words the infant acquires. Nevertheless, for the sake of completeness, in a final set of analyses we correlated the age of emergence of the various social-cognitive measures from Study 1 with the quantitative monthly measures of joint engagement from Study 2.

As expected, although there were a few reliable positive (at earlier months) and negative (at later months) correlations, the correlations as a group were not consistently high. When the ages of emergence of the social-cognitive measures were correlated with infants' production of gestures and comprehension and production of language from Study 2, we found no significant correlations with gestures and only one significant, positive correlation for comprehension (between the AOE of attention following and the number of words comprehended at 10 months). For word production, however, there were several significant correlations between the AOE of attention following and the number of words produced from 12 to 24 months (five of the six correlations for these months were significant; r's ranged from $-.36$ to $-.38$). Similarly, the AOE of communicative gestures (from Study 1) and the number of words produced from 12 to 24 months were also often significantly correlated (five of the six correlations for these months were significant; r's ranged from $-.35$ to $-.43$). Note that the negative value of these correlations actually has a positive meaning: the earlier infants displayed attention following and communicative gesture skills (the smaller the AOE), the more words they produced from 12 through 24 months.

DISCUSSION

As in Study 1, the age of emergence and developmental progression of the individual measures of this study were overall very similar to those found in other studies in which similar measurement procedures were used, with the possible exception of productive language. Thus, on average, there was a gradual increase over the period between 9 and 15 months in the amount of time that infants and their mothers spent in joint attentional engagement—an increase due mostly to increasing numbers of joint-engagement episodes of similar duration (this contrasts to some degree with Bakeman & Adamson's, 1984, finding that episode duration increased during this time). In the 10-minute free-play session with their mothers, 60% of infants participated in some joint engagement at 9 months, and all infants participated in some joint engagement by 11 months of age. These findings place the age of emergence of joint engagement a bit earlier than do those of Bakeman and Adamson (1984), but, as Figure 18 above illustrates, the general developmental trend is very similar in the two studies. We also found some marked individual differences (and not much intraindividual stability over time) in joint engagement across dyads: the ages at which infants consistently spent 5% or more of their time in joint engagement (30 seconds) were spread across the entire age range of the study (9 months for three infants; between 9 and 15 months for 15 infants; and, presumably, after 15 months for the remaining six infants).

This pattern of interindividual differences and intraindividual differences across time clearly indicates that the ability to engage in a particular kind of social interaction on one or a few occasions does not translate directly into large or stable quantities of that type of social interaction. Many variables come together to produce extended periods of mother-infant joint engagement, including mothers' skill at identifying and manipulating infants' focus of attention, infants' engagement with the objects available, and the particular motivational predispositions of both mother and infant on a particular occasion.

In terms of language skills, as measured by the MacArthur CDI, our sample of infants was almost exactly at the 50th percentile in their production of gestures and comprehension of words, but in their production of words they were a bit later than most samples (e.g., Fenson et al., 1993). The reason for this is very likely the instructions that we gave mothers to count only words that infants used referentially and flexibly. Our rationale was that we were using very strict criteria for all the other social-cognitive skills and that our criteria for the communication measures should therefore likewise be strict (for a justification of this procedure, see also Tomasello & Mervis, 1994). Apparently, this procedure had its strongest effect on the production measure, perhaps because it is easier to tell when an infant is producing a word in only one narrow context, whereas context-bound usage is more difficult to discern in the case of comprehension.

The most important findings of this second study concern the strong positive relation between the amount of time that mother-infant dyads spent in joint attentional engagement and infants' very earliest skills of nonlinguistic and linguistic communication. With regard to production of gestures, mother-infant dyads who spent more time in joint engagement at 9 and 11 months had infants with more gestures some months later, mostly between

11 and 13 months (this was still true when maternal language was factored out). A similarly strong relation was found between joint engagement and word comprehension. Joint engagement in the middle months of the study (months 11–13) correlated positively with word comprehension at the same time and beyond, mostly between 11 and 15 months (this was still true when maternal language was factored out).

The relation between joint engagement and language production was not as clear as that between joint engagement and the gesture and comprehension measures. Initially, the only relation found was between joint engagement at 14 months and concurrent and later language production, including strong correlations with both 18- and 24-month productive vocabulary size. This suggests that the window of time in which joint engagement begins to influence language production opens at 14 months. The data at 15 months did not support this trend, however, as there were no significant correlations at 15 months. The reason for this very likely involves the fact that the joint-engagement measure was lower at this age than would be expected, reflecting some confluence of unusual events for the measurement of this variable at this age. In any case, when we employed a different procedure in which we considered, not infants' chronological age, but rather the age of their first significant amount of joint engagement (the "calibrated analyses"), strong correlations were found between joint engagement and language production.

These findings suggest that the window of time in which joint engagement is associated with language production is specific, not to a particular age, but rather to a particular amount of time spent in joint engagement. They also reveal a significant measurement issue when the target of investigation is the initial emergence of some skill or skills: there can be no overall correlation as long as the majority of the sample is still "on the floor," as was the case in the earliest months of the current study. In general, it is possible to obtain strong correlations in cases of initial developmental emergence only when the skills being correlated have both gotten started for the majority of infants—which is precisely the rationale for our calibrated analyses of language production.

A related finding was that maternal language that followed into infants' focus of attention was related to infants' linguistic but not their gestural development. Maternal language that followed into the infants' attention did not relate in any significant way to the infants' gestural communication at any time between 9 and 15 months of age. On the other hand, maternal following language was consistently related to infants' concurrent and later comprehension of language from the middle months of the study on: the more mothers used their language to follow into their infant's attention, the more words the infant comprehended at the same and later months (this was still true when time in joint engagement was factored out). In terms of language production, maternal following language used at 9 months related to infants' later production at 13–15 months (this was still true when time in joint engagement was factored out). However, the predictive value of maternal following language in the current study did not continue after 15 months, suggesting that adults' following into children's attentional focus is most beneficial at younger ages, when children are less skilled at following into and directing the attention of others (see also Smith et al., 1988; Tomasello, in press).

It should be noted that, in the current study, we did not find that maternal language used to redirect the infant's attentional focus (often called *maternal directiveness*) correlated consistently negatively with infant language, as has been found by other researchers (e.g., Dunham et al., 1993; Tomasello & Farrar, 1986a)—although we did find a fairly large number of nonsignificant negative correlations. However, recall that Akhtar et al. (1991), using the same coding scheme as the current study, did not find significant correlations between total maternal leading language and vocabulary size; only a subset of leading language, attention directives, significantly predicted a smaller vocabulary. Perhaps one other issue is that we used total number of leading utterances, whereas some previous studies have used proportions of utterances, thus factoring out any positive effects of total amount of maternal language.

When joint engagement and maternal following language were used in concert to predict infants' early language skills, a very large amount of the variance was accounted for. In predicting word comprehension and word production (using the calibrated analyses), approximately 50% of the variance was accounted for in several different cases. This is noteworthy because language development depends on a number of factors not measured at all in this study that presumably contribute as well. Most notably, there was no measure of vocal-auditory processing, clearly a key skill in language acquisition, or of the ability to categorize, also a key skill in learning the referential extensions of words (Gopnik & Meltzoff, 1987). We thus think that accounting for over half the variance in some cases with basically two measures of social interaction—one of the tendency of mother-infant dyads to enter into joint attentional engagement and one of mothers' tendency to use language to follow into their infant's attentional focus—is an amazing outcome.

The current study is thus the first to establish a relation between joint engagement, maternal language, and children's communicative competence during the initial stages of communicative development. This is important for a number of reasons, the more theoretical of which will be discussed in Chapter V below. For now, the important point is a methodological one. Direction of influence has always been an issue in studies of the relation between joint attentional engagement and language since children's ability to communicate with language (as well as through other means) is obviously an important factor in their ability to establish and maintain joint attentional engagement with adults (Tomasello, 1988). Indeed, the child's use of a piece of language during joint focus with the adult is used by most researchers as an indicator, equivalent to a look to the adult's face, of the child's appreciation that the adult is actively participating in the interaction—raising the concern that the measures of joint engagement and language are not truly independent.

The point is that, in our study, the strongest correlations of joint engagement were with language comprehension—which was not correlated with language production—which obviates the methodological concern that an infant who talks more provides researchers with more opportunities to establish that the infant and the adult are jointly focused on something. In general, our argument (following Tomasello, 1988, 1992) is that the causality involved in the current study is transactional: as adult and infant become better able and more motivated to enter into extended periods of joint engagement, the infant's communicative skills become more sophisticated, and, as those skills become more sophisticated, the dyad is better able to establish and maintain extended periods of joint engagement—which leads to the acquisition of more new language, and so on, across time. However, we also believe that the current study has established that the first step in this process is when adult and infant begin to enter into periods of nonlinguistic joint engagement, which gets the process moving initially.

With regard to future studies of relations between joint engagement and communication, it is important to extend the age range for some of the measures, although more important than the actual age range may be the stage of language development of the children. Measurement of joint engagement beginning at the age of children's first words and continuing past the age of their vocabulary spurt may be most illuminating. This period may reveal a changing relation between joint engagement and language development before and after the understanding of referentiality. It is also important to increase the specificity of the measures. For example, an ideal measure of gestures would include a greater variety than that measured here and should include symbolic, or representational, gestures as these are thought to emerge within the context of joint engagement, much like first words (Acredolo & Goodwyn, 1988). In addition, vocabularies should be examined by types of words (e.g., nominals vs. other types). Perhaps calibration of joint-engagement and production data to the onset of referential language, as measured by first nominal production or onset of vocabulary spurt, would reveal a pattern or amount of joint engagement that consistently precedes the use of referential language.

There is also a need to study the relation between joint engagement and language in a variety of contextual and cultural settings as this relation appears to be highly sensitive to situational demands. Studies almost exclusively have observed the mother and child in an uninterrupted free-play situation without the distractions that typify the daily routines of the mother and child at home. The presence of other children, such as siblings in the home or a group of children in a day-care setting, reduces the amount of undivided attention that a mother or a caregiver can devote to any one child, and it also affects the style of interaction; for example, when caring for more than one child, a caregiver's speech is more directive than when caring for a single child (Schaffer & Liddell, 1984; Tomasello et al., 1986). Thus, findings from mother-child free play in laboratory settings may not generalize as robustly as might be hoped to other settings found in the home or day-care center. We will briefly address the issue of other cultures in Chapter V below.

V. GENERAL DISCUSSION

In the current study, we have attempted to investigate young children's earliest social-cognitive skills in two ways: (*a*) from the perspective of early social cognition as infants first learn to tune in to adults and to get adults to tune in to them in individual behavioral acts and (*b*) from the point of view of communication and language as infants begin to acquire the conventional communicative signals and symbols of their cultures in relatively extended periods of joint attentional engagement with adults. These two perspectives were taken simultaneously on the same group of 24 infants, longitudinally from 9 to 15 months of age at monthly intervals, and thus the current study represents the most broadly based investigation to date of infants' earliest skills of social cognition and communication. Because we observed a wider range of behaviors and processes than previous studies, and because we observed those behaviors and processes at more closely spaced longitudinal intervals than many studies, we were able to document in some detail the various developmental interrelations among these fundamentally important skills.

In this general discussion, we first review the main findings of our investigation. We then discuss some of the important theoretical implications of these findings for theories of social-cognitive development and the early acquisition of communicative competence. We conclude with a brief discussion of the ways in which infants' emerging skills of social cognition enable them, early in the second year of life, to become fully active and contributing participants in the cultural and communicative practices into which they are born.

SUMMARY OF THE MAIN FINDINGS

The main findings from our current sample of 24 American middle-class infants from 9 to 15 months of age, across both studies, may be summarized as follows:

1. *The age of emergence and developmental progression of each of the individual*

116

social-cognitive and communicative skills were for the most part comparable to those found in previous studies using similar operational definitions, procedures, and scoring criteria. As a whole, our findings strongly support the generally held view that the age period from 9 to 12 months is a crucially important one in the emergence of infants' initial skills of social cognition and communication, with the acquisition of language skills (in either comprehension or production) following closely behind. The majority of our infants displayed all the skills that we measured, with the exception of productive language, by 12 months of age—despite the fact that we took great pains to devise stringent criteria that, in our view, ensured that children really understood the intentions or attention of their social partner for each skill measured.

2. *The most common order of emergence of the five major social-cognitive and communicative skills measured was: joint engagement → communicative gestures → attention following → imitative learning → referential language.* This was true on average as well as on the level of individual infants, as almost two-thirds of the infants followed this exact pattern of emergence and over 80% followed it when attention following and imitative learning are allowed to alternate (since both involve following into the attention/behavior of others). The two object-related skills measured—object permanence and spatial relations— did not fit into this sequence in a consistent way across infants. When we look at individual tasks and their requirements, we may reconfigure this sequence slightly into the theoretically more meaningful sequence share attention → follow attention/behavior → direct attention/behavior. To share attention, infants simply look to the adult's face (check for the adult's attention) when the two of them are interacting in relatively close proximity with an object; to follow or direct attention/behavior, infants must take into account precisely what the adult is attending to, or needs to attend to, in relatively distal space.

3. *These social-cognitive and communicative skills intercorrelated positively, although in some cases only at moderate levels and only when individual tasks were considered.* Significant positive correlations were found between the ages of emergence of each pair of the main social-cognitive skills or one of their constituent tasks (with the exception of joint engagement, which had emerged for all infants by 9 months at the beginning of the study and therefore had no variation). These correlations were found even though the skills emerged in a relatively rapid manner for most infants (almost 60% in 3 months or less and almost 80% in 4 months or less), thus creating little variability that could be correlated.

4. *On average, there was a gradual increase over the period between 9 and 15 months in the amount of time that infants and their mothers spent in joint attentional engagement, but there were marked individual differences (and not much intraindividual stability over time) in this pattern.* This pattern of interindividual and intraindividual differences clearly indicates that the child's possession of a certain

117

social-cognitive skill does not translate directly into large or stable quantities of particular types of social interaction. Many variables, many of them mainly due to the adult partner, must come together to enable infants to participate in extended periods of adult-child joint attentional engagement.

5. *The amount of time that mother-infant dyads spent in joint attentional engagement was reliably related to infants' very earliest skills of nonlinguistic and linguistic communication.* The relation between joint engagement and gesture production was strongest at the earliest months when gestures were first emerging, the relation between joint engagement and language comprehension was strongest during the middle months when the comprehension of language was first emerging, and the relation between joint engagement and language production was strongest during the later months when language production was first emerging—beginning in those months in which individual infants had significant amounts of joint engagement with their mothers.

6. *Maternal language that followed into infants' focus of attention was related to the infants' linguistic but not to their gestural development.* No aspects of maternal language related significantly to the infants' gestural communication at any time between 9 and 15 months of age. On the other hand, maternal language that followed into children's already-established attentional focus was consistently related to infants' comprehension and production of language during the middle months of the study, with weaker relations later in the study. This weakening of the relation presumably comes about because children become better able to determine adults' focus of attention more reliably, even when it is discrepant with their own, at older ages. Maternal following language combined with the joint-engagement measure to account for over half the variance in infants' linguistic competence at several time periods.

These results have important implications for our understanding of children's early social cognition, for our understanding of children's nascent skills of gestural communication and language, and, in general, for our understanding of the process by which children become fully participating members of cultures. We discuss these points each in turn.

INFANT SOCIAL COGNITION

The major theoretical hypothesis motivating the current study was that the different social-cognitive skills in late infancy that have been of central concern to many recent investigators are all manifestations of infants' emerging understanding of other persons as intentional agents whose attention and behavior to outside objects and events may be shared, followed into, and directed in various ways (Tomasello, 1995a; Tomasello, Kruger, & Ratner, 1993). This view does not imply that understanding others as intentional agents is an all-or-nothing affair, all infants' interactions with others being totally transformed instantaneously—in a stage-like fashion, for example. Much more compatible with the current view are such ideas as Bates's (1979) "homology through shared origins," in which a new cognitive competence becomes manifest in particular behaviors at different developmental periods depending on a number of context-specific factors, and Fisher and Silvern's (1985) notion that new levels of cognition do not by themselves determine particular behavioral skills but merely open possibilities that still must be individually worked out through behavioral interactions with different environments in different contexts.

Our view of early social cognition contrasts sharply with the two other currently influential views in which these different skills are seen as developmentally unrelated or at least not dependent on a new form of social understanding. First, Baron-Cohen (1993, 1995) has proposed that infants' social cognition during the first 2 years of life is composed of three "mind-reading" mechanisms/modules, each of which has its own developmental timetable. These are an intention detector, an eye direction detector, and a shared attention mechanism. Part of the evidence for positing the modularity of these mechanisms is that, according to Baron-Cohen, they emerge at different ages (he also invokes other evidence, such as patterns of breakdown in children with atypical cognitive profiles).

First, Baron-Cohen claims that children detect the intentions of others at least by 6 months of age. However, recent research by Gergely and his colleagues (Gergely et al., 1995; Csibra et al., in press), using habituation techniques, has found that 9- and 12-month-old infants, but *not* 6-month-old infants, take the intentional stance toward inanimate objects that are moving with respect to one another in particular ways. Research on children's more natural behaviors—such as those investigated in our Study 1 and others reviewed above—provides no more evidence that 6-month-olds are capable of intention detection. Second, Baron-Cohen claims that 6-month-old infants also follow the gaze of other persons (detect their eye gaze direction). However, recent research by Corkum and Moore (1995), along with our results in Study 1, indicates that a more realistic age (when all the appropriate experimental controls are in place) is 10–12 months (although the recent results of D'Entremont et al., 1997, provide still another age). Third, Baron-Cohen claims that it is not until 14 months of age that infants know that they are sharing attention with a social partner. However, the current results demonstrate that 9-month-old infants can enter into joint engagement with others (we found this for all 24 of our 9-month-olds in the hour-long session) and that, by 10–11 months, they can even actively show objects to others in a ritualized manner. Our view is thus that Baron-Cohen's ages of emergence are not correct in any of these three cases. If more accurate ages of emergence are used, there is a strong developmental synchrony among these different social-cognitive skills—with the relatively small decalages among them to be explained below.

The other main view is that of Moore and his colleagues (Barresi & Moore, 1993, 1996; Corkum & Moore, 1995; Moore, 1996; Moore & Corkum, 1994). Moore does not believe that what is happening at 9–12 months of age reflects a new understanding of other persons; rather, he argues that it is only at 18 months of age that infants truly understand others as intentional agents (an argument based on such things as their ability to recognize themselves in mirrors and their more skillful use of language). According to Moore and his colleagues, the behaviors that we have observed in this study are indeed the raw material out of which this understanding is constructed, but they themselves are independent behavioral skills each of which has its own critical stimuli, environmental contingencies, and learning history that do not depend on understanding others as intentional agents. To explain the developmental synchrony and interrelatedness of the different social-cognitive skills, Moore invokes the emergence of a new information-processing ability to focus attention on two things simultaneously. But, to our knowledge, this information-processing ability has never been independently measured and related to early social cognition, and, indeed, our object-related tasks, which might be expected to depend to some degree on this same information-processing skill, did not fit well into the observed developmental sequence, and they correlated with the social-cognitive measures in only a sporadic manner.

We nevertheless have some sympathy with Moore's view in the sense that each of the social-cognitive skills that we have observed does indeed require some specific learning experiences. For example, it is almost surely the case that, if infants were prevented from observing others look at things from birth to 18 months of age, they would not follow the gaze of others on first exposure at that time and that, if they were prevented from experiencing others communicating with them linguistically during this period, they would not immediately communicate with others linguistically at 18 months. But the fact that joint engagement, attention following, imitative learning, and communicative gestures all emerge for most infants during a very brief developmental window and in a correlated fashion—with the consistent developmental ordering among these skills having a theoretically coherent explanation (see below) and with the object-related skills not fitting well into this picture—is best explained, in our view, by invoking some specifically social developments that open up new interactional possibilities.

We thus believe that the current results accord best with our hypothesis of the shared origins of all these different skills of social cognition from children's emerging understanding of other persons as intentional agents. The idea is simply that the different behaviors and skills that fall under the general rubric of early social cognition, joint attention, and communication all involve social interaction with other persons. If the way that infants understand other persons changes, all these behaviors and skills are likely to be affected as well—just as a new understanding of objects is likely to show itself in all infants' interactions with physical objects. The current studies provide strong evidence for this view by demonstrating that the changes that occur in a number of theoretically interrelated behaviors and skills at the end of the first year take place in a relatively brief developmental period, are correlated, and are all of the same basic type. Each of the changes basically transforms a social interaction that was previously dyadic, between child and adult, into one that is triadic in the sense that the child incorporates into the interaction an understanding of the adult's intentions and attention toward external entities (perhaps including the self; Tomasello, 1996b).

The developmental ordering of the different behavioral manifestations of this new social understanding has a fairly straightforward explanation. The basic idea is that, in social cognition, we may first understand *that* others have some kind of psychological stance that is different from our own without knowing precisely *what* that stance is or how to go about identifying it; only later do we acquire means for determining the specific content of the psychological stances of others. This distinction is similar in spirit to that of Flavell (1992) between Level 1 and Level 2 perspective taking as manifest in children's understanding of visual perception (see also Flavell & Miller, 1998). But, since it deals with the understanding of the psychological relations of others to outside entities more generally, we will simply refer to the first level of understanding as "understanding *that*" others have psychological relations to the world and to the second level of understanding as "understanding *what*" particular contentful psychological relation obtains in a particular case.

Thus, the most basic level (understanding *that*) is an understanding that others attend to and have intentions toward outside entities. It is this level of understanding that underlies the skills that emerged earliest in the current study (on average 9–10½ months): joint engagement, proximal declarative gestures (shows), and checking others' facial expressions in the social obstacle task. What is characteristic of these three behaviors is that they all consist almost entirely of a look to the face of the other person: either spontaneously in play (joint engagement), or when holding up an object (showing), or when the other person has intervened in a behavioral sequence (blocking and teasing).

It is very difficult to determine what the infants understand of the other person's specific intentions or attention from these interactions (i.e., their content) because in all cases they are simply looking up to the adult's face. Indeed, with respect to showing, we have come to believe, on the basis of the many show gestures that we saw from infants who did not do such things as follow adult gaze, that, when infants of 9 and 10 months hold up objects and

121

look to the face of the adult, they expect that the adult already is looking—just as they do when they look up in joint-engagement sequences. This is suggested by the fact that, when infants show objects to others, they generally do so in close social interactions by bringing them into a space between themselves and the adult, with no change of gaze direction on the part of the adult either expected or needed.

Overall, then, following Gómez et al. (1993) and others, we believe that the fact that infants look to others' faces in these early interactions, and not to their hands or somewhere else, clearly indicates that they understand that other persons are psychological beings or, perhaps, intentional agents. But infants do not show any ability at this early age to follow into or direct the specific psychological orientations of other persons to specific objects and events.

As infants look to adults to check for their attention and intentions, it must happen often that the adult is focused or directed elsewhere. The second level of understanding (understanding *what*) thus reflects infants' attempts to determine what the adult is actually focused on or directed to—given that it is not what she herself is focused on or directed to. Infants thus seek to identify adults' specific behavioral intentions to change the state of the world in some specific way (i.e., their goals) and their specific perceptual intention to attend to some things, but not others, in the ambient environment (if, following Gibson & Rader, 1979, attention may be thought of as a kind of intentional perception). Once infants possess this level of understanding, they may then begin to follow into the specific focus of attention and behavioral intentions of others and, ultimately, to attempt to manipulate or influence those specific psychological states.

It is this level of understanding that underlies the kind of attention following, imitative learning, and distal communicative acts (both gestural and linguistic) that emerged in our children after 11½ months of age. It should be noted that all these later behaviors involve infants detecting adults' psychological relations to entities that are located in more distal space, as compared with the more proximal space involved in the earlier joint attentional behaviors. The distinction between proximal and distal joint attentional behaviors is thus also an important one and may explain the developmental sequence that we observed as well. But, in our view, the proximal-distal distinction is simply one aspect of our distinction between understanding the *that* and the *what* of others' intentional states, in the sense that understanding *what* someone else is attending to necessarily involves following that individual outside the current cocoon of shared proximal attention.

Within the *what* level of understanding, we found that infants' ability to follow into the attention and intentions of others emerged before their ability to direct the attention and intentions of others in acts of intentional communication toward distal entities, either gesturally or linguistically. Thus, on average, infants were first able to follow into the attention and behavior of others—via either gaze following or point following for attention and via imitative learning of either instrumental or arbitrary actions for behavior—between 11 and 12 months of age. On the other hand, they were first able to use distal gestures such as pointing to direct the adult's attention to something new—either imperatively or declaratively--only 1 month later, on average, between 12 and 13 months of age. In a sense, acquiring the productive use of linguistic symbols—which emerged in our sample several months later—requires all these skills; that is, it requires the ability to follow into the adult's attention as she uses a word and the ability imitatively to learn to use that word to direct the attention of others in specific ways. Indeed, the main advantage of language over gestures from a communicative point of view is precisely the level of specificity that it allows in directing the attention of others.

It is not clear how seriously to take this observed developmental sequence of attention/behavior following preceding attention/behavior directing within the *what* level of infant social understanding. One way to view it is as a kind of comprehension versus production question, and comprehension is well known to precede production in many domains of cognitive and communicative development. However, in some cases, this may not hold. Thus, some infants may actually point to distal entities before they follow the gaze or pointing of others to distal entities. The logical question is how they could do this: How could infants point to direct the attention of another person when they do not seem to comprehend that the other has attentional states that they may follow into?

The answer, we believe, is as follows. As Moore (1996) has argued, infants do indeed need to learn specific behavioral skills in specific behavioral contexts. In the months around their first birthdays, this may be done either with or without an understanding of others as intentional agents. This difference is manifest in the type of learning process involved, of which there are two. First, infants may behave for their own reasons and, owing to the reactions of others, have that behavior "socialized" in the sense that they come to see its social effects. This is a mechanism (proposed by Kaye, 1982, and Vygotsky, 1978) in which, in a sense, production precedes comprehension. Thus, an infant may extend her index finger toward an object as a kind of self-directing behavior, but, when adults repeatedly respond by either fetching the object or otherwise attending to it, the infant may learn that her index finger extension leads to some predictable social results. Initially, this may be accomplished without an understanding of others as intentional agents, in much the manner Moore (1996) proposes. This is essentially the learning mechanism dubbed "ontogenetic ritualization" by Tomasello (1990, 1994), and it accounts for infants' acquisition of many gesture productions (e.g., hands over head to be picked up) as well as the gesture productions of at least some nonhuman primates (Tomasello & Camaioni, 1997).

On the other hand, infants may learn a new social behavior or skill by observing the intentional actions of others and going through a process of imitative learning in which they understand that, for example, Mom is trying to get Dad to look over there by pointing toward that location and that, if I have the same goal, I can use that same behavioral means (the same applies to such things as infants watching someone trying to open a box using a key and understanding that, when they have the same goal, they can use the same means). The point is that this kind of imitative learning (one form of cultural learning; Tomasello, Kruger, & Ratner, 1993) requires that the infant understand something of the intentions and attention of others, especially the fact that the behavior of others may be partitioned into ends (goals) and behavioral means. The current results are that, before their first birthdays, infants are able to engage in this kind of imitative learning in at least some instances, including the imitative learning of linguistic symbols, which, because of their conventional nature, can be learned only by means of imitation. When this form of imitative learning is involved, it is fair to say that attention following (comprehension) precedes attention directing (production).

We are aware of very little evidence that speaks directly to the question of which of these two processes might be at work in specific cases, and, indeed, we believe that infants' gestures such as pointing may potentially be learned in either of these ways. In some cases, infants may even learn a gesture by ritualization and then, at some later point, come to understand the correspondence between their own gesture and that of other persons—thus transforming it, belatedly, into a shared communicative convention. Our view of the ordering of attention following and attention directing within the *what* level, then, is that there may be some variability depending on the specific ontogenetic histories of specific individuals.

Finally, we may ask the question of where this new understanding of other persons comes from ontogenetically. Some would claim that it is innate and present from birth and that it is only the infant's skills of behavioral expression that develop (e.g., Trevarthen, 1979b). We believe that there is social-cognitive development involved, however, and that there are two key developmental precursors: (*a*) infants' ability to identify with others—to perceive others as "like me"—and (*b*) infants' experience of their own intentionality. These must come together for infants to understand that other persons are intentional agents who experience the world in ways similar to the ways in which they themselves do.

With regard to the first precursor, Meltzoff and Gopnik (1993) argue that the infant's identification with others is present in nascent form from birth, as evinced by neonatal mimicking or imitation. From the very beginning, infants identify with and imitate others—and know when others are imitating them—so that their growing understanding of others is applied to themselves and, conversely, their knowledge of themselves is applied to others (see also Gopnik & Meltzoff, 1993). On the other hand, citing Anisfeld's (1991) skeptical review of neonatal imitation research, Barresi and Moore (1996) believe that a certain type of social experience is necessary for children to learn the kind of self-other correspondences that Meltzoff and Gopnik posit as innate. Key in Barresi and Moore's account are situations in which adult and infant take similar intentional stances toward an outside entity and the infant attends to this convergence; for example, they both look to the same place or fear the same object. It is in such interactions, and only in such interactions, that children have available both first-person information about their own intentional states and third-person information about the intentional states of the other (e.g., through their facial expressions and behavior) simultaneously. Through these kinds of convergence experiences infants come both to identify and to differentiate first- and third-person perspectives in much the same way as they come to differentiate and coordinate their sensorimotor schemes from the world in general.

The problem is that neither of these theories of how infants come to identify with others is very specific about how their understanding of others develops and changes, and this brings us to the second precursor concerning intentionality. In this connection, there is one very important developmental fact that has not typically been connected with infants' social cognition: at around 8–9 months of age, infants for the first time differentiate in their *own* behavior between the ends and the means of instrumental acts; that is, they begin to behave in ways that are clearly intentional. In Piaget's (1952) formulation, infants begin down this path when they begin removing obstacles and performing other acts whose function it is to enable other acts (see also Frye, 1991, and the current findings with regard to the physical obstacle task). Such hierarchically organized behavior indicates the infant's understanding of the relativity of means and ends—that an activity that is an end in one context may be a means in another. The essential point is that this dissociation of means and ends enables infants to formulate a goal independently of and prior to actually acting, and thus this new mode of behavior is the child's first experience with a mental entity (i.e., a goal) that is at least somewhat independent of direct sensorimotor action.

It is not an accident, we would argue, that, very soon after infants begin behaving in this clearly intentional way (i.e., at 8–9 months), they begin seeing the behavior of others as intentional as well, as evinced by the findings of many studies, including the current one. Our proposal is thus that it is in their own intentional behavior that infants first experience intentionality as they formulate independent goals and then act on them, either attaining them or not. This experience then provides the basis for an understanding

125

that others also act intentionally in this same way. Exactly how it does so is not clear at this time, but it is obviously based in some way on the first precursor: infants' previous identification with other persons in the months leading up to this new development (by either the Meltzoff-Gopnik or the Barresi-Moore developmental pathway). In either case, the proposal is that children's knowledge of their own behavior—from the inside as it were—is the impetus for new levels in the understanding of the behavior of others (for a defense of this view in the form of simulation theory, see Gordon, 1986, 1992). Although we have not focused on the role of emotions in all this, one hypothesis might be that children do this most readily with respect to shared emotions and thus that social referencing (which we did not assess in the current study) might be the leading edge of the transition from understanding the self's psychological states to understanding the psychological states of others.

To make this a complete account of children's social-cognitive development, it would have to be extended to children's understanding of the thoughts and beliefs of others, what we have called the *understanding of mental agents,* sometime in their fourth year of life (Tomasello, Kruger, & Ratner, 1993). The idea would have to be that children come to understand first that their own beliefs are sometimes different from the way things "really" are, and this understanding could then be extended to others. Although we do not know the basis for the initial discovery at this time, in our view it is likely that the raw material for this discovery is the kind of conflicting conceptual perspectives that are the stuff of linguistic interaction and discourse in the second and third years of life (see Harris, 1996).

THE EMERGENCE OF LANGUAGE

The study of language acquisition has been very much influenced by formal linguistic models that are fundamentally inimical to analyses focused on psychological process (Tomasello, 1995b). In opposition to this view, and following the general hypothesis of the current study, our view is that children's initial skills of linguistic communication are a natural outgrowth of their emerging understanding of other persons as intentional agents—given that they regularly experience adults using a set of linguistic conventions (each with its own cultural history) to communicate both with them and with other people. Perhaps surprisingly, language is seldom considered in the context of children's other skills of social cognition, but our view is that, when language is viewed as a set of social conventions whose primary function is to enable one person to manipulate the attention of other persons in very specific ways, the use of language for purposes of communication is perhaps the most powerful social-cognitive skill that young children are acquiring in their second year of life and beyond. This may be called the *social-pragmatic view* of language acquisition.

There are two main views of early language development that are in opposition to our view of linguistic communication as fundamentally a skill of social cognition. First is the view that the structure of language is innate and highly modularized. Although different nativistic theories are concerned with different aspects of language structure, there are some views in which children have a priori knowledge of even the most elementary aspects of language from the beginning. This knowledge emanates from the language module, which has its own developmental timetable (for a broad summary of some of these views, see Pinker, 1994). Although many nativists confine their hypotheses to syntax and the more abstract aspects of language, other theorists have attempted to extend this general line of reasoning to more basic aspects of linguistic competence. For example, some theorists recognize that much of language is acquired through individual acts of learning, but they still contend that infants have a head start on the process by having some kind of built-in "constraints" that guide, for example, their initial hypotheses about the meanings of words (e.g., Markman, 1989, 1992).

The most obvious question for this view in the current context is why language emerges directly on the heels of the dawning of many of children's other skills of social cognition and communication. A reasonable response might be that many things emerge in children's development during this same age period. But then the question becomes why the emergence of language is correlated with the emergence of these other skills of social cognition, as found by many other studies as well as this one (e.g., Bates, 1979)—perhaps especially the tight intercorrelation of early language skills with skills of joint attentional engagement. Experimental studies in which children use social-pragmatic cues to learn new words also support this view (for a review, see Tomasello, in press).

The other opposing view is one in which language is viewed as just another learned behavior, with the acquisition of language depending on nothing other than very general skills of perception, memory, and learning. Thus, in a recent paper, Smith (1995; see also Smith & Samuelson, 1997) argues that word learning takes place as children associate words with whatever is most salient to their attention in the general situational context, with language structure emerging from complex and dynamic developmental processes (there have also been a variety of prior behavioristic approaches in the same spirit, but with less sophisticated theories of development). This is a reasonable view that has the advantage of highlighting the individual learning processes that are clearly an integral part of the language-acquisition process. But the question again in this case is why linguistic skills emerge when they do, correlated with other skills of social cognition. Perhaps there is some general process explanation in terms of different subskills maturing or the like, but our view is that a new element is needed. The new element that is needed is children's newly emerging ability to understand other persons as individuals "like me" who have psychological relations to the world that can be shared, followed into, and manipulated with both gestures and language.

Language acquisition is a very complex phenomenon, and we can provide here only very brief characterizations (perhaps caricatures) of two approaches to language acquisition that do not consider language as primarily a manifestation of social-cognitive skills. But we would like to be very clear about one thing. The social-pragmatic view of language acquisition is sometimes characterized as focusing on the influences of the social environment on language. We are not arguing here for the influence of social factors on language acquisition—for example, the role of "input" or the influence of social setting—important though these may be. What we are doing is making the stronger claim that language *is* a social skill, not some separate entity to be influenced by social factors (Tomasello, 1992). As such, language should be considered as just another social skill, like the others that we have investigated in the current two studies. This is perhaps clearest when we consider what a linguistic symbol is in psychological terms and how children might go about acquiring one.

Suppose the following: an adult addresses a novel expression to a child, perhaps while pointing to an interesting event, for example, "A tractor!" For a child to understand this novel expression, she must understand that the adult is making this unfamiliar noise in an effort to get her to focus her attention on some aspect of the ongoing event; that is, she must understand that the adult has intentions toward her attentional state. We may thus describe the social situation as the adult focusing on some aspect of an ongoing event and then attempting to get the child to do the same. For her part, the child must have some way of understanding that this is what the adult is trying to do without relying on the new linguistic expression *tractor*—which she, by stipulation, does not yet comprehend. To achieve this understanding, she may use her knowledge of the adult's likely focus of attention in such situations, her understanding of adult gestures, her knowledge of the surrounding language that she does understand, or anything else in the situation that might help her zero in on the adult's communicative intention.

Once the child does understand the adult's communicative intention in using the new expression *tractor*, a symbol is created when she then acquires appropriate use of the expression herself. That is, as in all types of cultural learning, the process is something like the following: (*a*) the child understands that the adult's intention is for her to focus on the tractor, and (*b*) she also realizes that when she wishes to do as the adult is doing—when she wishes to focus someone else's attention on the tractor—she may use this same means of expression. There is thus a role reversal in cultural learning as the child identifies with the adult and adopts the adult's behavioral strategy for this specific function. As the child does this, she retains her understanding that the adult also comprehends and uses this same linguistic expression. The child's use of the expression thus creates a communicative *convention,* or symbol, whose essence is its intersubjectivity: the child simultaneously produces the symbol and appreciates that the recipient comprehends the symbol. We may thus think of this bidirectionality of linguistic symbols as simply the quality of being socially "shared" (Akhtar & Tomasello, in press; Tomasello, in press).

In terms of the two levels of social understanding that we have already posited—a *that* level in which infants recognize that other persons have intentions and attention toward the world and a *what* level in which they begin to determine precisely what those intentions and attention are—we believe that the *what* level is necessary for language acquisition. That is, simply understanding that another person may have a psychological relation to the world is not enough to acquire linguistic symbols, whose function is to pick out a very specific entity or aspect of a situation. Our prediction is thus that, at the first level, at 9 or 10 months, infants can do only something very basic, like look up to another or hold up an object to another who is already looking. They cannot direct the attention of others to particular locations and entities, either gesturally or linguistically, or follow others' attention to particular entities because they do not understand that they can share with others aspects of the world with such specificity. A corollary of this view is that the skills of linguistic comprehension that some infants seem to show at 9–10 months of age are not of the same nature as their later linguistic skills in that they are not intersubjective in the same way. They are more associatively based and resemble in fundamental structure the skills possessed by household pets who comprehend such linguistic expressions as "Dinner" and "Go for a walk."

But the *what* level of social-cognitive understanding of intentional agents is not by itself sufficient for the acquisition of a language; learners must also be exposed to particular linguistic conventions. That is, although many gestural skills might develop from general social interactions alone, in which the infant directs the attention of the adult to something in their shared environment, a language is a cultural artifact that has undergone many thousands of years of historical development. The acquisition of language can occur only when young children encounter other people using the communicative conventions of a particular language (given that they are in possession of the appropriate social-cognitive skills). Furthermore, it might be that, to acquire linguistic conventions at a very early age, say 12–13 months of age as was reported for some of the infants in our study and others, particular kinds of social environments and cultural routines may be required in which the adults' communicative intentions are made especially salient for children

(Tomasello, 1992). Indeed, we believe that this is precisely what we have shown here. Mother-infant dyads who knew how to enter into joint attentional engagement produced children with larger vocabularies, and, moreover, mothers following into their infant's immediate attentional focus was also associated with larger vocabularies for children. Both these relations held from as early as we could reliably measure the infants' language and social-cognitive skills.

However, it may be that, later in their second year of life, children may go on to acquire linguistic symbols in a wide array of less user-friendly environments in which they have to work much harder to discern the adult's communicative intentions (Tomasello, in press). That is to say, the relations that we have found here between joint attentional engagement, maternal following language, and children's language development may be especially relevant for—or perhaps even confined to—the earliest stages of language development, before children have found ways intersubjectively to enter into more complex social and communicative situations.

Of special importance in this regard are reports of the language development of children in many non-Western societies (e.g., Scheffelin & Ochs 1986), who are not engaged in the same intensive way as Western children in joint-engagement interactions and whose mothers do not use their language to follow into the child's current attentional focus. Indeed, there are recent reports that children in some cultures seem to acquire language almost exclusively as they observe, from the outside as it were, third parties interacting with and talking to one another (Brown, in press)—in which case the kinds of joint attentional engagement processes that we have described here are not really operative. Nevertheless, in the current view, these children must have some way of establishing joint attention with others; it is just that they may have to use more sophisticated social-cognitive skills to do so. The process may thus unfold at a somewhat later age than in Western middle-class families—mostly in children's third year of life, for example—and, indeed, there is some initial evidence that this is the case (Brown, in press).

The most general point is thus that language acquisition requires both specific social-cognitive skills on the part of the child and specific types of social interaction in which the child is exposed to the social conventions that constitute her native language. Our hypothesis is that children must reach the *what* level in the understanding of other persons as intentional agents before language acquisition can begin in earnest and that, at very early ages (12–14 months), they may require adults to scaffold the process by following into their already-established attentional focus. As children develop in their ability to identify the specific referents that adults intend when using new pieces of language, adult scaffolding may become unnecessary.

THE HUMAN CAPACITY FOR CULTURE

The cognitive skills that most clearly differentiate human beings from other animal species are those that allow them to take advantage of the knowledge and skills of conspecifics. It is not clear that human skills of spatial cognition, for instance, are more sophisticated than those of other primates, in the absence of maps and compasses. It is not clear that human skills of mathematics would be so different from those of other primates in the absence of a symbol system for indicating numbers and skillful practitioners to teach novices. It is not clear that human skills of categorization would be so different from those of other primate species in the absence of language (Tomasello & Call, 1997).

What we have investigated in this *Monograph* are the social-cognitive skills that enable infants and young children to begin participating in the collectivity of culture in an active way and thereby to amplify their cognitive skills by tuning in to others who have other skills. Certainly, young infants are cultural beings from the beginning in the sense that their development takes place within a particular cultural context that influences many aspects of their cognitive development (Kruger & Tomasello, 1996). But it is only with the emergence of the kinds of social-cognitive abilities that we have investigated here that they become able to tune in to other persons and their cognitive skills directed to outside entities, that is, in a way that fosters acquisition of the conventional use of cultural artifacts such as tools and language—which then serve to mediate their subsequent interactions with their environments in cognitively meaningful ways. This is the essence of the process of enculturation.

Perhaps the most compelling evidence of the importance of early social-cognitive skills is the case of children with autism, who have many cognitive competencies but appear to be deficient in one way or another (with wide individual differences) in just the social-cognitive skills studied here. This means that they do not tune in to the knowledge and skills of others in the same way as normally developing children and that they do not therefore become enculturated in the same way either (again with very large individual differences; Baron-Cohen, 1993; Hobson, 1993).

The uniqueness of the human adaptation for culture is also brought into stark relief when a comparison is made to our nearest primate relatives. Although there are population differences in the behavior of, for example, different groups of chimpanzees, these primates may be said to have *culture* in only an extended sense of that term (Tomasello, 1994). The reason that they have not created cultures of the human kind is that it appears as though they do not understand their conspecifics as intentional agents like themselves who experience the world in ways similar to the ways in which they themselves do. Thus, in their communication with conspecifics, apes do not point to distal entities in the environment, they do not hold up objects for others to see and share, and they do not actively give or offer objects to other individuals. They also do not actively teach one another with any regularity, and the kinds of cooperation in which they engage are very simple and basic (i.e., they very likely do not involve an understanding of the role of the other). Chimpanzees do not do these things because they do not have an understanding of their conspecifics as intentional agents whose mental lives they may affect through their own communicative, pedagogical, or cooperative efforts. This means that these apes will not be able, at least not in the manner of humans, to pool their cognitive resources and create cultural artifacts that all members of the group can exploit for cognitive purposes.

Apes raised by humans in human-like cultural environments may be somewhat different. These "enculturated" apes develop some human-like skills that they do not develop in their natural habitats or under more typical captive conditions, for example, imperative pointing, some skills with language-like symbols, and some skills of imitative learning (for a review, see Call & Tomasello, 1996). But they do not thereby turn into human beings. For example, it is still a rare event for an enculturated ape to simply show something to a human or an ape companion or to point to something just for the sake of sharing attention to it (Gómez et al., 1993). Also, in tasks in which they must cooperate with conspecifics, their skills of collaborative learning are very limited as well, and there is still very little, if any, behavior of enculturated apes that qualifies as teaching. What is common to all these activities is that they are all motivated by a desire simply to share experience with others, without any immediate concrete goal, as demonstrated daily by human infants from around their first birthdays. This may be a uniquely human motivation that not even human rearing can instill in nonhuman primates.

In conclusion, in the two studies reported here, we have provided evidence that, by their first birthdays, infants have begun to understand some aspects of the minds of other persons. At the very least, they understand that people attend to things of interest and behave intentionally toward them. This understanding manifests itself in a number of ways, for example, in attention following, intentional communication, and imitative learning. Understanding others in this way is foundational for almost all the uniquely human aspects of cognition because it allows human infants and young children to begin making use of the knowledge, skills, and artifacts that others have created, perhaps especially language. In this way, young children may begin to amplify their own individual cognitive skills in a manner unique to the species—a manner that, sadly, seems to be unavailable to some atypically developing children. This does not mean, of course, that later forms of social cognition such as understanding the thoughts and beliefs of others—"theory of mind"—are not also important. It is just that they are most appropriately conceived, in our view, as icing on the cake in the ontogeny of human social cognition. The origins of the species-unique aspects of human social cognition lie in the kinds of simple acts that we have observed in the current studies in which infants share, follow into, and direct the attention and behavior of others.

TABLE A1

IMITATIVE LEARNING ACTIONS

Instrumental Actions[a]	Arbitrary Actions
Compress spring	Hit the side of the box
Detach parts of PVC pipe	Kick the top of the box
Lift doorstop	Kiss the top of the box
Open hinge	Pat one hand on top of the box
Press doorbell	Pat both hands on top of the box
Pull ring	Rub one hand on top of the box
Slide bolt	Rub both hands on top of the box
Turn spinner	Touch head to top of the box

NOTE.—All actions were performed several times during each model with the exception of turning the spinner (which, incidentally, was almost never modeled because most infants did this action spontaeously), kissing the box, and touching the head to the box. The latter two actions were done in an exaggerated way.

[a] Alternate actions were move swing on or around stand, move straw on covered cup, twang small spring, and twist lid off covered cup.

REFERENCES

Abacus Concepts. (1989). *SUPERANOVA: Accessible general linear modeling*. Berkeley, CA: Abacus Concepts.

Abravanel, E., & Gingold, H. (1985). Learning via observation during the second year of life. *Developmental Psychology, 21*(4), 614–623.

Abravanel, E., Levan-Goldschmidt, E., & Stevenson, M. B. (1976). Action imitation: The early phase of infancy. *Child Development, 47*, 1032–1044.

Acredolo, L. P., & Goodwyn, S. W. (1988). Symbolic gesturing in normal infants. *Child Development, 59*, 450–466.

Adamson, L. B. (1995). *Communication development during infancy*. Madison, WI: Brown & Benchmark.

Adamson, L. B., & Bakeman, R. (1985). Affect and attention: Infants observed with mothers and peers. *Child Development, 56*, 582–593.

Ainsworth, M. (1973). The development of infant-mother attachment. In B. Caldwell & H. Ricciuti (Eds.), *Review of child development research* (Vol. 3). Chicago: University of Chicago Press.

Akhtar, N., Carpenter, M., & Tomasello, M. (1996). The role of discourse novelty in early word learning. *Child Development, 67*, 635–645.

Akhtar, N., Dunham, F., & Dunham, P. J. (1991). Directive interactions and early vocabulary development: The role of joint attentional focus. *Journal of Child Language, 18*, 41–49.

Akhtar, N., & Tomasello, M. (1996). Twenty-four month old children learn words for absent objects and actions. *British Journal of Developmental Psychology, 14*, 79–93.

Akhtar, N., & Tomasello, M. (in press). Intersubjectivity and early language. In S. Braaten (Ed.), *Intersubjective communication and emotion in ontogeny*. Cambridge University Press.

Anisfeld, M. (1991). Review: Neonatal imitation. *Developmental Review, 11*, 60–97.

Bakeman, R., & Adamson, L. (1984). Coordinating attention to people and objects in mother-infant and peer-infant interactions. *Child Development, 55*, 1278–1289.

Bakeman, R., & Adamson, L. (1986). Infants' conventionalized acts: Gestures and words with mothers and peers. *Infant Behavior and Development, 9*, 215–230.

Bakeman, R., & Gottman, J. (1986). *Observing interaction: An introduction to sequential analysis*. Cambridge: Cambridge University Press.

Baldwin, D. (1991). Infants' contribution to the achievement of joint reference. *Child Development, 63*, 875–890.

Baldwin, D. (1993a). Early referential understanding: Young children's ability to recognize referential acts for what they are. *Developmental Psychology, 29*, 1–12.

Baldwin, D. (1993b). Infants' ability to consult the speaker for clues to word reference. *Journal of Child Language, 2*, 395–418.

Baldwin, D. (1995). Understanding the link between joint attention and language. In C. Moore & P. Dunham (Eds.), *Joint attention: Its origins and role in development*. Hillsdale, NJ: Erlbaum.

Baldwin, D., & Moses, L. (1996). The ontogeny of social information gathering. *Child Development*, **67**, 1915–1939.

Baron-Cohen, S. (1993). From attention-goal psychology to belief-desire psychology: The development of a theory of mind and its dysfunction. In S. Baron-Cohen, H. Tager-Flusberg, & D. J. Cohen (Eds.), *Understanding other minds: Perspectives from autism*. New York: Oxford University Press.

Baron-Cohen, S. (1995). *Mindblindness: An essay on autism and theory of mind*. Cambridge, MA: MIT Press.

Baron-Cohen, S., & Ring, H. (1994). A model of the mindreading system: Neuropsychological and neurobiological perspectives. In C. Lewis & P. Mitchell (Eds.), *Children's early understanding of mind: Origins and development*. Hove: Erlbaum.

Barresi, J., & Moore, C. (1993). Sharing a perspective precedes the understanding of that perspective. *Behavioral and Brain Sciences*, **16**, 513–514.

Barresi, J., & Moore, C. (1996). Intentional relations and social understanding. *Behavioral and Brain Sciences*, **19**, 107–154.

Bart, W. M., & Airasian, P. W. (1974). Determination of the ordering among seven Piagetian tasks by an ordering-theoretic method. *Journal of Educational Psychology*, **66**, 277–284.

Bates, E. (1979). Intentions, conventions, and symbols. In E. Bates (Ed.), *The emergence of symbols: Cognition and communication in infancy*. New York: Academic.

Bates, E., Benigni, L., Bretherton, I., Camaioni, L., & Volterra, V. (1979). Cognition and communication from nine to thirteen months: Correlational findings. In E. Bates (Ed.), *The emergence of symbols: Cognition and communication in infancy*. New York: Academic.

Bates, E., Camaioni, L., & Volterra, V. (1975). The acquisition of performatives prior to speech. *Merrill-Palmer Quarterly*, **21**, 205–224.

Bretherton, I., McNew, S., & Beeghly-Smith, M. (1981). Early person knowledge as expressed in gestural and verbal communication: When do infants acquire a "theory of mind"? In M. E. Lamb & L. R. Sherrod (Eds.), *Infant social cognition: Empirical and theoretical considerations*. Hillsdale, NJ: Erlbaum.

Brown, P. (in press). The conversational context for language acquisition: A Tzeltal (Mayan) case study. In M. Bowerman & S. Levinson (Eds.), *Language acquisition and conceptual development*. Cambridge: Cambridge University Press.

Bruner, J. (1975a). From communication to language. *Cognition*, **3**, 255–287.

Bruner, J. (1975b). The ontogenesis of speech acts. *Journal of Child Language*, **2**, 1–20.

Bruner, J. (1977). Early social interaction and language acquisition. In H. R. Schaffer (Ed.), *Studies in mother-infant interaction*. New York: Academic.

Bruner, J. (1981). The pragmatics of acquisition. In W. Deutsch (Ed.), *The child's construction of language*. New York: Academic.

Bruner, J. (1982). The organization of action and the nature of the adult-infant transaction. In E. Z. Tronick (Ed.), *Social interchange in infancy: Affect, cognition, and communication*. Baltimore: University Park.

Bruner, J. (1983). *Child's talk: Learning to use language*. New York: Norton.

Butterworth, G. (1991a, April). *Evidence for the "geometric" comprehension of manual pointing*. Paper presented at the meeting of the Society for Research in Child Development, Seattle.

Butterworth, G. (1991b). The ontogeny and phylogeny of joint visual attention. In A. Whiten (Ed.), *Natural theories of mind: Evolution, development and simulation of everyday mindreading*. Cambridge, MA: Blackwell.

Butterworth, G., & Cochran, E. (1980). Towards a mechanism of joint visual attention in human infancy. *International Journal of Behavioral Development*, **3**, 253–272.

Butterworth, G., & Grover, L. (1988). The origins of referential communication in human infancy. In L. Weiskrantz (Ed.), *Thought without language*. Oxford: Clarendon.

Butterworth, G., & Grover, L. (1990). Joint visual attention, manual pointing, and preverbal communication in human infancy. In M. Jeannerod (Ed.), *Attention and performance XIII*. Hillsdale, NJ: Erlbaum.

Butterworth, G., & Jarrett, N. (1991). What minds have in common is space: Spatial mechanisms serving joint visual attention in infancy. *British Journal of Developmental Psychology*, **9**, 55–72.

Call, J., & Tomasello, M. (1996). The role of humans in the cognitive development of apes. In A. Russon (Ed.), *Reaching into thought: The minds of the great apes*. Cambridge: Cambridge University Press.

Camaioni, L. (1993). The development of intentional communication: A re-analysis. In J. Nadel & L. Camaioni (Eds.), *New perspectives in early communicative development*. New York: Routledge.

Campos, J., & Stenberg, C. (1981). Perception, appraisal, and emotion: The onset of social referencing. In M. Lamb & L. Sherrod (Eds.), *Infant social cognition: Empirical and theoretical considerations*. Hillsdale, N.J: Erlbaum.

Carpenter, M., Akhtar, N., & Tomasello, M. (1998). Fourteen- through 18-month-old infants differentially imitate intentional and accidental actions. *Infant Behavior and Development*, **21**, 315–330.

Chomsky, N. (1968). *Language and mind*. New York: Harcourt Brace.

Churcher, J., & Scaife, M. (1982). How infants see the point. In G. Butterworth & P. Light (Eds.), *Social cognition: Studies of the development of understanding*. Chicago: University of Chicago Press.

Cole, M. (1996). *Cultural psychology: A once and future discipline*. Cambridge, MA: Harvard University Press.

Collis, G. M. (1977). Visual co-orientation and maternal speech. In H. R. Schaffer (Ed.), *Studies in mother-infant interaction*. New York: Academic.

Corkum, V., & Moore, C. (1995). Development of joint visual attention in infants. In C. Moore & P. Dunham (Eds.), *Joint attention: Its origins and role in development*. Hillsdale, NJ: Erlbaum.

Corrigan, R. (1979). Cognitive correlates of language: Differential criteria yield differential results. *Child Development*, **50**, 617–31.

Csibra, G., Gergely, G., Biró, S., & Koos, O. (in press). The perception of pure reason in infancy. *Cognition*.

Decasper, A. J., & Fifer, W. P. (1980). Of human bonding: Newborns prefer their mothers' voices. *Science*, **208**, 1174–1176.

Della Corte, M., Benedict, H., & Klein, D. (1983). The relationship of pragmatic dimensions of mothers' speech to the referential-expressive distinction. *Journal of Child Language*, **10**, 35–43.

D'Entremont, B., Hains, S., & Muir, D. (1997). A demonstration of gaze following in 3- to 6-month-olds. *Infant Behavior and Development*, **20**, 569–572.

Desrochers, S., Morissette, P., & Ricard, M. (1995). Two perspectives on pointing in infancy. In C. Moore & P. Dunham (Eds.), *Joint attention: Its origins and role in development*. Hillsdale, NJ: Erlbaum.

Dunham, P. J., Dunham, F., & Curwin, A. (1993). Joint-attentional states and lexical acquisition at 18 months. *Developmental Psychology*, **29**, 827–831.

Fantz, R. L. (1963). Pattern vision in newborn infants. *Science*, **140**, 296–297.

Fenson, L., Dale, P. S., Reznick, S., Thal, D., Bates, E., Hartung, J. P., Pethick, S., & Reilly, J. S. (1993). *MacArthur Communicative Development Inventories: User's guide and technical manual.* San Diego, CA: Singular.

Fisher, K., & Silvern, L. (1985). Stages and individual differences in cognitive development. *Annual Review of Psychology,* **36,** 613–648.

Flavell, J. H. (1992). Perspectives on perspective taking. In H. Beilin & P. B. Pufall (Eds.), *Piaget's theory: Prospects and possibilities.* Hillsdale, NJ: Erlbaum.

Flavell, J., & Miller, P. (1998). Social cognition. In D. Kuhn & R. Siegler (Eds.), W. Damon (Series Ed.), *Handbook of child psychology: Vol. 2. Cognition, Perception, and Language.* New York: Wiley.

Franco, F., & Butterworth, G. (1996). Pointing and social awareness: Declaring and requesting in the second year. *Journal of Child Language,* **23,** 307–336.

Frye, D. (1991). The origins of intention in infancy. In D. Frye & C. Moore (Eds.), *Children's theories of mind.* Hillsdale, NJ: Erlbaum.

Gergely, G., Nádasdy, Z., Csibra, G., & Biró, S. (1995). Taking the intentional stance at 12 months of age. *Cognition,* **56,** 165–193.

Gibson, E., & Rader, N. (1979). Attention: The perceiver as performer. In G. A. Hale & M. Lewis (Eds.), *Attention and cognitive development.* New York: Plenum.

Gómez, J. C., Sarriá, E., & Tamarit, J. (1993). The comparative study of early communication and theories of mind: Ontogeny, phylogeny, and pathology. In S. Baron-Cohen, H. Tager-Flusberg, & D. J. Cohen (Eds.), *Understanding other minds: Perspectives from autism.* New York: Oxford University Press.

Gopnik, A. (1984). The acquisition of *gone* and the development of the object concept. *Journal of Child Language,* **11,** 273–292.

Gopnik, A., & Meltzoff, A. (1987). The development of categorization in the second year and its relation to other cognitive and linguistic developments. *Child Development,* **58,** 1523–1531.

Gopnik, A., & Meltzoff, A. (1993). Imitation, cultural learning, and the origins of "theory of mind." *Behavioral and Brain Sciences,* **16,** 521–23.

Gordon, R. (1986). Folk psychology as simulation. *Mind and Language,* **1,** 158–71.

Gordon, R. (1992). The simulation theory: Objections and misconceptions. *Mind and language,* **7,** 87–103.

Green, B. F. (1956). A method of scalogram analysis using summary statistics. *Psychometrika,* **21**(1), 79–88.

Guttman, L. (1950). The basis for scalogram analysis. In S. A. Stouffer et al. (Eds.), *Measurement and prediction.* Princeton, NJ: Princeton University Press.

Hannan, T. E. (1987). A cross-sequential assessment of the occurrences of pointing in 3- to 12-month-old human infants. *Infant Behavior and Development,* **10,** 11–22.

Harding, C. G., & Golinkoff, R. M. (1979). The origins of intentional vocalizations in prelinguistic infants. *Child Development,* **50,** 33–40.

Harris, P. (1996). Desires, beliefs, and language. In P. Carruthers & P. Smith (Eds.), *Theories of theories of mind.* Cambridge: Cambridge University Press.

Harris, M., Jones, D., Brookes, S., & Grant, J. (1986). Relations between non-verbal context of maternal speech and rate of language development. *British Journal of Developmental Psychology,* **4,** 261–268.

Hobson, P. (1993). *Autism and the development of mind.* Hillsdale, NJ: Erlbaum.

Jones, S. (1996). Imitation or exploration? Young infants' matching of adults' oral gestures. *Child Development,* **67,** 1952–1969.

Kaye, K. (1982). *The mental and social life of babies: How parents create persons.* Chicago: University of Chicago Press.

Killen, M., & Uzgiris, I. C. (1981). Imitation of actions with objects: The role of social meaning. *Journal of Genetic Psychology,* **138,** 219–229.

Kruger, A., & Tomasello, M. (1996). Cultural learning and learning culture. In D. Olson (Ed.), *Handbook of education and human development: New models of teaching, learning, and schooling.* Cambridge, MA: Blackwell.

Lempers, J. D. (1979). Young children's production and comprehension of nonverbal deictic behaviors. *Journal of Genetic Psychology,* **135,** 93–102.

Lempers, J. D., Flavell, E. R., & Flavell, J. H. (1977). The development in very young children of tacit knowledge concerning visual perception. *Genetic Psychology Monographs,* **95,** 3–53.

Leung, E. H. L., & Rheingold, H. L. (1981). Development of pointing as a social gesture. *Developmental Psychology,* **17**(2), 215–220.

Lewis, C., & Mitchell, P. (1994). *Children's early understanding of mind: Origins and development.* Mahwah, NJ: Erlbaum.

Markman, E. (1989). *Categorization and naming in children.* Cambridge, MA: MIT Press.

Markman, E. (1992). Constraints on word learning: Speculations about their nature, origins, and word specificity. In M. Gunnar & M. Maratsos (Eds.), *Modularity and constraints in language and cognition.* Hillsdale, NJ: Erlbaum.

Masur, E. F. (1983). Gestural development, dual-directional signaling, and the transition to words. *Journal of Psycholinguistic Research,* **12**(2), 93–109.

Masur, E. F., & Ritz, E. G. (1984). Patterns of gestural, vocal, and verbal imitation performance in infancy. *Merrill-Palmer Quarterly,* **30**(4), 369–392.

McCabe, M. A., & Uzgiris, I. C. (1983). Effects of model and action on imitation in infancy. *Merrill-Palmer Quarterly,* **29**(1), 69–82.

McCall, R. B., Eichorn, D. H., & Hogarty, P. S. (1977). Transitions in early mental development. *Monographs of the Society for Research in Child Development,* **42**(3, Serial No. 108).

McCall, R. B., Parke, R. D., & Kavanaugh, R. D. (1977). Imitation of live and televised models by children one to three years of age. *Monographs of the Society for Research in Child Development,* **42**(5, Serial No. 173).

Meltzoff, A. N. (1988a). Infant imitation after a 1-week delay: Long-term memory for novel acts and multiple stimuli. *Developmental Psychology,* **24,** 470–476.

Meltzoff, A. N. (1988b). Infant imitation and memory: Nine-month-olds in immediate and deferred tests. *Child Development,* **59,** 217–225.

Meltzoff, A. N. (1995). Understanding the intentions of others: Re-enactment of intended acts by 18-month-old children. *Developmental Psychology,* **31**(5), 1–16.

Meltzoff, A. N., & Gopnik, A. (1993). The role of imitation in understanding persons and developing a theory of mind. In S. Baron-Cohen, H. Tager-Flusberg, & D. J. Cohen (Eds.), *Understanding other minds: Perspectives from autism.* New York: Oxford University Press.

Meltzoff, A. N., & Moore, M. K. (1977). Imitation of facial and manual gestures by human neonates. *Science,* **198,** 75–78.

Meltzoff, A. N., & Moore, M. K. (1989). Imitation in newborn infants: Exploring the range of gestures imitated and the underlying mechanisms. *Developmental Psychology,* **25,** 954–962.

Moore, C. (1996). Theories of mind in infancy. *British Journal of Developmental Psychology,* **14,** 19–40.

Moore, C., & Corkum, V. (1994). Social understanding at the end of the first year of life. *Developmental Review,* **14,** 349–372.

Moore, C., & Dunham, P. (Eds.). (1995). *Joint attention: Its origins and role in development.* Hillsdale, NJ: Erlbaum.

Morissette, P., Ricard, M., & Gouin-Décarie, T. (1995). Joint visual attention and pointing in infancy: A longitudinal study of comprehension. *British Journal of Developmental Psychology*, **15**, 163–77.

Morton, J., & Johnson, M. (1991). CONSPEC and CONLEARN: A two-process theory of infant face recognition. *Psychological Review*, **98**, 164–181.

Murphy, C. M., & Messer, D. J. (1977). Mothers, infants and pointing: A study of a gesture. In H. R. Schaffer (Ed.), *Studies in mother-infant interaction*. New York: Academic.

Murray, L., & Trevarthen, C. (1985). Emotional regulation of interactions between two-month-olds and their mothers. In T. M. Field & N. A. Fox (Eds.), *Social perception in infants*. Norwood, NJ: Ablex.

Nelson, K. (1973). Structure and strategy in learning to talk. *Monographs of the Society for Research in Child Development*, **38**(1–2, Serial No. 149).

Nelson, K. (1981). Individual differences in language development: Implications for development and language. *Developmental Psychology*, **17**, 170–187.

Ninio, A., & Bruner, J. (1978). The achievement and antecedents of labelling. *Journal of Child Language*, **5**, 1–15.

Pawlby, S. J. (1977). Imitative interaction. In H. R. Schaffer (Ed.), *Studies in mother-infant interaction*. New York: Academic.

Perucchini, P., & Camaioni, L. (1993, September). *When intentional communication emerges? Developmental dissociations between declarative and imperative functions of the pointing gesture.* Paper presented at the Developmental Conference of the British Psychological Society, Birmingham.

Phillips, W., Baron-Cohen, S., & Rutter, M. (1992). The role of eye contact in goal detection: Evidence from normal infants and children with autism or mental handicap. *Development and Psychopathology*, **4**, 375–383.

Piaget, J. (1952). *Origins of intelligence in children.* New York: Norton.

Piaget, J. (1962). *Play, dreams, and imitation in childhood.* New York: Norton.

Pinker, S. (1994). *The language instinct.* New York: Morrow.

Povinelli, D. J., & Eddy, T. J. (1996). What young chimpanzees know about seeing. *Monographs of the Society for Research in Child Development*, **61**(3, Serial No. 247).

Ratner, N., & Bruner, J. (1978). Games, social exchange and the acquisition of language. *Journal of Child Language*, **5**, 391–401.

Reissland, N. (1988). Neonatal imitation in the first hour of life: Observations in rural Nepal. *Developmental Psychology*, **24**, 464–469.

Rocissano, L., & Yatchmink, Y. (1984). Joint attention in mother-toddler interaction: A study of individual variation. *Merrill-Palmer Quarterly*, **30**, 11–31.

Rodgon, M. M., & Kurdek, L. A. (1977). Vocal and gestural imitation in 8-, 14-, and 20-month-old children. *Journal of Genetic Psychology*, **131**, 115–123.

Rogoff, B. (1990). *Apprenticeship in thinking.* Oxford: Oxford University Press.

Ross, H. S., & Lollis, S. P. (1987). Communication within infant social games. *Developmental Psychology*, **23**(2), 241–248.

Ruddy, M., & Bornstein, M. (1982). Cognitive correlates of infant attention and maternal stimulation over the first year of life. *Child Development*, **53**, 183–188.

Rutter, D. R., & Durkin, K. (1987). Turn-taking in mother-infant interaction: An examination of vocalizations and gaze. *Developmental Psychology*, **23**(1), 54–61.

Saxon, T., Frick, J., & Colombo, J. (1997). A longitudinal study of maternal interactional styles and infant visual attention. *Merrill-Palmer Quarterly*, **43**, 48–66.

Scaife, M., & Bruner, J. S. (1975). The capacity for joint visual attention in the infant. *Nature*, **253**, 265–266.

Schaffer, H. R., & Liddell, D. (1984). Adult-child interaction under dyadic and polyadic conditions. *British Journal of Developmental Psychology*, **2**, 33–42.

Scheffelin, B., & Ochs, E. (1986). *Language socialization across cultures*. Cambridge: Cambridge University Press.

Smith, C. B., Adamson, L. B., & Bakeman, R. (1988). Interactional predictors of early language. *First Language, 8,* 143–156.

Smith, L. (1995). Self-organizing processes in learning to learn words. In C. A. Nelson (Ed.), *Basic and applied perspectives on learning, cognition, and development* (Minnesota Symposium on Child Psychology, Vol. 28). Mahwah, NJ: Erlbaum.

Smith, L., & Samuelson, L. (1997). Perceiving and remembering: Category stability, variability, and development. In K. Lamberts & D. Shanks (Eds.), *Knowledge, concepts, and categories*. Cambridge: Cambridge University Press.

Snow, C., & Goldfield, B. (1983). Turn the page please: Situation-specific language acquisition. *Journal of Child Language, 10,* 551–570.

Sugarman, S. (1984). The development of preverbal communication: Its contribution and limits in promoting the development of language. In R. L. Schiefelbusch & J. Pickar (Eds.), *The acquisition of communicative competence*. Baltimore: University Park.

Sugarman-Bell, S. (1978). Some organizational aspects of pre-verbal communication. In I. Marková (Ed.), *The social context of language*. New York: Wiley.

Tamis-LeMonda, C., & Bornstein, M. (1989). Habituation and maternal encouragement of attention in infancy as predictors of toddler language, play, and representational competence. *Child Development, 60,* 738–751.

Tomasello, M. (1988). The role of joint attentional processes in early language development. *Language Sciences, 10,* 69–88.

Tomasello, M. (1990). Cultural transmission in the tool use and communicatory signaling of chimpanzees? In S. Parker & K. Gibson (Eds.), *"Language" and intelligence in primates: Developmental perspectives*. Cambridge: Cambridge University Press.

Tomasello, M. (1992). The social bases of language acquisition. *Social Development, 1*(1), 67–87.

Tomasello, M. (1994). The question of chimpanzee culture. In R. Wrangham, W. McGrew, F. de Waal, & P. Heltne (Eds.), *Chimpanzee cultures*. Cambridge, MA: Harvard University Press.

Tomasello, M. (1995a). Joint attention as social cognition. In C. Moore & P. Dunham (Eds.), *Joint attention: Its origins and role in development*. Hillsdale, NJ: Erlbaum.

Tomasello, M. (1995b). Language is not an instinct. *Cognitive Development, 10,* 131–156.

Tomasello, M. (1996a). Do apes ape? In C. Heyes & B. Galef (Eds.), *Social learning in animals: The roots of culture*. New York: Academic.

Tomasello, M. (1996b). Self as social agent. In P. Rochat (Ed.), *The self in infancy: Theory and research*. Amsterdam: Elsevier.

Tomasello, M. (in press). Understanding intentions and learning words in the second year of life. In M. Bowerman & S. Levinson (Eds.), *Language acquisition and conceptual development*. Cambridge: Cambridge University Press.

Tomasello, M., & Akhtar, N. (1995). Two-year-olds use pragmatic cues to differentiate reference to objects and actions. *Cognitive Development, 10,* 201–224.

Tomasello, M., & Barton, M. (1994). Learning words in nonostensive contexts. *Developmental Psychology, 30,* 639–650.

Tomasello, M., & Call, J. (1997). *Primate Cognition*. Oxford: Oxford University Press.

Tomasello, M., & Camaioni, L. (1997). A comparison of the gestural communication of apes and human infants. *Human Development, 40,* 7–24.

Tomasello, M., & Farrar, M. J. (1986a). Joint attention and early language. *Child Development, 57,* 1454–1463.

Tomasello, M., & Farrar, M. J. (1986b). Object permanence and relational words: A lexical training study. *Journal of Child Language, 13,* 495–505.

Tomasello, M., Kruger, A. C., & Ratner, H. H. (1993). Cultural learning. *Behavioral and Brain Sciences,* **16,** 495–552.

Tomasello, M., Mannle, S., & Barton, M. (1989). The development of communicative competence in twins. *Revue Internationale de Psychologie Sociale,* **2,** 49–59.

Tomasello, M., Mannle, S., & Kruger, A. (1986). The linguistic environment of one to two year old twins. *Developmental Psychology,* **22,** 169–176.

Tomasello, M., & Mervis, C. B. (1994). Commentary: The instrument is great, but measuring comprehension is still a problem. In L. Fenson et al., *Variability in Early Communicative Development. Monographs of the Society for Research in Child Development,* **59**(5, Serial No. 242).

Tomasello, M., Savage-Rumbaugh, S., & Kruger, A. C. (1993). Imitative learning of actions on objects by children, chimpanzees, and enculturated chimpanzees. *Child Development,* **64,** 1688–1705.

Tomasello, M., & Todd, J. (1983). Joint attention and lexical acquisition style. *First Language,* **4,** 197–212.

Trevarthen, C. (1979a). Communication and cooperation in early infancy: A description of primary intersubjectivity. In M. M. Bullowa (Ed.), *Before speech: The beginning of interpersonal communication.* New York: Cambridge University Press.

Trevarthen, C. (1979b). Instincts for human understanding and for cultural cooperation: Their development in infancy. In M. von Cranach, K. Foppa, W. Lepenies, & D. Ploog (Eds.), *Human ethology: Claims and limits of a new discipline.* Cambridge: Cambridge University Press.

Trevarthen, C., & Hubley, P. (1978). Secondary intersubjectivity: Confidence, confiding and acts of meaning in the first year. In A. Lock (Ed.), *Action, gesture, and symbol: The emergence of language.* New York: Academic.

Tronick, E. Z. (1989). Emotions and emotional communication in infants. *American Psychologist,* **44,** 112–119.

Uzgiris, I. C., & Hunt, J. M. V. (1975). *Assessment in infancy: Ordinal scales of psychological development.* Urbana: University of Illinois Press.

Vibbert, M., & Bornstein, M. (1989). Specific associations between domains of maternal-child interaction and toddler referential language and pretense play. *Infant Behavior and Development,* **12,** 163–184.

Vygotsky, L. (1978). *Mind in society: The development of higher psychological processes.* Cambridge, MA: Harvard University Press.

Vygotsky, L., & Luria, A. (1993). *Studies on the history of behavior.* Hillsdale, NJ: Erlbaum.

Walden, T., & Ogan, T. (1988). The development of social referencing. *Child Development,* **59,** 1230–1240.

Zentall, T. (1996). An analysis of imitative learning in animals. In C. Heyes & B. Galef (Eds.), *Social learning in animals: The roots of culture.* New York: Academic.

Zinober, B., & Martlew, M. (1985). Developmental changes in four types of gesture in relation to acts and vocalizations from 10 to 21 months. *British Journal of Developmental Psychology,* **3,** 293–306.

ACKNOWLEDGMENTS

This research was supported by a grant from the Spencer Foundation to Michael Tomasello and by a National Institute of Mental Health Postdoctoral Training Grant to Malinda Carpenter. We thank Laura Rekau for help collecting and coding data, Nameera Akhtar and Danielle Weir for help with the analyses of mothers' speech, Steve Cole and Josep Call for help with data analysis, and the parents and children who participated in the study. We also thank three anonymous reviewers for very helpful comments. Please address correspondence to Malinda Carpenter at School of Biological Sciences, Nicholson Building, University of Liverpool, Liverpool L69 3BX, United Kingdom; or at mcarpent@liverpool.ac.uk.

COMMENTARY

ORIGINS OF JOINT VISUAL ATTENTION IN INFANCY

George Butterworth

Introduction

To take the "intentional stance" toward persons (or other complex systems) is to attribute rationality, beliefs, and desires to them (Dennett, 1987). When do human infants attribute rationality to other people? When do they take the intentional stance with respect to the shared objects of their own and other's experience? Is the intentional stance the sine qua non of human communication? Carpenter, Nagell, and Tomasello claim that the intentional stance emerges toward the end of the first year of life, as the infant progresses from sharing attention, to following attention, and finally to directing the attention of others. Their argument, which is well made, is that social cognitive skills, rather than nonsocial actions on objects, lie at the heart of the transition from preverbal communication to language. Their evidence comes from the pattern of intercorrelation of emerging abilities in the period from 9 to 15 months, in particular, the emerging ability of the infant intentionally to redirect other's attention, which they take as evidence for attributing mind to others.

However, another possibility exists, namely, that unambiguously intentional communication arises in development when cognitive developmental changes begin to supplement the infant's direct experience of the communicative intentions of others. If this is true, then a rather different time-

Much of the research reported here was funded by the Economic and Social Research Council of Great Britain in grants to the author and his colleagues. This Commentary was written with the support of a Leverhulme Foundation research fellowship, which is gratefully acknowledged.

table for the emergence of joint visual attention in relation to referential communication and pointing seems possible. This Commentary will address the question of whether there is evidence for joint visual attention prior to the timetable proposed by Carpenter et al. It will be argued that, while the developmental changes that Carpenter et al. observe at 9–12 months are not themselves in dispute, they do not constitute the origin of joint visual attention. The widespread changes that they observe reflect a new ability to integrate events across progressively larger gaps in space and time. This new ability serves the comprehension and production of pointing, but joint visual attention is already in place and has been for many months.

Carpenter et al.'s finding that joint visual attention actually begins toward the end of the first year, just before the production of pointing, is inconsistent with much recent data and probably reflects the robust criteria that they adopted for emergence and their spatial conditions of testing. Further evidence will be reviewed concerning the relation between joint attention, pointing, and the development of language, and an alternative theory to that of pointing acquisition by ritualization will be proposed. Finally, the relation between a perceptual-ecological approach and a cognitive developmental approach to early communicative development will be addressed. These approaches are not mutually exclusive, and both types of account are needed to understand the origins of communicative competence. Indeed, referential communication, even among adults, may depend at least in part on ecological factors that assist in determining the precise objects of reference.

On the Origins of Intentionality

Carpenter et al. take rather a conservative stance on the emergence of joint visual attention. Although their description of the onset of robust triadic attention at 13 months agrees broadly with that reported by most observers, and although they offer useful new information on the interrelations among constituent skills, their specific theoretical proposals concerning the development of pointing are open to alternative interpretations. Carpenter et al. do not directly research the mechanisms that may underlie the emergence of joint visual attention, and their concluding account of the possible relations between pointing onset and language is speculative. Alternative theoretical scenarios will be sketched, but first it is necessary to address the central question of the origins of intentionality.

In common with Piaget (1952), Carpenter et al. attribute intentionality to infants at around 9–12 months. Piaget argued that intentions are first seen in coordinated secondary circular reactions, when the infant performs a sequence of actions as a means to an end. Piaget did not deny that infants may have intentions before 9–12 months; he merely said that it is difficult to rule out nonintentional explanations for behavior until infants coordinate separate activities in a goal-directed fashion. Thus, Carpenter et al. are essentially following Piaget's timetable in tracing the origins of intentionality to the period of secondary circular reactions. Where they differ from Piaget, however, is in distinguishing social cognitive development from physical cognition and in arguing that the baby not only controls her own actions intentionally but also attributes intentions to others. Taking the intentional stance is the first step in attributing mind to others, and this emergent ability separates human cognition from that of the higher primates. Although human infants are comparable to other primates in the development of physical cognition, they rapidly outstrip higher primates in social cognition, especially as language develops.

The theory is fully spelled out in Tomasello and Call (1997), and it will be useful to be clear on the details. The infant's newly emergent intentional stance on communication and imitation is thought to allow her to tune in to others' focus of attention by gaze following, to do what someone else is doing through imitative learning, and to engage in emotional communication through social referencing. Babies also become intentional agents themselves and act in such a way that others come to tune in to their own focus of attention, through gestures such as pointing. All these skills emerge concurrently because they are manifestations of the newfound ability to understand others as intentional agents. An intentional agent is "an animate being that chooses its own goals, [chooses] behavioural means for pursuing goals and [chooses] attentional foci for monitoring progress toward goals" (Tomasello & Call, 1997, p. 405).

There are further ramifications of this cognitive revolution, including the beginning of self-consciousness. The distance between humans and higher primates increases as humans engage in imitative learning and teaching, whereas higher primates emulate (i.e., they may learn through observation how to achieve a particular goal but without paying close attention to the precise means). Humans communicate through symbols, and they recognize attention as a mental state, whereas animals communicate through signals and recognize attention merely as a bodily orientation. Human gestures are said to be acquired by imitation, and they are socially transmitted, whereas higher primates acquire gestures by ontogenetic ritualization, a process in which the signal function of the gesture arises idiosyncratically in social interaction. Such gestures are neither socially nor transgenerationally transmitted among the higher primates, but they are transmitted in precisely those ways between humans.

These extensive qualitative distinctions between different levels of organization are helpful in differentiating the mechanisms supporting similar surface behaviors across species and at different stages of development. However, since Carpenter et al.'s emphasis is almost exclusively on cognitive processes whose origins can be traced to the period 9–12 months, the precursors of joint visual attention tend to be neglected. The focus on cognitive attribution as a core ability may give a misleading picture of the species-typical foundations for communication. Of particular concern are those aspects of human embodiment that serve as signals and that are deeply involved in the development of referential communication. The intentional stance is presented by Carpenter et al. as both necessary and sufficient for joint visual attention, but this is to sideline the role of perception and action systems in the emergence of human communication.

An alternative theoretical approach, one that also recognizes intentionality, among other factors, would be to argue that intentionality itself admits of degrees. On this view, intentionality includes innate aspects based on the direct perception of physical and social objects, goal-directed activity (i.e., intentions expressed in and read from instrumental actions), and deliberation and forethought (i.e., intentions expressed in cognition and also revealed through language). The emergent intentionality observed in the period 9–12 months could be considered an intermediate form bridging earlier "perceptual," current (9–12 months) "instrumental," and future "represented" intentions. Goal-directed action can be observed even in newborns (e.g., Butterworth & Hopkins, 1989; Lew & Butterworth, 1995, 1997), in 2-month-old babies (e.g., Kalnins & Bruner, 1974), and in numerous well-researched examples in early infancy, such as visually guided reaching (e.g., Bower, Broughton, & Moore, 1970; Von Hofsten, 1990).

In the interpersonal realm, newborn babies imitate oral movements, vowel sounds, and finger movements (see Butterworth, in press). Two-month-olds in interaction with their mothers are said to show social communicative protointentions (e.g., Trevarthen, 1990). These abilities need to be explained, not only in terms of the underlying mechanisms for social participation, but also in terms of the infant's intrinsic motives for communication.

Such early appearing forms of intentionality have been described by Vedeler (1994) as object-directed intentions. That is, the intended objects of action and interaction are in the physical and social environment: they are not the purely mental objects that are emphasized by traditional philosophy of mind and on which the theory of the intentional stance is based. From the outset, object-directed intentionality is a property of behavior, whereas intentions as "purely mental" objects take time to develop. Thus, evidence that babies may attribute intentionality (rather than perceive intentionality in the communicative actions of others) comes only later in infancy.

Similarly, even though the weight of modern evidence suggests that imitation is innate and based on perception (Butterworth, in press), it is only in the second year that babies will imitate an intended action when they have simply observed a failed action, once the requisite representational ability is available (Meltzoff, 1995). This later appearing ability requires the infant to foresee the intended outcome; it occurs at an age when language is becoming well established, and some would call this insight. Carpenter et al. call it the intentional stance. The first theoretical disagreement, then, with Carpenter et al. is that there is no graduation ceremony in development at which intentionality is first conferred on the infant. Similarly, joint attention admits of development, and it can be shown to be present, in an honest form, long before the 9–12-month watershed.

The Emergence of Joint Attention

From the outset, the major theoretical effect of Scaife and Bruner's (1975) pioneering study was on received theories of infant egocentrism. Their observation suggested that very young babies share perspectives with others, that they are not locked into a solipsistic universe, and that they rely on perception for information about physical and social reality. The fact that infants as young as 2 months follow a change in the orientation of gaze of an adult is not possible in traditional theories, such as Piaget's (1952, 1954; see Butterworth, 1987). Carpenter et al. maintain that joint attention in gaze following is not observed consistently until 13 months, 1.3 months later than babies follow pointing (at 11.7 months in their data) and at about the time that they produce declarative pointing (at 12.6 months). Corkum and Moore (1995), Moore and Corkum (1994), and Morissette, Ricard, and Gouin-Decarie (1995) also offer a similar timetable for the emergence of joint visual attention. That is, between Scaife and Bruner's (1975) original observation and the present, the developmental timetable for the origins of joint visual attention has been set back by about a year! The consequence is that the significance for developmental theory of an early form of perceptually based perspective sharing is in danger of being overlooked.

One reason why the age of emergence of joint visual attention has been progressively delayed in successive studies is that conservative diagnostic criteria have often been adopted. The criterion for success in Carpenter et al.'s study was that babies should show a correct response to each of two targets on either side of the room. That is, babies must accurately localize a target at approximately 45 degrees, at a distance of either 6 feet or 6 feet, 6 inches (to the baby's right or left), and they must also localize a more peripheral target at about 80 degrees, at a distance of between 4 feet and 4 feet, 6 inches, also to the right and the left (see Carpenter et al.'s Figure 1). This spatial arrangement requires the baby to ignore the 45-degree target in order correctly to localize the more peripheral referent on the same side of the room.

Similarly, Corkum and Moore (1995) applied a stringent criterion that infants should show spontaneous gaze following and make a run of five consecutive correct responses in order to be credited with the capacity for joint visual attention. Even so, they were unable to train infants to make eye movements in the opposite direction to an adult's signal, which suggests that directional cues are important even at 6 months. Morissette et al. (1995) also used large spatial separations of the targets and stringent scoring criteria in their study, which showed joint visual attention to be coincident with comprehension of pointing at 12–15 months.

Stringent performance criteria and demanding spatial conditions will certainly show when a *robust* ability for joint visual attention is available, but these procedures do not allow for early appearing joint visual attention. The consequence is that they also conflate the later developing pointing system with the early appearing capacity for joint visual attention.

There are a number of methodological reasons that may make it appear that gaze following, comprehension, and production of pointing are coincident in development, even though gaze following actually occurs much earlier. In Carpenter et al.'s relatively informal tests, the visual environment was cluttered and asymmetrical, and, on the adult's cue, infants must break off from attending to an attractive toy. While this may be more typical of the conditions under which joint attention occurs in everyday life, the test makes strong demands on the babies' capacity to regulate attention and to inhibit attention at one focus of activity in favor of a new one. Furthermore, to reach the performance criterion for joint visual attention, not only must the babies look in the correct direction, but they must also single out the correct target on each of two trials to the near and far locations. The far location requires the child to inhibit any tendency to fixate the near location on the scan path from the adult. Not until all these conditions are satisfied are infants credited with joint attention on the basis of gaze following, which turns out to be after they comprehend pointing.

Others, using different procedures, have consistently claimed that joint visual attention can be observed at least as early as 6 months, long before there is evidence for the comprehension of pointing (e.g., Butterworth & Cochran, 1980; Butterworth & Jarrett, 1991; D'Entremont, Hains, & Muir, 1997; Scaife & Bruner, 1975). How can these conflicting studies be reconciled? Experimental and naturalistic studies differ widely in their parameters and their criteria for when joint attention may be first observed. Babies at 6 months are notoriously flighty, but that does not mean that joint attention is impossible.

For example, Butterworth and Cochran (1980) and Butterworth and Jarrett (1991) carried out studies with participants as young as 6 months, in an undistracting laboratory, with the walls screened by curtains to form a neutral background. Identical targets were systematically, symmetrically located, relatively close to the experimenter and infant (minimum and maximum distances in the infant's visual field were approximately 1 meter at 60 degrees from the midline and 2.60 meters at 30 degrees from the midline), who were seated "en face," at the same height as the targets. Whether babies were correct in reorienting their attention to particular target positions at different ages could be assessed. Distracting objects were not permitted to be held by the infant, the adult changed her focus of attention by reorienting her head, eyes, and trunk, without speaking, and she held the posture for approximately 5 seconds. The aim was to establish the spatial conditions under which 6-month-old babies could "follow into" a change in the adult's direction of gaze. Under these conditions there was no doubt that infants would accurately respond to the spatial direction (left or right) of the adult's signal. Nor were the babies imitating the adult since there was a measurable delay between the adult's signal and the infant's response and the placement of targets often required asymmetrical rather than mirror-image responses by the infant.

The scoring protocol compared infant responses to targets in the correct direction with those in the incorrect direction, and babies at 6 months showed significantly more responses to targets on the correct side. At 6 months, the probability of a response was less than among older babies, and infants were not necessarily accurate in locating the correct target. However, they were clearly capable of reorienting attention on the basis of an adult's signal (Butterworth & Jarrett, 1991). Babies at 6 months code the general direction in which to look from the adult's change of orientation, but the adult's signal does not carry precise information for the location of the target. Further studies showed that babies younger than 1 year could be accurate (i) if the correct target was stationary and first along the baby's scan path into the periphery of vision or (ii) if both targets were simultaneously in motion and the correct target was the more peripheral of the two (Grover, 1988). That is, attention-worthy object attributes in the periphery of vision may assist the young baby to establish a common focus for joint attention, on the basis of a change in the adult's direction of gaze.

Other important factors (some mentioned by Carpenter et al.) included whether the visual field was empty or contained potential targets. With an empty visual field, babies at 12 months searched through about 40 degrees from their own midline and then gave up (Butterworth & Cochran, 1980). That is, the infant takes the adult's signal to refer to a potential object somewhere within a shared visual space, into which she will follow the adult's change of gaze. However, when the infant's own change in focus of attention fails to terminate in an object (because the shared visual field is empty), the process of achieving joint visual attention terminates. Changes in the adult's direction of gaze, accompanied by reorientation of head and body posture, were sufficient to lead to a statistically reliable response of the infant's direction of gaze to the appropriate side of the room. Adding pointing was actually counterproductive for babies of 6 and 9 months since it did not increase accuracy of target localization and often resulted in the baby fixating the adult's hand (Butterworth & Grover, 1989). At 12 months, however, adding pointing did improve the accuracy of target localization, and, by 15 months, there was a definite advantage when pointing was added to head and eye movements in a relatively large-scale environment with targets at distances up to 4.7 meters (Butterworth, 1991; Butterworth & Grover, 1989).

In Scaife and Bruner's (1975) original study, babies followed the adult's direction of gaze, to the left or the right, into an empty visual field. The requirement for success at this most elementary developmental level was that the infant need only look in the appropriate direction, and the absence of objects may have made the effect particularly fragile. Collis (1977) was unable to replicate joint visual attention in such young infants. D'Entremont et al. (1997), however, have successfully demonstrated that 4-month-old babies can look in the same direction as an adult. These investigators ensured that target objects were directly in front of the baby, just to the left and the right, within her span of apprehension. There was no requirement to single out a particular target among many potential targets, and joint attention was inferred from the fact that the response terminated at the target located in the appropriate direction. That is, the process may be one in which the infant encodes the direction of the object of the adult's gaze and/or head orientation and the specific referent singles itself out as it comes into the periphery of vision. Hood, Willen, and Driver (1998) showed that babies of 4 months who were cued to look in a particular direction by the orientation of the eyes on a face presented as a computer display would do so. For adults, the eye movements in such displays take precedence in allocating attention, even when their direction does not predict the location of a subsequent event. Hood et al. (1998) suggest that the same mechanisms may be involved in directing eye movements as in allocating visual attention. Thus, following gaze may indeed give access to attention as "intentional perception" (Gibson & Rader, 1979).

The theory that joint visual attention may presuppose intentional objects within the visual field is supported by a series of studies in which the number and dynamic characteristics of the targets available to babies were varied (Grover, 1988). The number of targets in the baby's visual field influenced the probability of a response, with two targets reliably eliciting more responses than just one. Caron, Krakowski, Liu, and Brooks (1996) also showed that 14-month-old infants are sensitive to the presence or absence of potential targets in joint visual attention tasks. This suggests that joint visual attention depends, at least in part, on the adult's signal helping resolve uncertainty about the aspect of the environment that is being referred to. Indeed, as Carpenter et al. point out, not only may checking between object and adult reveal communicative intent, but it may also be important in providing confirmation that attention has been reoriented to the appropriate referent, an important consideration in making definite reference.

How the infant's responses are scored is also important in determining what mechanism may be involved in joint visual attention at any particular age. The evidence already reviewed suggests that joint attention as signaled by changes in head, body, and gaze orientation precedes comprehension of pointing. Differences in scoring procedures may have led to some confusion in the literature. Where the scoring procedure directly compared spatially incorrect with correct responses, there was evidence that at 6 months babies look in the correct direction significantly more often than they look in the incorrect direction (Butterworth, 1991; Butterworth & Cochran, 1980; Butterworth & Jarrett, 1991). Where responses in the incorrect horizontal direction are summed with other incorrect responses (e.g., looking down or otherwise disengaging from the task), the first evidence for robust joint visual attention comes at about 12 months (Morissette et al., 1995).

Therefore, once the competing evidence is carefully analyzed, it is clear that joint visual attention is possible, under appropriate conditions, before the 9–12-month watershed. In postulating that an "ecological" mechanism serves the earliest form of joint attention, Butterworth and Jarrett (1991) were suggesting something more subtle than that the baby's attention is merely "grabbed" by something entering the periphery of vision. The argument is that, at root, joint visual attention is an object-directed process that relates to the real world. The fundamental mechanism therefore requires real-world objects in which otherwise unrelated minds can meet. The ecological mechanism depends on a two-part process, in which the adult's change of orientation carries information for a potential object in a particular hemifield of visual space. A triangulation then occurs, in which the meeting of minds is completed by the intentional encounter with the object itself. That is, the interesting object can be considered as the terminus of an intentional action on the part of both the adult and the infant. The baby perceives the adult's reorienting of gaze and posture as an object-relevant signal. Then the object or event that first attracted the adult's interest also captures the infant's interest, thus allowing both minds to meet in the same object. This is a presymbolic mechanism that enables communication within the spatial constraints that apply to the 6-month-old infant. The question of resolving uncertainty also raises the important issue of how links between joint visual attention and the species-typical expression of emotions in humans may assist in explaining the origins of human communication (Baldwin & Moses, 1996; Campos et al., 1983).

The Transition to Pointing Comprehension

If joint visual attention is possible from early in development, why does comprehension and production of manual pointing occur only toward the end of the first year, as Carpenter et al. and others have shown? Among the most important constraints on joint attention in early infancy is the capacity to integrate actions and events across gaps in space and time. Millar and Schaffer (1972, 1973) showed that babies of 6 months of age readily learned to bang on a canister for contingent light reinforcement, which occurred at the same place where they were banging (i.e., under conditions of complete contiguity between stimulus and response). Infants at 6 months also learned such a response when the location of the reinforcer was more distant than the location of the response, so long as there was a spatial cue to assist the infant to attend to the reinforcer within the same visual field as the response (i.e., under conditions of linear noncontiguity). However, they failed to learn this simple operant if the light reinforcer was displaced by 60 degrees from the site of the response (i.e., under conditions of displaced noncontiguity). Millar and Schaffer found that, before 9 months, dividing attention between an action and its consequences presents major difficulties for the infant because attention must be coordinated between separate foci.

Evidence is widespread that a rapid, stage-like change occurs in the ability to bridge such gaps in space and time between 9 and 12 months, including the study of joint visual attention by Carpenter et al. This change may be linked with maturation of frontal lobe functions that allow infants to make rapid progress in solving delayed-response tasks. Diamond (1991), for example, reports that babies can successfully search for hidden objects in delayed-response Piagetian Stage IV search tasks with a delay of 3 seconds at 9 months, which increases to 12 seconds by 12 months. In these tasks, the infant must keep track of the successive positions of the hidden object across a small spatial gap, typically just a few centimeters, between the hiding locations. There is therefore a very rapid change in the capacity to integrate successive attentional foci over space and time at this stage of development (see also Diamond, Werker, & Lalonde, 1994).

Given such a rapidly developing capacity to integrate attention to separate loci, the precise spatiotemporal demands of different tasks may be sufficient to account for the variety of estimates of the age of pointing comprehension. Both Morissette et al. (1995) and Carpenter et al. found that pointing comprehension occurred earlier for nearby than for more distant targets. Morissette et al. (1995) found that the angle subtended by the targets, relative to the baby, influenced the probability of pointing comprehension. Targets at 20 degrees from the midline and 0.85 meters distance were localized at 12 months, whereas targets at 70 degrees and 2.11 meters were localized at 15 months.

Others have also found similar effects of the particular spatial conditions of testing (Lempers, 1976; Murphy & Messer, 1977). Carpenter et al. also note that babies showed joint visual attention to targets on their right 2 months before showing it to targets on their left. Butterworth and Jarrett

(1991) did not find any advantage to the right side of the room in the case of gaze comprehension, but Butterworth and Morissette (1996) found a strong right-hand and right-side advantage in the production of pointing. These observations could be important in implicating cerebral asymmetries in joint visual attention, which would allow further links with language-specific precursors. However, such spatially asymmetrical effects seem to require another level of explanation than the "intentional stance," which is presumably not restricted to the right half of the visual field.

In summary, the ability to integrate information across spatiotemporal gaps may be one of the basic underlying processes that allow the comprehension of pointing. The increasing distance of targets that are accessible to joint visual attention may simply reflect changes in the ability to integrate attention to events at different foci across space and time. This may also account for developmentally coincident changes in the ability to sequence actions as a means to an end.

The Signal Values of Different Joint-Attention Cues

Butterworth and Jarrett (1991) describe a transition at about 12 months from an "ecological" mechanism (in which the attentioncapturing characteristics of the object complete the reference triangle) to a "geometric" mechanism, which enables the baby to single out targets at more peripheral locations among multiple objects. This new factor in joint visual attention was operationally defined as the ability to ignore the first object along the scan path in favor of a more peripheral target. The mechanism was called *geometric* because it appeared to involve extrapolation of vectors through visual space, an ability that seemed to require greater precision than before.

Recent studies have examined just how precisely babies, children, and adults can locate where someone else is looking or pointing (Butterworth, 1997a; Itakura & Butterworth, 1997). One study with young adults enabled precise determination of the accuracy of spatial localization of various joint visual attention signals. Participants were 72 female Japanese college students aged 18–20 years. The experimenter was seated at a distance of 2.7 meters from six targets, blue, red, and green discs positioned at eye height (each with a diameter of 17.8 centimeters), placed facing the participants, equidistant to the left and the right of the midline. These distances were similar to those that had been used with babies by Butterworth (1991). Twelve participants were tested at each angular separation between targets of 4, 6, 8, 10, 15, and 45 degrees, and each was tested when seated both to the left and to the right of the experimenter. There were four conditions for each angle of target separation: (i) the experimenter pointing with the right hand, with head and eye movements (P + H + E); (ii) head and eye movements alone (H +

E); (iii) eye movements alone (E); and (iv) head movements alone, with the experimenter wearing dark sunglasses (H + S). The participant simply had to state the color and side (left or right) of the disc being designated.

Adults were accurate as to the side of the visual field to which reference was being made. Within each hemifield, and whatever the type of signal, they were almost completely accurate with spatial separations of 45 degrees. Errors began to be made at 15 degrees target separation, and performance was inaccurate in more than 50% of participants at or below 10 degrees of spatial separation. Pointing (P + H + E) assisted in improving accuracy most for the target located in the extreme right periphery (perhaps because all pointing was carried out right-handed). However, it did not increase accuracy for the intermediate targets within either visual hemifield. In general, head movements with sunglasses (E + S) were more accurate than head movements with eye movements (H + E), which was interesting since this suggested that the motion of the spectacle frame was assisting the observer to localize the referent. Eye movements alone (E) gave the widest spread of error among the internal targets in each hemifield and the lowest correct identification of targets at the periphery.

These results suggest that, for adults, right-handed pointing assists in accurately localizing a target placed at the right periphery of a set of alternatives. In fact, all four signal types carried information for the periphery, with eye movements alone being the least useful in a crowded environment. Localization of targets through pointing did not depend on extrapolating precise linear vectors through visual space since, at separations of 10 degrees or less, adults were likely to choose an incorrect target in the intermediate positions and they were correct only for the most peripheral targets on each side. This suggests that target selection occurred in broad zones specified by each type of signal. Pointing was the most effective cue to direct adults' attention to targets in the extreme periphery, especially when the angular separation was very small (4, 6, or 8 degrees). Eye movements alone were less effective than head and eye movements or pointing in eliciting an accurate response. This might be because eye movements can specify only a relatively broad region of space for an observer, to the left or the right (and perhaps in the vertical plane), whereas the larger-scale orienting movements involving head, hand, and eye may be less ambiguous. Such a limitation on the spatial informativeness of another's eye movements may explain why it is relatively difficult to find evidence for eye movements alone being effective in joint attention before about 18 months (Butterworth & Jarrett, 1991; Corkum & Moore, 1995). It also explains why other postural subsystems, such as the extended arm and index finger, are necessarily involved in precise referential communication since the pointing gesture increases the efficiency of joint attention to the periphery.

A similar study with children aged 4 years compared accuracy of target localization at 10-degree separations with head movements and pointing, head and eye movements, eye orientation alone, or head orientation alone (Butterworth, 1997a). In this study, the children were accurate only to the peripheral targets and only when the signal included pointing. These findings suggest that, in the absence of object-specific factors that differentiate possible referents from each other, absolute accuracy of reference does not occur, either among babies, children, or adults, in cluttered environments. This leads to the hypothesis that the "ecological" mechanism must necessarily collaborate with the "geometric" mechanism if a specific referent is to be successfully singled out. This has particularly important implications for language acquisition since, unlike the verbally fluent adult, the preverbal child cannot rely on the adult's speech to disambiguate the intended referent. Rather, the nonverbal referential actions of the adult must serve, in collaboration with the structure of the environment, to assist the infant identify the referent so that referential communication through speech can begin.

The conclusion from these studies is that babies, children, and adults are partially dependent on target qualities to identify the specific referent of the gaze or pointing signal. That is, joint visual attention is a two-part process, one part being specified by change in gaze or postural orientation, which define the broad zones of visual space likely to be of mutual interest, and the other part depending on the object to single itself out in a crowded environment. Thus, what attracts the adult's attention and leads her to turn eventually also captures the infant's attention and enables a meeting of minds at the location of the object. Head and eye movements, which are understood as referential actions from early in development, come to be supplemented by the pointing gesture, which carries attention further into the periphery once the infant can integrate experience across the greater distances involved. The pointing gesture is more effective than head and eyes alone in carrying attention to the extreme periphery, especially when the environment is crowded. This account of the developmental transition to pointing does not preclude the possibility that older babies attribute intentions to others, but it does not require the infant to make such attributions. The infant's ability to integrate experience across larger and larger spatiotemporal intervals may be sufficient for the well-attested changes in joint attention that begin at about 9 months and that herald the comprehension and production of pointing.

Pointing Comprehension

Detailed naturalistic studies are needed to establish exactly how babies come to comprehend the pointing signal itself. Butterworth and Grover (1988, 1989) showed that pointing was understood by 12 months, which agrees closely with Carpenter et al.'s age of 11.7 months for pointing comprehension. Butterworth and Grover (1988) found that infants at 6 or 9 months were as likely to fixate the pointing hand as the designated target. If babies at 6 and 9 months succeeded in fixating the target, they did so in two steps, pausing first at the adult's hand, then alighting on the target, whereas 12-month-old babies looked to the target rapidly and smoothly. Indeed, it has sometimes been noted that mothers go to a great deal of trouble, with exaggerated hand movements, to lead the young infant's gaze from her hand to the target (Murphy & Messer, 1977). Grover (1988) showed that the infant's latency to fixate the correct target significantly decreases between 9 and 12 months. She also showed that manual pointing is a more potent signal than a simple change in head and eye orientation. At 12 months, babies were significantly more likely to respond when the signal included a point and more likely to fixate a target further into the periphery of vision, even if this meant ignoring an identical target seen earlier along their scan path.

Ecological factors also influenced the form and incidence of the infant's response to pointing. The likelihood of a response to pointing increased from 69% to 80% of trials when the number of targets in the field of view was increased from one to two. When the salience of the targets was experimentally manipulated by setting them in motion, either singly or in pairs, the infant's response to pointing increased to ceiling level. Target motion was sufficient to eliminate fixation on the pointing hand in 9-month-old infants, although babies then went on to fixate only the first target along their scan path from the adult's hand. Thus, attention may be "plucked" from the hand to the object by the attention-worthy properties of the object itself, which alert the baby to the referential significance of the manual gesture (Grover, 1988).

By 15 months, however, babies will sometimes alight on the second, more peripheral target in a sequence of fixations. Thus, by this age, infants were not merely fixating the first object that they encountered along the line from the adult's hand. Rather, they appear to be extrapolating along the pointing arm (often before the pointing arm comes to rest in a stationary posture) until their own gaze arrives in the more peripheral region of visual space. Once there, babies search for the potential object of joint attention by scanning between the potential (identical) targets or by singling out the most attention-worthy thing. It is possible that the infant's relative familiarity with the target contributes to the process of achieving joint visual attention. It might be predicted that babies would be more likely to attend to a novel item if such a target is encountered in an otherwise familiar setting. Studies varying the novelty of the objects for joint attention have not yet, however, been published.

Other cognitive processes have been postulated in pointing comprehension. Piaget (1954) noted that babies who do not search manually for hidden objects before about 9 months do not comprehend telltale signs that an object has been hidden at a particular place, such as bumps in the cloth occluder. He traced the beginnings of signification, the "semiotic function," to the period 9–12 months and related it to object permanence. It is interesting, therefore, that Carpenter et al. found the relation between object permanence and communication development to be less direct than is the range of social-cognitive skills. Perhaps the signal function of pointing is somehow inherent to the social aspects of the gesture? Butterworth (1997b, 1998) has argued that manual pointing is a species-typical signal in which a part of the body (the hand and arm) substitutes for the whole-body-orienting movements observed in other species. This implies that, as manual signification, pointing depends on a part-whole analysis in which the pointing hand takes on the signal function that until then has been served by the postural complex of head, eyes, and trunk. Furthermore, such an analysis gives renewed significance to the anatomical aspects of achieving joint visual attention through bodily reorientation. On this view, cognitive development operates in collaboration with perception and action in species-typical fashion to underpin the comprehension and production of pointing.

The Production of Pointing

The onset of pointing production is also subject to vagaries of estimation, although the range is less extreme than for joint visual attention. For clarity, pointing is here defined as extending the index finger and the arm, with the remaining fingers curled toward the palm and the thumb tucked in. A number of studies now converge on the emergence of canonical pointing at an average age of 11–12 months, although babies as young as 8½ months have been observed to point and there are precursors in the manual actions of babies even younger (Butterworth & Morissette, 1996; Fogel & Hannan, 1985; Schaffer, 1984). About 33% of parents of 8-month-old babies in the MacArthur study state that their babies already point (L. Fenson, 1997, personal communication; Fenson et al., 1994). Carpenter et al. did not observe proximal pointing, but they found that distal pointing occurred on average at 12.6 months, with no sex differences in their sample of 24 infants.

In a similar longitudinal study of 27 babies, Butterworth and Morissette (1996) found pointing production onset to be in the 11th month. There was a not quite significant sex difference in average age of onset of 11.2 months for females and 11.7 months for males. However, the sample size may not have been sufficiently large to offer the power needed reliably to detect the sex difference. In the standardization sample for the MacArthur test, with 60 children at each month, Fenson (1997, personal communication) found an accelerated pointing onset for female babies until 12 months, when the number of males who are said to point catches up. Sex differences in pointing onset could have important implications for understanding female advantage in aspects of language acquisition, further strengthening the link between joint visual attention and communication development.

As Carpenter et al. suggest, it is possible that comprehension of pointing (which they found as early as 11.7 months) may precede the production of pointing (which they found on average at 12.6 months). However, differential timing may simply reflect relative lack of knowledge about the antecedents of pointing production. Possible antecedents of pointing have been observed in the isolated extensions of the index finger of the 3-month-old baby that occur in close association with "speech-like" sounds in the infant engaged in social interaction (Fogel & Hannan, 1985; Masataka, 1995). Thus, it is possible that components of the pointing gesture that are particularly closely linked to syllabic vocalization can be observed very early in development and that pointing production is actually developing in parallel with comprehension.

There are also isolated reports that babies can sometimes be observed making pointing movements before they engage in pointing for others. Such phenomena may be involuntary orienting movements or expressions of interest that are perhaps related to the transitional phenomena observed by Franco and Butterworth (1996). Babies at 10 months sometimes point at an object, then turn to the mother as if to check, and then point at her. It is as if two preexisting but separate streams of behavior, visual checking and manual pointing, are now coming together in a new structure, one that is not fully sequentially organized.

Franco and Butterworth (1996) also found that further changes in the timing of checking occurred in relation to pointing. When babies first point, checking follows the gesture, whereas, by 16 months, they will first check to establish that they have the attention of the adult and only then point. Thus, there seems to arise an increasing flexibility in the sequential organization of checking and pointing that is consistent with developing intentionality.

Franco and Butterworth (1996) tested the Vygotskian hypothesis that pointing begins as an imperative gesture and only later comes to be socialized as a declarative gesture. Vygotsky argued that pointing develops out of failed grasping movements that become ritualized through social interaction with the mother. Franco and Butterworth (1996) compared the incidence of pointing and reaching gestures in 10–14-month-old babies in declarative and imperative communicative contexts. Pointing was never confused with reaching gestures. Pointing occurred primarily to distal targets and was accompanied by checking with the partner. Checking accompanied by pointing increased exponentially with age, thus revealing communicative intent. Reaching gestures were not strongly correlated with checking. These findings run against the ritualization view of the origins of pointing as propounded by Vygotsky (1988) since pointing was not derived from failed grasping. On the other hand, they are consistent with Carpenter et al. insofar as there was no evidence for the primacy of the imperative use of pointing, which Carpenter et al. observed at 14 months, a few weeks after the emergence of clearly declarative points, at 12.6 months.

Other studies investigated the social conditions for pointing (Franco & Butterworth, 1990). Pointing occurred only under conditions where a social partner was available for communication. Furthermore, pointing by the baby did not require that the adult also point, nor was the rate of infant pointing a function of the adult rate. That is, infant pointing implies an audience, even if the partner is another baby, but the incidence of pointing by the infant was not a function of whether the partner also pointed (Franco, Perruchini, & Butterworth, 1992). This evidence runs against the view that pointing is at first performed primarily for the self since it was accompanied by checking with the partner, who had to be present (Werner & Kaplan, 1963). Nor does it support the speculation that distal pointing is a conventional gesture developed by imitation of the mother, as suggested by Carpenter et al.

The results of Franco and Butterworth (1996) agree with Carpenter et al. that the pointing gesture in humans initially serves a protodeclarative purpose (i.e., look at that) rather than a protoimperative purpose (i.e., give me that). That is not to say that pointing has nothing at all to do with prehension, however, and this is where a radical alternative to the intentional stance, the ritualization, and the social transmission theories of pointing will be offered.

The argument to be advanced is that pointing and the pincer grip are coevolved but that these are different aspects of hand function that are specialized, respectively, for precise instrumental action and for precise communication (see Butterworth, 1997b, 1998). The characteristic hand posture observed in human pointing may be related to the pincer grip but as its "antithesis." Darwin (1904) first proposed the principle of antithesis to explain how animal communication often exploits visual signals to convey information. For example, an animal may signal readiness to attack by making "intention movements" that are preparatory to fighting. After a fight, the subdued posture of the defeated dog signals submission because the muscles are activated in the opposite configuration, or antithesis, to those involved in aggression. The opposition of the tip of the index finger and thumb in the pincer grip is postulated here to have pointing as its postural antithesis. This contrast in relative positions of index finger and thumb also involves a change in the focus of visual attention. In precise manual activities with tools, focal attention is on the hand, the tool, and the object in the service of precise control of manipulation. In pointing, by contrast, attention is outer directed and serves rather precisely to reorient the attention of another person so that an object at some distance can become a focus for shared experience.

On this theory, the emergence of pointing should be related to the development of other precise uses of the hand, and this, indeed, is what Butterworth and Morissette (1996) established. The pincer grip was invariably in the infant's repertoire approximately 1 month before pointing onset. Exploration of objects with the tip of the index finger (tipping) has also been linked to the onset of pointing (Shinn, 1900). Butterworth, Verweij, and Hopkins (1997) showed that "tipping" and the pincer grip are closely related in development, with the incidence of tipping declining as the pincer grip becomes established.

In summary, the theory that pointing develops at the same time as precise manual actions links pointing onset to "instrumental intentionality," which stresses less the purely cognitive aspects of the intentional stance. Species-specific aspects of hand anatomy and function, and the underlying processes for focused attention, are used in "antithesis" to support precise communication. On this argument, precise tool use and precise manual communication through the pointing gesture are coevolved, species-specific functions of the human hand.

Pointing and the Transition to Language

A variety of studies have linked preverbal referential communication with language acquisition (e.g., Baldwin, 1991, 1993). There is evidence that the amount of pointing at 12 months predicts speech production rates at 24 months (Camaioni, Castelli, Longobardi, & Volterra, 1991). Links between pointing onset and comprehension of object names have also been established, with infants understanding their first categorical object name in the same week as they point, which incidentally introduces yet another cognitive process, categorization, into the many factors involved in the emergence of referential communication (Harris, Barlow-Brown, & Chasin, 1995). Carpenter et al.'s study also adds important new information on the relation between persistent joint engagement. Maternal language following into the infant's focus of attention is the most important link with subsequent speech comprehension and production, but it should be noted that, for maternal following in to be effective, the joint visual attention system must already be operating reciprocally between mother and baby. After all, the mother already speaks the language, and it is therefore logical that the direction of transmission will be from her to the child. The duration of joint engagement proved diagnostic, and the joint visual attention window around 14 months seems particularly important for subsequent speech production. The question is whether there may be specific developmental changes in the baby at around this age that support the acquisition of speech.

Butterworth and Morissette (1996) studied the relation between age of pointing onset and the subsequent comprehension and production of speech

161

and gestures. A longitudinal study was carried out linking pointing, handedness, and onset of the pincer grip to early verbal and gestural communication, as measured by the MacArthur infant language inventory (Fenson et al., 1994). The earlier the onset of pointing, the greater were the number of different gestures produced, and the greater the number of animal sounds comprehended, at 14.4 months. That is, age of pointing onset appears to be related both to a gesture and to an auditory-vocal developmental pathway. The relative balance of use between left and right hands in unimanual tasks predicted MacArthur speech production and comprehension scores at 14.4 months. Girls showed more right-handed pointing than boys. The amount of right-handed pointing, and the relative balance of pincer grips between the left and the right hands (a measure of lateralized fine motor control), predicted speech comprehension and production at 14.4 months. Bimanual use of the hands, terminating in right-handed object retrieval, was significantly correlated with MacArthur speech production at 14.4 months. At this age, boys had relatively few words in production (about three), whereas girls had on average 12 words. Although the study stopped before 15 months, there is evidence from the MacArthur norms that, by 16 months, the sex difference in rate of speech production is marked. At 16 months, females have 95 words in production and males 25 words, although the sex difference begins to even out by 20 months (Fenson et al., 1994).

Thus, earlier onset of pointing, earlier right-handed pointing, and more rapid development of speech in girls may suggest that there is a link between pointing, cerebral lateralization, and the development of language and that there may be sex differences in this process. Carpenter et al. admit that a number of such language-relevant processes were not measured, and, clearly, there are limits to what can be done in any study. However, this sort of detail is needed to flesh out a viable theory of communication development that is based on the combined contributions of species-typical perception, action, and cognitive systems.

Conclusion

Carpenter et al. have presented important new information to show that joint visual attention is indeed related to the acquisition of language. The main purpose of this Commentary has been to propose an amended timetable for the origins of joint visual attention and to offer some theoretical alternatives for the development of pointing. First, and most important, infants are capable of joint attention in the period before comprehension and production of pointing even if this is not a robust ability. Second, relying on the intentional stance for theoretical unification of the data does not really solve the problem of defining intentionality. It was argued that there is no "graduation ceremony" for acquiring intentionality that is necessary and sufficient for communication development. A purely cognitive approach, perhaps inadvertently, downgrades the contribution made by perception and action systems to joint attention, to categorization, and to other precursors of speech (Rakison & Butterworth, 1998). Other species-typical aspects of human embodiment, such as lateralization or the development of precision grips, give rise to relations between motor control and communication development that also tend to be excluded. Although pointing is a simple, social means of reorienting attention, it is also intimately connected with species-typical right-handedness, which undergoes systematic, gender-linked changes in the period from 9 to 15 months. Thus, communication by means of the pointing gesture may make use of the same anatomical adaptations and attention mechanisms that serve precise tool use through the pincer grip. Pointing serves to identify the concurrent sound stream with a visual referent and thereby effects a link between the intentional objects of joint visual attention, language, and culture.

References

Baldwin, D. (1991). Infants' contribution to the achievement of joint reference. *Child Development,* **62,** 875–890.

Baldwin, D. (1993). Early referential understanding: Infants' ability to recognize referential acts for what they are. *Developmental Psychology,* **29**(5), 832–843.

Baldwin, D. A., & Moses, L. J. (1996). The ontogeny of social information gathering. *Child Development,* **67**(5), 1915–1939.

Bower, T. G. R., Broughton, J. M., & Moore, M. K. (1970). Demonstration of intention in the reaching behavior of neonate humans. *Nature,* **228,** 679–681.

Butterworth, G. E. (1987). Some benefits of egocentrism. In J. S. Bruner & H. Weinreich-Haste (Eds.), *Making sense of the world: The child's construction of reality.* London: Methuen.

Butterworth, G. E. (1991, April). *Evidence for the "geometric" comprehension of manual pointing.* Paper presented at the meeting of the Society for Research in Child Development, Seattle.

Butterworth, G. E. (1997a, December). *Did humans evolve pointing because gaze is not enough?* Paper presented at the conference of the British Psychological Society, London.

Butterworth, G. E. (1997b). Starting point. *Natural History,* **106**(4), 14–16.

Butterworth, G. E. (1998). What is special about pointing? In F. Simion & G. E. Butterworth (Eds.), *The development of sensory motor and cognitive capacities in early infancy: From perception to cognition.* Hove: Psychology Press.

Butterworth, G. E. (in press). Neonatal imitation: Existence, mechanisms, motives. In J. Nadel & G. E. Butterworth (Eds.), *Imitation in infancy.* Cambridge: Cambridge University Press, in press.

Butterworth, G. E., & Cochran, E. (1980). Towards a mechanism of joint visual attention in human infancy. *International Journal of Behavioural Development,* **3,** 253–272.

Butterworth, G. E., & Grover, L. (1988). The origins of referential communication in human infancy. In L. Weiskrantz (Ed.), *Thought without language.* Oxford: Oxford University Press.

Butterworth, G. E., & Grover, L. (1989). Joint visual attention, manual pointing and preverbal

163

communication in human infancy. In M. Jeannerod (Ed.), *Attention and Performance XII.* Hillsdale, NJ: Erlbaum.

Butterworth, G. E., & Hopkins, B. (1989). Hand-mouth co-ordination in the newborn human infant. *British Journal of Developmental Psychology,* **6**(4), 303–314.

Butterworth, G. E., & Jarrett, N. L. M. (1991). What minds have in common is space: Spatial mechanisms for perspective taking in infancy. *British Journal of Developmental Psychology,* **9**, 55–72.

Butterworth, G. E., & Morissette, P. (1996). Onset of pointing and the acquisition of language in infancy. *Journal of Reproductive and Infant Psychology,* **14**, 219–231.

Butterworth, G. E., Verweij, E., & Hopkins, B. (1997). The development of prehension in infants: Halverson revisited. *British Journal of Developmental Psychology,* **15**, 223–236.

Camaioni, L., Castelli, M. C., Longobardi, E., & Volterra, V. (1991). A parent report instrument for early language assessment. *First Language,* **11**, 345–360.

Campos, J. J., Barrett, K. C., Lamb, M. E., Hill, H., Goldsmith, H., & Stenberg, C. (1983). Socio-emotional development. In M. M. Haith & J. J. Campos (Eds), P. Mussen (Series Ed.), *Handbook of child psychology: Vol. 2. Infancy and developmental psychobiology.* New York: Wiley.

Caron, A., Krakowski, O., Liu, A., & Brooks, R. (1996, April). *Infant joint attention: Cued orienting or implicit theory of mind?* Paper presented at the International Conference on Infant Studies, Providence, RI.

Collis, G. (1977). Visual co-orientation and maternal speech. In H. R. Schaffer (Ed.), *Studies in mother infant interaction.* New York: Academic.

Corkum, V., & Moore, C. (1995). The origins of joint visual attention. In C. Moore & P. Dunham (Eds.), *Joint attention: Its origins and role in development.* Hillsdale, NJ: Erlbaum.

Darwin, C. (1904). *The expression of the emotions in men and animals.* London: John Murray. (Original work published 1872)

Dennett, D. (1987). *The intentional stance.* Cambridge, MA: MIT Press.

D'Entremont, B., Hains, S. M. J., & Muir, D. W. (1997). A demonstration of gaze following in 3 to 6 month olds. *Infant Behavior and Development,* **20**(4), 569–572.

Diamond, A. (1991). Frontal lobe involvement in cognitive changes during the first year of life. In K. R. Gibson & A. C. Petersen (Eds.), *Brain maturation and cognitive development: Comparative and cross-cultural perspectives.* New York: Aldine de Gruyter.

Diamond, A., Werker, J. F., & Lalonde, C. (1994). Toward understanding commonalities in the development of object search, detour navigation, categorization and speech perception. In G. Dawson & K. W. Fischer (Eds.), *Human behavior and the developing brain.* New York: Guilford.

Fenson, L., Dale, P. S., Reznick, J. S.., Bates, E., Thal, D. J., & Pethick, S. J. (1994). Variability in early communicative development. *Monographs of the Society for Research in Child Development,* **59**(5, Serial No. 242).

Fogel, A., & Hannan, T. E. (1985). Manual actions of nine to fifteen week old human infants during face to face interaction with their mothers. *Child Development,* **56**, 1271–1279.

Franco, F., & Butterworth, G. E. (1990, August). *Effects of social variables on the production of infant pointing.* Poster presented at the Fourth European Conference on Developmental Psychology, University of Stirling.

Franco, F., & Butterworth, G. E. (1996). Pointing and social awareness: Declaring and requesting in the second year of life. *Journal of Child Language,* **23**(2), 307–336.

Franco, F., Perruchini, P., & Butterworth, G. (1992, September). *Pointing for an age mate in 1 to 2 year olds.* Paper presented at the Sixth European Conference on Developmental Psychology, Seville.

Gibson, E., & Rader, N. (1979). Attention: The perceiver as performer. In G. A. Hale & M. Lewis (Eds.), *Attention and cognitive development.* New York: Plenum.

Grover, L. (1988). *Comprehension of the pointing gesture in human infants.* Unpublished Ph.D. dissertation, University of Southampton.

Harris, M., Barlow-Brown, F., & Chasin, J. (1995). Early referential understanding. *First Language,* 15(pt. 1, no. 43), 19–34.

Hood, B., Willen, J. D., & Driver, J. (1998). Adult's eyes trigger shifts of visual attention in human infants. *Psychological Science, 9,* 131–134.

Itakura, S., & Butterworth, G. E. (1997, April). *Role of head, eyes and pointing in joint visual attention.* Poster presented at the meeting of the Society for Research in Child Development, Washington DC.

Kalnins, I. V., & Bruner, J. S. (1974). Infant sucking used to change the clarity of a visual display. In J. Stone, H. T. Smith, & L. B. Murphy (Eds.), *The competent infant.* London: Tavistock.

Lempers, J. D. (1976). *Production of pointing, comprehension of pointing and understanding of looking behavior in young children.* Unpublished doctoral dissertation, University of Minnesota.

Lew, A., & Butterworth, G. E. (1995). Hand-mouth contact in newborn babies before and after feeding. *Developmental Psychology,* 31(3), 456–463.

Lew, A., & Butterworth, G. E. (1997). The development of hand-mouth co-ordination in 2 to 5 month old infants: Similarities with reaching and grasping. *Infant Behavior and Development, 20,* 159–169.

Masataka, N. (1995). The relation between index-finger extension and the acoustic quality of cooing in three month old infants. *Journal of Child Language, 22,* 247–257.

Meltzoff, A. N. (1995). Understanding the intentions of others: Re-enactment of intended acts by 18 month old children. *Developmental Psychology,* 31(5), 1–16.

Millar, W. S., & Schaffer, H. R. (1972). The influence of spatially displaced visual feedback on infant operant conditioning. *Journal of Experimental Child Psychology, 14,* 442–452.

Millar, W. S., & Schaffer, H. R. (1973). Visual manipulative response strategies in infant operant conditioning with spatially displaced feedback. *British Journal of Psychology, 64,* 545–552.

Moore, C., & Corkum, V. (1994). Social understanding at the end of the first year of life. *Developmental Review, 14,* 349–372.

Morissette, P., Ricard, M., & Gouin-Decarie, T. (1995). Joint visual attention and pointing in infancy: A longitudinal study of comprehension. *British Journal of Developmental Psychology,* 13(2), 163–177.

Murphy, C. M., & Messer, D. J. (1977). Mothers, infants and pointing: A study of gesture. In H. R. Schaffer (Ed.), *Studies of mother infant interaction.* London: Academic.

Piaget, J. (1952). *The origins of intelligence in children.* New York: Norton.

Piaget, J. (1954). *The construction of reality in the child.* New York: Basic.

Rakison, D., & Butterworth, G. E. (1998). Infants' use of object parts in early categorization. *Developmental Psychology,* 34(1), 49–62.

Scaife, M., & Bruner, J. S. (1975). The capacity for joint attention in the infant. *Nature, 253,* 265–266.

Schaffer, H. R. (1984) *The child's entry into a social world.* New York: Academic.

Shinn, M. (1900). *The biography of a baby.* Boston: Houghton Mifflin.

Tomasello, M., & Call, J. (1997). *Primate cognition.* Oxford: Oxford University Press.

Trevarthen, C. (1990). Growth and education in the hemispheres. In C. Trevarthen (Ed.), *Brain circuits and functions of the mind: Essays in honor of Roger W. Sperry.* Cambridge: Cambridge University Press.

Vedeler, D. (1994). Infant intentionality as object directedness: A method for observation. *Scandinavian Journal of Psychology, 35,* 343–366.

Von Hofsten, C. (1990). Development of manipulation action in infancy. In H. Bloch & B. I.

Bertenthal (Eds.), *Sensory-motor organizations and development in infancy and early childhood.* Dordrecht: Kluwer.

Vygotsky, L. S. (1988). Development of the higher mental functions. In K. Richardson & S. Sheldon (Eds.), *Cognitive development to adolescence.* Hove: Erlbaum. (Original work published 1931)

Werner, H., & Kaplan, B. (1963). *Symbol formation: An organismic-developmental approach to language and the expression of thought.* New York: Wiley.

SOCIAL COGNITION IN INFANCY

Chris Moore

Social Cognition in Infancy

For anyone interested in the social developments of the second half of infancy, the *Monograph* by Carpenter, Nagell, and Tomasello will be a pleasure to read. It undoubtedly provides the richest longitudinal description available of the development of social interactive behavior during approximately 8 months spanning the end of the first year of life. These behaviors serve as a fundamental context for much of the social communicative developments to come (Carpenter et al. show how early language is grounded in this context), and as such their description is immensely valuable. However, I use the term *description* advisedly here, for, while I believe that these data provide a rich texture for thinking about social development during this period, they ultimately tell us little definitively about the cognitive processes involved in these behaviors.

In this Commentary, I will focus on the theoretical account that the authors believe to be supported by these data. The title of the *Monograph* boldly asserts Carpenter et al.'s theoretical leanings: "Social Cognition. . . ." In addition to mapping out the development of the social interactive skills of the infant during the second half of infancy, Carpenter et al. want to make claims about infant social cognition. Their belief is that the pattern of evidence is consistent, indeed supports, the interpretation that infants have a concept of

Preparation of this commentary was supported by grant 410-95-1144 from the Social Sciences and Humanities Research Council of Canada. Correspondence should be addressed to Chris Moore, Department of Psychology, Dalhousie University, Halifax, Nova Scotia, Canada, B3H 4J1.

intentional agent and that this understanding develops by analogy from their awareness of their own intentional action. I will examine this interpretation, first, by considering whether the pattern of data does indeed provide support for Carpenter et al.'s claims for infant social cognition and, second, by examining their account of infant social cognition in the context of a more general consideration of infant cognition.

Theory and Data

Carpenter et al. propose that the behavior of infants around 12 months of age is based on the infants having a concept of an intentional agent. An intentional agent acts in relation to goals and has perceptual and emotional experience in relation to objects and states of affairs in the world. An intentional agent, then, is an entity that has both an objective identity (or who exists as an independent entity in a world of objects) and subjective experience (or for whom there are goals and objects with intentional inexistence). Because both self and others are members of the category *intentional agent,* having a concept of an intentional agent means appreciating the equivalence of self and other as agents who can take up intentional relations to objects or states of affairs. Significantly, such a conception of intentional agents is an individualistic one whereby agents are recognized to be individual centers of action and experience in relation to the world.

So what aspects of their data convince Carpenter et al. that an explanation in terms of the concept *intentional agent* is warranted? The reliable emergence of the social interactive phenomena without a coherent association with such object-related skills as object permanence and spatial relations implies to Carpenter et al. that "some specifically social developments" are responsible. While it is plausible to suggest that there is something intrinsically social about whatever is changing during this period, the inference that it is conceptual change in the area of intentional understanding is of course not necessary. The latter component rests more on the authors' interpretation of other types of evidence, in particular the reliable sequencing of types of skills and the patterns of gaze shown by infants.

Carpenter et al. are quite taken by the uniformity of the developmental picture. Because the various behavioral phenomena—joint engagement, attention and behavior following, attention and behavior directing—all emerge within a relatively short space of time and in a largely reliable sequence, it makes sense to postulate a single underlying change in development responsible for the overt behavioral changes. As such, the notion of a conceptual change is appealing. This change is not all or none. Carpenter et al. propose that the sequence from joint engagement and proximal declarative gestures to behavior following and distal gestures is the product of the infant, first, constructing the notion *that* others have intentions and, next, discovering *what* those intentions are about.

However, the proximal-distal sequence observed by Carpenter et al. is relatively straightforwardly interpreted without an attribution to infants of a concept of intentional agent of either the *that* or the *what* form. The sequence implies that infants first engage in triadic interactions when the object and adult are simultaneously part of perceptual experience. Such situations will inevitably place rather fewer demands on attentional resources than those in which the infant has to shift attention between objects that cannot be simultaneously within the visual field. In fact, a similar distinction appears to exist for gaze following, in that there is evidence that infants will follow gaze to a target that is within the visual field somewhat earlier than they will follow gaze to targets outside the visual field (Butterworth & Jarrett, 1991; D'Entremont, Hains, & Muir, 1997; Moore, in press).

Unfortunately, Carpenter et al. did not compare gaze following scenarios when the target was within or outside the visual field. However, there is some evidence in their work that is suggestive. In note 5, they report that the ages of onset of point and gaze following were significantly earlier to the left side of the room, which was closer to the infants, than they were to the right side of the room. Carpenter et al.'s suggested explanation for the reported proximal-distal difference in declarative gestures in terms of the distinction between understanding *that* and understanding *what* is seriously weakened if indeed there is an age-of-onset difference for proximal and distal gaze and point following.

There are also some more specific aspects of the behavioral phenomena that at first gloss imply conceptual understanding of intentional agents. Carpenter et al. are particularly impressed by gaze alternation and "checking," whereby the infant looks to the adult as if to determine what the latter's attentional or intentional orientation is. They suggest that such accompanying behaviors indicate more than rote learning of gaze following and the like, that they imply an understanding of the adult's intentions. Carpenter et al. put so much store in these kinds of behaviors that, for them, these behaviors "ensured that children really understood the intentions or attention of their social partner for each skill measured."

Personally, I find the use of gaze to faces to justify the notion of a concept of intentional agent unconvincing. In the first place, infants have been focusing their own attention on the faces of their interactive partners for some months prior to the onset of triadic interaction. Faces are salient stimuli from birth (e.g., Johnson, Dziurawiec, Ellis, & Morton, 1991) and play a significant role in the dyadic interactions evident from 2 months of age (e.g., Trevarthen, 1979). If we make the not unreasonable assumption that triadic interactions are developmentally continuous with these earlier face-to-face dyadic interactions, then there is no reason to imagine that infants would look anywhere else when they look at adults. The point is that triadic interactions may be seen as dyadic interactions into which a third element has been introduced, so of course infants will look at the adults' faces during these interactions. But there is no more reason to infer an understanding of intentional agency from gazing at faces at this stage than there is for the 2-month-old.

Now, clearly, it is not just that infants gaze at faces that is important; it is the pattern of facial gazing in association with other events, such as the adult blocking the infant's goal or the infant pointing at a target. It is appealing to infer that an infant whose goal is blocked and looks up at the adult's face, or who points at something to the side of the room and then turns "expectantly" to look at the adult, is attempting to determine the adult's intentional or attentional state. However, I think that this kind of evidence is at best only circumstantial—it cannot tell us directly anything about what the infant is looking *for*. It is worth noting that, in the literature, one and the same pattern of gaze has been interpreted in quite opposite ways. For example, Franco and Butterworth (1996) interpret infant looks to the interactive partner after pointing as indicating that the infant is checking whether the adult has seen or looked toward the target. In contrast, we (Moore & Corkum, 1994) and others (e.g., Desrochers, Morissette, & Ricard, 1995) have suggested that such a pattern is more consistent with the infant expecting some response from the adult (see also Bates, Camaioni, & Volterra, 1975). In general, then, it is difficult to see how patterns of gaze alone can distinguish between infants looking to see what the adult's intentional state is and infants simply shifting attention between object and adult because both are interesting sources of stimulation.

In sum, while there is appeal to the explanatory use of conceptual development to account for the phenomena that are so well laid out by Carpenter et al., I believe that this appeal is largely illusory. However, if a concept of intentional agent is not particularly warranted by the evidence, how should one think about the developmental changes seen during this period? To answer this question, it is worth considering the nature of infant cognition in more general terms.

The Nature of Infant Cognition

There is a long tradition in the developmental literature in which a distinction is made in type or level of cognition between infancy and the postinfancy years. For Piaget (e.g., 1962), infancy was characterized by sensorimotor schema where action was organized with respect to immediate perceptual input. The end of infancy was marked by the development of conceptual schemas where action could be internalized into thought in such a way that actions no longer had to be performed but could now be imagined or represented. In the more recent literature, a number of authors (e.g., Leslie, 1987; Olson, 1989, 1993; Perner, 1991) have argued that the end of infancy marks a watershed in cognition. While there are obviously differences between these authors' theoretical accounts, for all of them, infants are limited to basing action on a single representation, typically provided by immediate perceptual information. In a nutshell, the idea of infant cognition is that action is in response to immediate experience. The action that may be produced develops in organization and complexity through the period of infancy, and it clearly is modified by previous experience, but, ultimately, the infant is limited to dealing with information that is provided perceptually.

With the end of infancy comes the cognitive capacity to attend to more than one thing at a time. Olson (1989, 1993) characterizes this capacity as being able to hold one thing in mind while attending perceptually to something else. Perner (1991) talks of multiple models guiding action and Leslie (1987) of secondary representation. In each case, the idea is that action is no longer governed by the immediately provided experience but that the child can bring a different representation to bear on the determination of action. It is unfortunate that the language used by different authors does not allow a uniform labeling of the levels of cognition. For my purposes here, however, I shall refer to infant cognition as *sensorimotor* and postinfancy cognition as *imaginal*.

So how does the characterization of the cognitive development from infancy to the postinfancy period fit with the proposal of Carpenter et al.? Although they do not address the issue in these terms, I suggest that the kind of concept that they invoke to explain infant behavior in triadic interactions is not consistent with a sensorimotor level of cognition. Rather, it depends on an imaginal form. It is imaginal because, at the very least, attributing subjective experience to others and objective existence to self depends on an interpretation of perceptual experiences as something else. Thus, when I observe another person turn his head and point, I attribute to that person attention to an object in the world (i.e., I imagine information that is not given in my perceptual experience). At the same time, to interpret my own experience as that of an independent intentional agent like those others I observe around me, I must imagine myself, as it were, from the outside. In short, the recognition of the equivalence of the third-person experience of another's intentional activity and of my own first-person experience when acting intentionally requires interpreting two very different kinds of experience as manifestations of the same thing, namely, the intentional activity of an agent in relation to a goal or an object. And, in order to do such interpretation, imaginal information has to be involved. Thus, the concept *intentional agent* requires an imaginal level of cognition (see Barresi & Moore, 1996).

Because Carpenter et al.'s account attributes to 12-month-olds a form of cognitive ability usually reserved for children at the end of infancy, I think that it is worth exploring the alternative in more detail. Can a sensorimotor account serve to explain the phenomena that Carpenter et al. report? I believe that it can. The way to think about triadic interactive behavior is in terms of the infant's attention to people's activity and to the world of objects becoming coordinated. Critically, one must allow that infants can participate in social interactive structures in which their attention to others' action is linked to their attention to other objects and events. From a Piagetian point of view, such linkages would be seen as the coordination of schemes. While I think that there is reason to believe that there may be some general developmental pacing (hence the general emergence at the end of the first year of life), I do not think that necessarily one should expect extremely high correlations between tasks in social and nonsocial domains. These tasks may make quite different demands on the infants' information-processing skills and motivations. Indeed, given that the correlations between the social-cognitive tasks were quite low in some cases in Carpenter et al.'s study, to expect high correlations with tasks that are quite different in demands would be unreasonable.

Because infants show both following and directing behaviors, one has to allow that the coordinating structures can operate in either direction so that, within such interactive structures, the observation of the partner's head turn or point is linked to the expectation that something of note is available in the corresponding location in space. In addition, the infant's own observation of something of interest leads her to perform a gesture with the expectation that the adult will then provide some interesting feedback. Notice that this type of interpretation is consistent with a sensorimotor level of cognition because the infant is acting in relation to the currently experienced events and is not presumed to be interpreting either her own or another's behavior in terms of a concept.

My view is that this kind of sensorimotor account of triadic interactions is preferable, not only because it is consistent with the kind of cognition usually ascribed to infants, but also because it provides a potential solution to how an individualistic conception of intentional agency is acquired. By this account, infants' initial participation in triadic interactions reflects an interpersonal level of understanding of intentional activity. It is interpersonal because the infant's participation in interactive events provides experiences in which the necessary components for understanding intentional relations to objects are present as a result of the participation. Thus, the infant has first-person experience of goals and intentional objects and third-person experience of agentive action. However, because the infant is limited to acting in relation to immediately provided perceptual experience, intentional activity cannot be attributed independently to either self or other.

With the end of infancy and the development of the imaginal level of cognition, these interactive experiences can form the foundation for the acquisition of an individualistic understanding of intentional activity. Now the first-person experience of goals and intentional objects can be represented as the intentions of self, and the third-person experience of the activity of others can be represented as their intentions toward goals. In short, both kinds of experience can be represented as the intentional activity of an agent in relation to a goal. It is worth noting, I think, that this account is truly Vygotskian because the proposal is that the initial level of understanding of intention is thoroughly interpersonal and that it becomes individualistic only later through interactive experience and the ability to reflect on those interactive experiences.

Final Note

If older infants and young toddlers are different in their type of understanding of intention, then it should be possible to demonstrate the difference. Carpenter, Nagell, and Tomasello have provided us with a rich picture of the development of social communicative behavior in the latter half of infancy, and their work will provide a reference for thinking about sequence and developmental relations in this area. However, in the end, descriptive data of the kind that they provide will not allow us to decide issues of social cognition. What is needed is experimental evidence in which the behavior of children at the relevant ages is compared under different conditions. For example, we know that, when gaze-orientation cues are manipulated, 12-month-olds follow head orientation but pay little attention to eye direction, whereas, from 18 months, children will follow eye orientation (e.g., Butterworth & Jarrett, 1991; Corkum & Moore, 1995; Moore & Corkum, in press). While not conclusive on its own, such evidence may, in combination with data from various manipulations, ultimately provide us with a clear picture of the nature of infant social cognition.

References

Barresi, J., & Moore, C. (1996). Intentional relations and social understanding. *Behavioral and Brain Sciences,* **19,** 107–154.

Bates, E., Camaioni, L., & Volterra, V. (1975). The acquisition of performatives prior to speech. *Merrill-Palmer Quarterly,* **21,** 205–224.

Butterworth, G., & Jarrett, N. (1991). What minds have in common is space: Spatial mechanisms serving joint visual attention in infancy. *British Journal of Developmental Psychology,* **9,** 55–72.

Corkum, V., & Moore, C. (1995). Development of joint visual attention in infants. In C. Moore & P. Dunham (Eds.), *Joint attention: Its origins and role in development.* Hillsdale, NJ: Erlbaum.

D'Entremont, B., Hains, S., & Muir, D. (1997). A demonstration of gaze following in 3- to 6-month-olds. *Infant Behavior and Development,* **20,** 569–572.

Desrochers, S., Morissette, P., & Ricard, M. (1995). Two perspectives on pointing in infancy.

In C. Moore & P. Dunham (Eds.), *Joint attention: Its origins and role in development*. Hillsdale, NJ: Erlbaum.

Franco, F., & Butterworth, G. (1996). Pointing and social awareness: Declaring and requesting in the second year. *Journal of Child Language, 23,* 307–336.

Johnson, M., Dziurawiec, S., Ellis, H., & Morton, J. (1991). Newborns' preferential tracking of face-like stimuli and its subsequent decline. *Cognition, 40,* 1–19.

Leslie, A. (1987). Pretense and representation: The origins of "theory of mind." *Psychological Review, 94,* 412–426.

Moore, C. (in press). Gaze following and the control of attention. In P. Rochat (Ed.), *Infant social cognition*. Hillsdale, NJ: Erlbaum.

Moore, C., & Corkum, V. (1994). Social understanding at the end of the first year of life. *Developmental Review, 14,* 349–372.

Moore, C., & Corkum, V. (in press). Infant gaze following based on eye direction. *British Journal of Developmental Psychology*.

Olson, D. (1989). Making up your mind. *Canadian Psychology, 30,* 617–627.

Olson, D. (1993). The development of representations: The origins of mental life. *Canadian Psychology, 34,* 293–306.

Perner, J. (1991). *Understanding the representational mind*. Cambridge, MA: MIT Press.

Piaget, J. (1962). *Play, dreams, and imitation in childhood*. London: Routledge & Kegan Paul.

Trevarthen, C. (1979). Communication and cooperation in early infancy: A description of primary intersubjectivity. In M. Bullowa (Ed.), *Before speech: The beginnings of interpersonal communication*. Cambridge: Cambridge University Press.

Malinda Carpenter (Ph.D. 1995, Emory University) currently is a postdoctoral researcher at the University of Liverpool Department of Psychology. Her research interests include social-cognitive development in typically developing infants, children with autism, and nonhuman primates.

Katherine Nagell (Ph.D. 1996, Emory University) has research interests that focus on joint attention and language acquisition in early development.

Michael Tomasello (Ph.D. 1980, University of Georgia) is codirector of the Max Planck Institute of Evolutionary Anthropology in Leipzig. His research interests focus on processes of communication, social cognition, and cultural learning in children and nonhuman primates—with a special focus on the language acquisition of children and the gestural communication of chimpanzees. He is the author of *First Verbs: A Case Study of Early Grammatical Development* and the coauthor (with Josep Call) of *Primate Cognition*.

George Butterworth (D.Phil. 1975, University of Oxford) is professor of psychology at the University of Sussex. His research interests are in the development of perception, action, and cognition in babies. Most recently, he has been investigating the species-specific origins of index finger pointing in human infants. He is the coauthor (with Margaret Harris) of *Principles of Developmental Psychology* and the editor of the journal *Developmental Science*.

Chris Moore (Ph.D. 1985, Cambridge University) is a professor of psychology at Dalhousie University. His research focuses on social understanding and social behavior in infancy and the preschool years. He is the editor (with Philip Dunham) of *Joint Attention: Its Origins and Role in Development* (1995).

STATEMENT OF EDITORIAL POLICY

The *Monographs* series is intended as an outlet for major reports of developmental research that generate authoritative new findings and use these to foster a fresh and/or better-integrated perspective on some conceptually significant issue or controversy. Submissions from programmatic research projects are particularly welcome; these may consist of individually or group-authored reports of findings from some single large-scale investigation or of a sequence of experiments centering on some particular question. Multiauthored sets of independent studies that center on the same underlying question can also be appropriate; a critical requirement in such instances is that the various authors address common issues and that the contribution arising from the set as a whole be both unique and substantial. In essence, irrespective of how it may be framed, any work that contributes significant data and/or extends developmental thinking will be taken under editorial consideration.

Submissions should contain a minimum of 80 manuscript pages (including tables and references); the upper limit of 150–175 pages is much more flexible (please submit four copies; a copy of every submission and associated correspondence is deposited eventually in the archives of the SRCD). Neither membership in the Society for Research in Child Development nor affiliation with the academic discipline of psychology are relevant; the significance of the work in extending developmental theory and in contributing new empirical information is by far the most crucial consideration. Because the aim of the series is not only to advance knowledge on specialized topics but also to enhance cross-fertilization among disciplines or subfields, it is important that the links between the specific issues under study and larger questions relating to developmental processes emerge as clearly to the general reader as to specialists on the given topic.

Potential authors who may be unsure whether the manuscript they are planning would make an appropriate submission are invited to draft an outline of what they propose and send it to the Editor for assessment. This mechanism, as well as a more detailed description of all editorial policies, evaluation processes, and format requirements, is given in the "Guidelines for the Preparation of *Monographs* Submissions," which can be obtained by writing to the Editor, Rachel K. Clifton, Department of Psychology, University of Massachusetts, Amherst MA 01003.